PROFILING VIOLENT CRIMES

Third Edition

Donald Leo French (1926-2000)
We will miss you

PROFILING VIOLENT CRIMES

An Investigative Tool

Third Edition

RONALD M. HOLMES • **STEPHEN T. HOLMES**
University of Louisville   *University of Central Florida*

SAGE Publications
International Educational and Professional Publisher
Thousand Oaks ▪ London ▪ New Delhi

For information:

Sage Publications, Inc.
2455 Teller Road
Thousand Oaks, California 91320
E-mail: order@sagepub.com

Sage Publications Ltd.
6 Bonhill Street
London EC2A 4PU
United Kingdom

Sage Publications India Pvt. Ltd.
M-32 Market
Greater Kailash I
New Delhi 110 048 India

Printed in the United States of America

Library of Congress Cataloging-in-Publication Data

Holmes, Ronald M.
  Profiling violent crimes: An investigative tool / Ronald M. Holmes,
Stephen T. Holmes.—3rd ed.
    p. cm.
  ISBN 0-7619-2593-7 (c)
  ISBN 0-7619-2594-5 (p)
  1. Criminal investigation—Psychological aspects. 2. Criminal
behavior—Research—Methodology. 3. Criminal
methods—Research—Methodology—Case studies. I. Holmes, Stephen T. II.
Title.
  HV8073.5 .H65 2002
  364.3—dc21

                                                        2002000283

This book is printed on acid-free paper.

  03 04 05 10 9 8 7 6 5 4 3 2

CONTENTS

PREFACE AND ACKNOWLEDGMENTS   ix

1. PSYCHOLOGICAL PROFILING: AN INTRODUCTION   1

Inductive Versus Deductive Profiling   5
Goals in Profiling   7
Profiling: An Art, Not a Science   10
Conclusion   15

2. PROFILING IN FANTASY AND FACT   16

Sherlock Holmes: The Master Detective   16
Will Graham and *Red Dragon*   18
Clarice Starling and *The Silence of the Lambs*   20
Zoe Koehler: A Female Serial Murderer   21
Dr. Laszlo Kreizler: *The Alienist* and *The Angel of Darkness*   23
Other Works of Fiction and Psychological Profiling   23
Profiling in Fact   25
Profile of a Rape Case   31
An Actual Profile: Mrs. Charlene L. Miller   32
Conclusion   35

3. THE RATIONALE FOR PSYCHOLOGICAL PROFILING   37

Personality and Crime   37
New Ways of Viewing the Personality   40
Assumptions of the Profiling Process   40
Conclusion   46

4. CRIMINAL THEORIES AND PSYCHOLOGICAL PROFILING   47

   Theories of Crime and Criminality   49
   Individual Theories of Crime   50
   Social and Ecological Theories of Crime   65
   Combining the Disciplines   68
   Key Terms   69

5. ANALYZING THE CRIME SCENE   71

   Beyond the Physical Evidence   71
   Psychological Profiling Typology   72
   Crime Scene Differences   80
   Conclusion   84

6. ARSON AND PSYCHOLOGICAL PROFILING   85

   What Is Arson?   85
   Statistics on Arson   87
   A View of the Firesetter   89
   Typologies of Firesetters   90
   The Pyromaniac's Firesetting Experience   98
   Types of Arsonists   100
   Organized Versus Disorganized Personality   104
   Conclusion   108

7. PROFILING SERIAL MURDERERS   109

   Typology of Serial Murderers   110
   Spatial Mobility of Serial Killers   111
   Serial Murderers: General Characteristics   115
   Profiling a Serial Murder Case   126
   Conclusion   137

8. PSYCHOLOGICAL PROFILING AND RAPE   139

   Definitions of Rape   139
   Statistics on Rape   140
   Selected Characteristics of Rapists   142
   Psychology and Rape   143
   Typology of Rapists   144
   Conclusion   157

9. PEDOPHILIA AND PSYCHOLOGICAL PROFILING   158

Child Molester or Pedophile   158
Types of Pedophiles   161
Profiling Child Molester Types   168
Conclusion   171

10. AUTOEROTICISM   172

What Is Autoerotic Sex Behavior?   173
Traits and Characteristics of Autoerotic Practitioners   176
Autoerotic Scene Indicators   179
Evidence of Past Autoerotic Behaviors   182
Conclusion   184

11. PROFILING SATANIC AND CULT-RELATED MURDERS   185

Roots of Satanism   186
Satanism in the United States   186
The Satanic Bible   187
Types of Personal Involvement in Satanism   188
General Beliefs in Satanism   195
Satanic Masses   199
Satanic Ceremonies   200
Crime Scene Elements   202
Conclusion   206

12. GEOGRAPHY, PROFILING, AND PREDATORY CRIMINALS   208

The Role of Geography   208
The Nature of Geographic Profiling   215
Computerized Geographical Analyses   220
Conclusion   222

13. JACK THE RIPPER: A CASE FOR PSYCHOLOGICAL PROFILING   223

Victim: Mary Ann "Polly" Nichols   224
Victim: Annie Chapman   228
Victim: Elizabeth Stride   231
Victim: Catharine Eddowes   234
Victim: Mary Kelly   236
Who Was Jack the Ripper?   240
Conclusion   242

14. JONBENET RAMSEY: THE MURDER OF A BEAUTY QUEEN   **243**

The Principal Players in the Ramsey Murder Case   243

The Morning of the Murder, December 26, 1996   247

Aftermath of the Investigation   255

The Autopsy Report   255

Conclusion   266

15. THE VICTIM IN PSYCHOLOGICAL PROFILING   **268**

Elements in the Victim Profiling Process   268

Conclusion   274

16. PROFILING AND THE FUTURE   **275**

Additional Uses for Profiling   275

Education and Training for Profiling   276

Computerized Monitoring   277

Computerized Profiling   279

Conclusion   279

REFERENCES   **281**

INDEX   **292**

ABOUT THE AUTHORS   **299**

PREFACE AND ACKNOWLEDGMENTS

Within the past 20 years, interest in psychological profiling has increased. If profiling had ever been expected to resolve all difficulties in bringing to justice the perpetrators of violent personal crimes, it would be classified as an abject failure. In its role as yet another forensic tool to complement thorough investigation by competent and educated law enforcement professionals, however, it can be very useful.

Profiling has been practiced on many levels for years. Hitler was profiled in the latter days of World War II. The Boston Strangler and Mad Bomber were both profiled, with different degrees of accuracy. Fictional murderers have maintained the popularity of profiling for years. Such detectives as Sherlock Holmes, Charlie Chan, and Will Graham, the retired federal agent in Thomas Harris' novel *Red Dragon* (1981), are as popular today as ever. Over the past several years, law enforcement agencies have begun to recognize the possible benefits of profiling. Even in 2001, when the Metro Police Department of Washington, D.C. had no leads to investigate in the disappearance of Chandra Levy, they turned to profilers.

During the past several years, we have profiled more than 600 homicide and rape cases, almost all of which were submitted by police agencies. Although this may appear to be a shift in the faith of these officers in the ability of profilers, it must be said that these same agencies seek help from astrologers, psychics, and others who enjoy a similar dubious reputation with many in the general public and criminal justice system.

Despite the reputation of many profilers in the business today, we have and will continue to combine the knowledge of both social and forensic sciences. Although no profile is entirely accurate, we have done surprisingly well given the limited information contained in many of the case files that we have worked on. This is not to say that we are special by any means. Rather, it simply means that by relying on common sense, a keen sense of perception, and an understanding of aberrant behavior, we have been successful. This is not a skill that we have developed on our own. There have been many people who have shed light on what to look for and what not to focus on. These people have included numerous police officers, homicide detectives, fellow academics, and many offenders in prison convicted of a plethora of violent offenses. Our interviews have probably taught us more about the ability of getting inside of the perpetrators head than any other source. After all, because we do think of ourselves as rational people (although some would argue that), it is difficult—if not impossible—to understand the actions and behaviors of the irrational unless it is explained to you in lay terms.

We would also like readers of this volume to note that throughout the text we often use the term psychological profiling; however, what we mean is *sociopsychological* profiling. We attach the prefix *socio* because what a thorough profile offers is more than a personality sketch. A thorough profile includes sociodemographic data, which are not usually part of the classic definition of psychological profiling. Age, race, gender, occupation, education, and other factors make up the *social core variables* addressed in the profiling process. Because *sociopsychological* is rather a large and unwieldy term, in this volume we often refer to it as simply *psychological profiling*. The reader should keep that in mind.

Since the first edition of this book, much has changed. In this edition we have beefed up the theory chapter, added chapters on autoeroticism, satanic and cult related murders, and added a separate chapter on the victims so that readers will not become callous to the true nature of the crimes that many of these violent criminals commit. We have also included two chapters on famous unresolved crimes: the Jack the Ripper and the JonBenet Ramsey cases. In these chapters we make no assessment but rather leave it up to the readers to construct their own profiles of the killer based on the evidence presented. We think that these changes not only strengthen this edition but make it useful for our audience as they begin to hone their own profiling skills.

Finally, no work of this nature takes place in a vacuum. Special people deserve special thanks: Dr. Al Carlisle, Utah State Prison; Jerry

Thompson [Retired], Salt Lake County (Utah) Sheriff's Department; Norman Pomrenke, former director of the Southern Police Institute; Jim Massie, Kentucky Parole Office; Don Patchen [Retired], Tallahassee Police Department; Sergeant David Rivers [Retired], Metro Dade (Florida) Police Department; Corporal Jay F. Whitt, Greensboro (North Carolina) Police Department; Lieutenant George Barrett, Louisville (Kentucky) Police Department; Sheriff Charles Cox, Miami (Ohio) Sheriff's Office; Eric Hickey, California State University, Fresno; Steve Egger, Illinois State University; David Fabianic and Bernie McCarthy of the University of Central Florida; Robert Langworthy of the University of Alaska, Anchorage; and Drs. Edward Latessa, James Frank, and Lawrence Travis of the University of Cincinnati. If there are others whom we have neglected to list, we are sorry.

In addition, we have also gained a great deal of insight into crimes of a violent nature from the offenders themselves. Ted Bundy, Douglas Clark, and others have given us tremendous understanding into the minds of the very violent. Other incarcerated offenders to whom we have written and corresponded have given us more insight than could have ever been gleaned from academic texts.

It is our sincere hope that the information in this book will aid those who must investigate various types of predatory crimes. If it helps in just one case, then it was indeed worth the effort.

Ronald M. Holmes
Stephen T. Holmes

PSYCHOLOGICAL PROFILING

An Introduction

Historically, crime and criminals have galvanized the attention of law-abiding citizens. Whatever the reason—be it the romance of a Capone or a Dillinger, or the utter lack of any understanding of how or why criminals can do what they do—books, TV, and movies flood the market with police and crime. Russell Vorpagel, an ex-FBI agent, speaks of his own contributions to the development of psychological profiling in his early years with the FBI (Vorpagel, 1998). According to his testimony, he along with Ressler, Douglas, and others were pioneers in the process of crime scene analysis. Indeed, Vorpagel claims in his book *Profiles in Murder: An FBI Legend Dissects Killers and Their Crimes* (1998) that he was instrumental in helping Detective Ray Biondi in Sacramento, California, with the Richard Trenton Chase murder case. Unfortunately, Vorpagel was not able to profile Chase's suicide by pills while in Vacaville prison.

Robert Ressler, another retired FBI agent, discusses the same case of Richard Chase in his book coauthored with Tom Shachtman, *Whoever Fights Monsters* (1992), but with only one line devoted to the help of Vorpagel in developing a separate profile—amazingly similar to Ressler's profile. "The fact that Chase so precisely fit the profile (of Chase) that I had drawn up in conjunction with Russ Vorpagel was gratifying to me" (Ressler & Shachtman, 1992, p. 9). Ressler continues to mention other serial killers such as Ted Bundy, John Wayne Gacy, David Berkowitz, Edmund Kemper, Peter Sutcliffe, Jeffrey Dahmer, and mass killer Richard Speck. Unfortunately, there is no mention of an interviewing methodology of the meetings. Ressler has published another book, also with Shachtman, called *I Have Lived in the Monster: Inside the Minds of*

1

the World's Most Notorious Serial Killers (Ressler & Shachtman, 1997). In this book, interesting stories abound that relate to Ressler's career in the FBI and his work with many serial killers during his career.

Not to be outdone, John Douglas and his coauthor Mark Olshaker wrote *Mind Hunter: Inside the FBI's Elite Serial Crime Unit* (Douglas & Olshaker, 1995). In this book, Douglas lays claim to a friendship with Tom Harris, the author of *Red Dragon, The Silence of the Lambs*, and *Hannibal* (Harris, 1981, 1988, 1999). He takes the reader along the steps in his work in several major cases and the effects that the profiling work has on mind and health. The book jacket claims that he is the model for Jack Crawford in *The Silence of the Lambs*, a claim that Harris denies (T. Harris, personal communication, June 20, 2000). The book jacket also claims that Douglas has interviewed dozens of serial killers and assassins—including Richard Speck, Charles Manson, and James Earl Ray. He has published two other books, *The Cases That Haunt Us: From Jack the Ripper to JonBenet Ramsey, the FBI's Legendary Mindhunter Sheds Light on the Mysteries That Won't Go Away* and *The Anatomy of Motive: The FBI's Legendary Mindhunter Explores the Key to Understanding and Catching Violent Criminals* (Douglas & Olshaker, 1999, 2000). Both books address Douglas's law enforcement career and his involvement with serial murderers. In *The Cases That Haunt Us*, Douglas and Olshaker lead the reader through several celebrated unsolved homicides; one is the JonBenet Ramsey case. Douglas offers reasons for his belief that JonBenet's parents were not involved in the murder of the young beauty queen. He reacts with some vigor to the criticisms of his own professionalism and to the criticism of his former colleagues in the FBI. He also offers a profile of his own on the infamous Jack the Ripper case.

The Evil That Men Do: FBI Profiler Roy Hazelwood's Journey Into the Minds of Sexual Predators is another book written by a retired FBI profiler, Roy Hazelwood along with Stephen Michaud (2001). Hazelwood was known as a profiler of sexual predators, especially rapists. In this publication, the reader is once again privy to the special talents of the FBI agents and the manner in which they helped police departments around the world in the successful resolution of their cases.

As profilers, we have met many people involved in the field. Some of these encounters have been pleasant and some not. As a general rule, we have found that those who do not advertise their rates on their Web pages are generally the most reputable. Colleagues like Eric Hickey, Steve Egger, and a few more enjoy favorable reputations in the criminal justice system. Regardless, a tremendous amount of interest surrounds the field of profiling. But we must remember that it is only one tool and by itself has never solved a murder case despite the statements made by some.

Profilers are also seen in the media. These programs illustrate the work of a profiler and how neatly the whole crime is resolved in an hour show. But unlike a vintage Dragnet episode, criminals are not always brought to justice. Every killer is not peacefully arrested with nothing more than an M.O. or a signature of the identity of the perpetrator. This M.O. (method of operation or modus operandi) holds to a basic principle: Each perpetrator commits a crime in a certain manner. Therefore, each time a person commits a crime, it will be done in the same, or at least similar, fashion. This is a prodigious step in logic, but one that has been validated by tradition and common sense, both with less than reliable sources of knowledge.

For the homicide investigator in which the motives of normal killings are absent, a psychological profile may be the investigative tool essential to a successful resolution of the case (Douglas & Burgess, 1986; Douglas, Burgess, Burgess, & Ressler, 1992; Palmiotto, 1994; Sears, 1991). How accurate are the profiles? This will obviously depend on the expertise of the persons involved in such an assessment. Kocsis, Orwin, and Hayes (2000) reported that when they compared how five different groups studied crimes—(a) 5 professional profilers, (b) 35 police officers, (c) 30 psychologists, (d) 31 students, and (e) 20 self-declared psychics—profilers appear to have higher skills. That the psychologists ranked second in the study suggested that psychologists were better at this endeavor than police officers, perhaps because of their understanding of human behavior. Psychics were the least reliable of the groups. They apparently depended more on the stereotypes of murderers than of a true understanding of the mind and mentality of a killer. Police probably would do better at profiling if they were educated in the principles of the process (Peterson, 1997).

Thus profiling, or criminal investigation assessment, is an educated attempt to provide investigative agencies with specific information about the type of individual who committed a certain crime (Gerberth, 1981, p. 46). Of course, profiles are not suitable in all cases, even in some murder cases (Holmes & Holmes, 1992, 2000). They are usually more efficacious in cases in which an unknown perpetrator has displayed indications of psychopathology (Gerberth, 1981; Holmes & Holmes, 2000). Crimes most appropriate for psychological profiling are those listed in Table 1.1.

TABLE 1.1   Crimes Suitable for Profiling

Suggested crimes for profiling include

Sadistic torture in sexual assaults
Eviscerations
Postmortem cases of slashing and cuttings
Motiveless fire settings
Lust and mutilation murders
Rapes
Occult crimes
Child sexual abuse including pedophilia
Bank robberies
Obscene and terroristic letter writings

SOURCE: From *Practical Homicide Investigation,* by V. Gerberth, 1983, New York: Elsevier. Reprinted with permission.

It is important to come to a general understanding of the type of person who would commit an offense such as lust murder. Inherent within the premise that a profile is valid and reliable is that the person who commits a lust murder, for example, has a personality that reflects pathology. Chaos, the lack of planning, mutilations, and so on all reflect this personality. Therefore, the crime scene itself reflects pathology. As we will mention later in this text, offenders will leave part of themselves at the crime scene. In addition, we have discovered in the crimes we have profiled for various police departments around the world, now at more than 600, that offenders commit their crimes in certain manners. If it is a serial crime, the crimes are similar although not always identical. It is the responsibility of the profiler to offer insight from the physical evidence of the pathology exhibited in the crime scene (Michaud, 1986).

Of course, a good criminal investigative assessment will also depend, to some extent, on the working relationship between the police agency desiring a profile and the profiler. This should be obvious, but nonetheless it is important to state and understand. One reason is that if the police agency has no faith in the process or the profiler, information may not be included that is vital to the profile itself. This omission can be simple negligence or it could be intentional. Ideally, most of the time it is unintentional.

INDUCTIVE VERSUS DEDUCTIVE PROFILING

There are two different postures to develop a profile. One is the inductive approach and the other is the deductive approach. At first glance they seem to be mutually exclusive, but on a closer examination they share some commonalities.

Inductive Criminal Investigative Assessments

The inductive approach to profiling rests with a simple premise, an assumption that if certain crimes committed by different people are similar, then the offenders must also share some common personality traits. The information gathered comes from past crimes, past known offenders, and other sources of information including media reports.

There are obvious advantages to this type of profile. It is quick, inexpensive, and there is no need to blend the academic disciplines of sociology, psychology, criminology, and psychiatry. Thus the profiler does not necessarily need any special skill or knowledge of human behavior. For example, this type of profiler would not need to know some of the early pioneers in the field of psychology such as Sigmund Freud (1856–1939), William James (1842–1910), John Watson (1878–1958), and B.F. Skinner (1904–1990), among others. Their valuable work in human behavior could be ignored. What happens in the inductive approach is that an assessment is offered simply from similar crime scenes.

Deductive Criminal Investigative Assessments

This method is actually slightly different. From a thorough analysis of the crime scene and the evidence left at that scene, the profiler is able to construct a mental picture of the unknown offender. As profilers, we know from experience that one of the most important elements in the analysis of a crime is victimology. Despite requests for the profiling package to include all that is known about the victim, these data are typically deficient. The more one knows about the victim, the more one knows about the offender. Thus, from this perspective, the profile is drawn from the physical and nonphysical evidence (love, hate, rage, and fear).

The profile drawn from this perspective is agonizingly slow. Much care is taken from the examination of forensic reports, victimology, and so forth and the report will take much longer to develop using only this approach. Looking at the crime scene evidence is imperative. This is one problem we have with the profile done for the Ramsey family on the murder of their young daughter, JonBenet. The crime scene was destroyed by the time the profiler was able to develop an assessment. It would have been important to know, for example, the exact positioning of the hands, the manner in which the garrote was found, the position of the body in relationship to the opening of the door to that small room. There are other questions that need to be addressed and the answers only could have been obtained from the examination of the physical evidence present at the scene. The physical evidence will also be some indicator of nonphysical evidence.

For example, in a southern state, an elderly white female was beaten to death in her home. The killer had been in the home when she returned from a night out with two companions. As she undressed in her unlit bedroom, the killer came on her from the back, hit her over the head, and bludgeoned her to death. From the crime scene it was apparent that the killer had been there for some time, perhaps knowing he would have to await her return from an evening of entertainment in town. He had a bottle of wine sitting in the hallway and it was uncorked. The victim, however, was known as a very clean housekeeper and would not have left a container of spirits in the hallway. The killer not only felt comfortable enough to drink some of the wine, he also apparently knew where the bottle had been kept in the pantry. Before the victim came home, the killer went into the bedroom and placed framed pictures of the victim's nieces and nephews facedown. When she arrived, he was hiding in a corner of the bedroom before he killed her.

From the description of this crime scene, it is easy to see a combination of inductive and deductive reasoning. Knowing something of the academic disciplines of psychology, sociology, criminology, and psychiatry, a clear picture of the mind and mentality of the unknown killer appears. Also, we can gather some information from other cases that involve elderly females. Because we know there was no sexual assault, we can presume that the victim was killed by a close friend or relative. Coupled with the facedown picture frames, other cases of this type, although not completely alike, can educate us to the possible identity of the perpetrator.

Ideally, then, we can use both methods to develop a psychological profile. It is important to use both methods simply because there are benefits to both. One may be quicker to develop whereas the other takes more time but can more thoroughly evaluate the unknown offender, thereby differentiating him or her from the other offenders who have committed similar crimes. Both the deductive approach and the inductive approach have assets to bring to an assessment. With the deductive approach, for example, one assumption is that any crime is accompanied by a fantasy. When examining the forensic evidence at one particular crime scene, a profiler can link that evidence to similar findings at other crime scenes in which the crimes have been solved. Using the deductive method, the profiler can "interpret" the crime scene and thus examine the fantasy present in the crime scene itself.

Although inductive profiling may not be as reliable as the deductive method, there is no reason to ignore the possible benefits derived from the use of this method. Combining the benefits of both is truly the correct response.

GOALS IN PROFILING

Some confusion arises when the topics of goals and objectives are discussed. Simply stated, goals are broad general statements of what is to be accomplished. Objectives are specific, measurable statements to be accomplished in a given time (Craig, 1980, p. 24). Goals are usually statements individuals or organizations offer to direct their efforts toward some reward. Obviously, these efforts take varied forms. It may be a certain number of units manufactured in a given time period or a number of violent personal crimes cleared by arrests. Objectives are means used to satisfy the goals of the organizations. Moreover, objectives must be measurable.

Goals in profiling are not distinctly unique. They exist to aid the criminal justice system in its battle against crime. As such, there are three major goals.

Goal 1: To provide the criminal justice system with a social and psychological assessment of the offender.   The purpose of this goal is very simple. It should contain basic and sound information concerning the social and psychological core variables of the offender's personality. This assessment should include race, age range, employment, religion, marital status, education, and so on.

This psychological packet will focus the investigation. Instead of dealing with a wide range of possible perpetrators, the profile will reduce the scope of the investigation. This will have a direct affect on the number of days and weeks spent on the case by positioning the police toward a successful resolution. A profile contains information that alerts the law enforcement professional to the possible psychological traits present in a crime scene. It can predict future possible attacks as well as probable sites of attacks.

Case Study

Recently a profile was completed for a police department in a southern city where in the course of four months four young women were attacked, their throats cut, and then murdered. None of the four women were sexually molested but there were several commonalities.

The profile offered information about the age, education, residence, and a predicted time when the perpetrator would strike again. The profile was accurate even to the day that the next attack would occur. The police department, with confidence in the profiling packet, redoubled their efforts with the positive benefit of the apprehension of the attacker on the night predicted.

Goal 2: To provide the criminal justice system with a psychological evaluation of belongings found in the possession of the offender. This particular goal is very important to investigators when they have a prime suspect. It may be that all of the physical evidence, witness reports, and all pertinent information point toward one suspect. The psychological profile may suggest items the offenders may have in their possession: souvenirs, photos, pornography, and so on. These items will serve as a reminder of the violent episode. In the case of a serial pedophile, for instance, we are very familiar with pedophiles' child pornography collections. By analyzing the collection, the profiler can offer the police interrogator a plan to interview the alleged offender about the choice of victim, seduction or capturing strategies, and other pertinent information gleaned from the collateral evidence found in the possession of the charged offender. This same statement can be said of other types of offenders undergoing interrogation, offenders such as arsonists, serial killers, rapists, and so forth.

Case Study

Jerry Brudos is a serial killer presently in Oregon State Penitentiary for the brutal and sadistic killing of young women in the late 1960s. Jerry has a shoe fetish. He stole a pair of high-heeled black shoes during the course of a robbery and rape. He often wore the shoes around his home and demanded his wife do the same. One victim, a young National Merit scholar, was forced to wear the shoes even as Brudos hung her from the rafter in his garage. In addition, Brudos was involved in triolism, a sexual behavior in which sexual gratification is gained by seeing oneself, others, or both in sexual scenes. Combining his transvestism with triolism, Brudos took pictures of himself wearing the high-heeled shoes, panties, bra, and stockings. He also took pictures of his wife nude and photographed three of his four victims. One victim was already dead when he photographed her (Stack, 1983).

If profiling had been popular and used by the Salem Police Department, such a profile might have alerted the police to the possibility of finding souvenirs or trophies in the possession of Brudos. This physical evidence, if listed on a search warrant, could have been invaluable at his trial. It might have also alerted police to the possibility of film that might display nude females or other suspicious pictures coming through local businesses for development. As it did transpire, Brudos convinced his wife that she could pose for him in the nude because "big labs process too much film to look at every picture. . . . They look at the first or the last and that's all" (Stack, 1983, p. 33). Brudos apparently used this same subjective rationale when he photographed his victims.

Goal 3: To provide interviewing suggestions and strategies.   Once a subject is apprehended, a profile packet should contain information regarding proper and effective methods of interviewing and interrogation. This can be crucial. The profile packet should contain information regarding different personalities and effective strategies in soliciting information from a diverse group of offenders. Not all people react to questioning in the same fashion. For one type of offender, one strategy may be effective, but it is a mistake to assume all offenders will respond to the same interviewing strategy. For example, not all serial murderers kill for the same reason and not all respond to the same type of interviewing strategy. Violent personal offenders also vary with their motives as well as their responses to interrogation.

Case Study

In a small midwestern town, 15-year-old Diana Harris and her boyfriend were shot. Their bodies were found in his car parked in a lonely lovers' lane area. She died of one shot to the left temple and her male companion was mortally wounded with a single shot entering under his left armpit. One additional bullet was fired through the passenger side window. No physical evidence other than the bullets was obtained.

The police department investigated this case thoroughly but unsuccessfully. After talking with the mother and stepfather, one detective believed that the stepfather was not telling all he knew. Most people feared Mr. Harris. A football coach, he carried himself in such a manner that defied anyone to doubt his virility, masculinity, or intelligence.

The detective interviewed the stepfather about the case. After questioning him for several hours, the police officer asked him pointedly if he had killed his stepdaughter and her boyfriend. Breaking into profuse perspiration, the man replied, "Not in my right mind did I kill them. You'll have to prove that I did." Instead of keeping some pressure on the stepfather, a coffee break was taken. After regrouping himself psychologically, Mr. Harris denied any knowledge or responsibility in this case. All progress stopped, and the investigation came to a halt. All strategies used provided no further information.

Finally, this police department requested direction in the interrogation of Mr. Harris. Suspecting he demanded to be in control but with a flaw in his personality, a far different strategy was offered. The suspect was taken into an interrogation room where pictures of the crime scene lined the four walls. A suggestion was made to the suspect that the police really wanted to solve the crime of the murder of his stepdaughter. Despite all they had done, they were getting nowhere. They needed help. The pictures of the crime scene served as constant reminders of what had occurred, not only to the boy but to Diana as well.

After the suspect believed that he was now in control of the investigation and could offer some helpful suggestions to the police, he became fully engrossed in the case. The more he talked, the more familiar he became with the details of the crime. After more than eight hours, the man broke down and cried. Then the detective resumed his questioning, and the man confessed to the double homicide.

PROFILING: AN ART, NOT A SCIENCE

Not everyone agrees that psychological profiling is of benefit to law enforcement (Jenkins, 1994). Indeed, not all crimes are suitable for the profiling process.

> While virtually any crime showing mental, emotional, or personality aberration can be analyzed for profiling purposes, certain crimes are particularly appropriate for the process; these crimes include a series of rapes, serial murders, child molesting, ritualistic crimes, threat communications, violence in the workplace, and serial arson. (Hazelwood & Burgess, 1995, p. 12)

Some crimes are suitable for profiling. Witness the ongoing murder case of JonBenet Ramsey. The alleged ransom note stated (See Figure 1.1 as well),

Mr. Ramsey,
   Listen carefully! We are a group of individuals that represent a small foreign faction. We respect your business but not the country that it serves. At this time we have your daughter in our possession. She is safe and unharmed and if you want her to see 1997, you must follow our instructions to the letter.
   You will withdraw $118,000.00 from your account. $100,000 will be in $100 bills and the remaining $18,000 in $20 bills. Make sure that you bring an adequate size attaché to the bank. When you get home you will put the money in a brown paper bag. I will call you between 8 and 10 am tomorrow to instruct you on delivery. The delivery will be exhausting so I advise you to be rested. If we monitor you getting the money early, we might call you early to arrange an earlier delivery of the money and hence a [sic] earlier pick-up of your daughter.
   Any deviation of my instructions will result in the immediate execution of your daughter. You will also be denied her remains for proper burial. The two gentlemen watching over your daughter do not particularly like you so I advise you not to provoke them. Speaking to anyone about your situation, such as Police, F.B.I., etc., will result in your daughter being beheaded. If we catch you talking to a stray dog, she dies. If you alert bank authorities, she dies. If the money is in any way marked or tampered with, she dies. You will be scanned for electronic devices and if any are found, she dies. You can try to deceive us but be warned that we are familiar with Law enforcement countermeasures and tactics. You stand a 99% chance of killing your daughter if you try to out smart us. Follow our instructions and you stand a 100% chance of getting her back. You and your family are under constant scrutiny as well as the authorities. Don't try to grow a brain John. You are not the only fat cat around so don't think that killing will be difficult. Don't underestimate us John. Use that good southern common sense of yours. It is up to you now John!
   Victory!
   S.B.T.C.

In a later chapter devoted to the Ramsey slaying, we will share some insights about the note as concerns suspected author, and what exactly is revealed about the writer from a content analysis of the letter itself, as well as some other details. Nonetheless, this letter contains information that is "nonphysical" evidence about the writer as well as the killer of the

(Text continues on page 13)

Mr. Ramsey,

Listen carefully! We are a group of individuals that represent a small foreign faction. We do respect your bussiness but not the country that it serves. At this time we have your daughter in our possesion. She is safe and unharmed and if you want her to see 1997, you must follow our instructions to the letter.

You will withdraw $118,000.00 from your account. $100,000 will be in $100 bills and the remaining $18,000 in $20 bills. Make sure that you bring an adequate size attache to the bank. When you get home you will put the money in a brown paper bag. I will call you between 8 and 10 am tomorrow to instruct you on delivery. The delivery will be exhausting so I advise you to be rested. If we monitor you getting the money early, we might call you early to arrange an earlier delivery of the

---

FIGURE 1.1 JonBenet Ramsey Ransom Note

SOURCE: Brugnatelli, F. (1999, July 4). *Ramsey Case: The Ransom Note* [Web]. Retrieved August 22, 2001, from the World Wide Web: http://web.fiscali.it/fuustobrugnatelli/

money and hence. d earlier delivery pick-up of your daughter. Any deviation of my instructions will result in the immediate execution of your daughter. You will also be denied her remains for proper burial. The two gentlemen watching over your daughter do particularly like you so I advise you not to provoke them. Speaking to anyone about your situation, such as Police, F.B.I., etc., will result in your daughter being beheaded. If we catch you talking to a stray dog, she dies. If you alert bank authorities, she dies. If the money is in any way marked or tampered with, she dies. You will be scanned for electronic devices and if any are found, she dies. You can try to deceive us but be warned that we are familiar with law enforcement countermeasures and tactics. You stand a 99% chance of killing your daughter if you try to out smart us. Follow our instructions

(Continued)

6-year-old beauty queen. Regardless, some may argue that professionals in criminal justice must realize that profiling is at best an art, not a science. It was maintained that (a) the profiles submitted to police departments as gospel testament to the type of offender committing an act of lust (murder,

FIGURE 1.1 (Continued)

and you stand a 100% chance
of getting her back. You and
your Family are under constant
scrutiny as well as the authoritie
Don't try to grow a brain
John. You are not the only
Fat cat around so don't think
that killing will be difficult.
Don't underestimate us John.
Use that good southern common
sense of yours. It is up to
you now John!

Victory!

S. B. T. C

rape, etc.) are probably little better than information one could obtain from the neighborhood bartender; (b) files are either too vague and ambiguous or else they are simple common sense; and (c) as long as police officers are impressed with the credentials, status, and education of the academicians, many academicians will continue to play their education guessing games (Campbell, 1976, pp. 110–119). Vernon Gerberth, a retired homicide commander with the New York Police Department, was misquoted in a newspaper stating that he was not aware of one serial murder case in which a profile led to an arrest. Gerberth said the actual quotation should have read, "Criminal profiling is an excellent law enforcement tool. However, it is just one of many tools and does not replace good investigative techniques. In fact, I don't know of any profile in and by itself that has resulted in an actual arrest" (Gerberth, personal communication, February 6, 1995). Although there may be some truth to this criticism, it is reasonable to expect that the profiler's years of education and training will be of value to law enforcement as it attempts to solve heinous and difficult crimes. But again, we agree with Gerberth. By itself, a profile does not solve any crime. It is only one forensic tool of many that should be used in the investigation of a crime.

There are a few discrete rules by which to adhere when profiling a difficult criminal case. Of course, educated guesses are made. They are, however, aided by knowledge gained from the profiler's experience in the criminal justice system and from familiarity with relevant concepts in criminology, sociology, psychology, and psychiatry. In addition, the profiler is assisted by an intuitive sense in the profiling process. That is, one develops a feel for the crime. This is the art dimension. Nonprofessional sources of information seldom have the mixture of competencies essential for efficient profiling.

CONCLUSION

Obviously, some cases are more suitable and appropriate for psychological profiling than others. The role of the profiler, then, is to assist the police department in its investigations of the cases in which additional aid is sought for the successful resolution of cases such as lust murder, rape, and so on. The successful profiler will blend educational and training backgrounds in order to offer insight into the type of person who would commit a given crime. It is, however, more than a simple list of suspected characteristics. Profilers will keep in mind their roles in assisting the police by fulfilling fundamental processes in the profiling endeavor. These processes, then, are reached as much through education and training as they are through the acquired art and skill in profiling itself.

PROFILING IN FANTASY AND FACT

Crime has long been of interest to popular readers. New crime books are steady additions to the bookshelves of local bookstores. *Hannibal, The Diary of Jack the Ripper, The Cases That Haunt Us*, and many others continue to feed the insatiable reading appetites for true and fictional crime genres (Douglas & Olshaker, 2000; Harris, 1999; Harrison & Maybrick, 1994). Obviously, this is nothing new. Since the 1880s, Sir Arthur Conan Doyle, G. K. Chesterton, Agatha Christie, Earl Biggers, Lawrence Sanders, Thomas Harris, Caleb Carr, Patricia Cornwell, and John Sandford, among others, have written novels that have influenced readers' impressions of criminals and their crimes.

Who are some of these fictional characters that have galvanized our interests in murder and mayhem? Let us examine some of the more popular.

SHERLOCK HOLMES: THE MASTER DETECTIVE

In the late 1800s, just before the horrific crimes of Jack the Ripper, a fictional master detective contributed the skills of his delving mind to police departments and citizens alike in the solving of particularly puzzling and horrible crimes. Accompanied by his good friend and associate, Dr. Watson, Sherlock Holmes solved case after case, rarely failing. This point is illustrated in Holmes's dialogue with a young wife who, in one story, asks his help.

Wife: He [Major Prendergast] said that you could solve anything.
Holmes: He said too much.
Wife: That you are never beaten.
Holmes: I have been beaten four times—three times by men, and once by a woman.

Wife: But what is that compared with the number of your successes?
Holmes: It is true that I have been generally successful. (Doyle, 1891c,
         p. 70)

Holmes solved his cases by deduction (note our descriptions of the inductive and the deductive methods described in the previous chapter). He recognized things that others missed. His colleague, Dr. Watson, was constantly amazed by what Holmes was able to see, many times recognizing the nonphysical evidence as presented through the physical evidence.

Watson says,

> But I was always impressed with a sense of my own stupidity in my dealings with Sherlock Holmes. Here I had heard what he had heard, I had seen what he had seen, and yet by his words it was evident that he saw clearly not only what had happened, but what was about to happen. (Doyle, 1891d, p. 35)

The consummate detective, Holmes took note of evidence that others neglected. On many occasions he remarked, "Perhaps I have trained myself to see what others overlook" (Doyle, 1891b, p. 42).

Sherlock Holmes maintained that the educated and trained mind of the detective is the most important forensic tool in the resolution of a crime. The master detective investigated his cases with great care, examining each minute detail. In *The Basecombe Valley Mystery*, for example, Holmes deduced from the manner in which a man has been struck over his left shoulder that the perpetrator is left handed and walks with a limp. When Holmes explains to Watson how he has reached this conclusion, the good doctor is once again astounded by what Holmes has seen and he (Watson) has not (Doyle, 1891a).

In *The Man With the Twister Lip*, Holmes investigates the case of a missing husband. One clue centers on the manner in which a letter has been addressed:

Holmes: I perceive that whoever addressed the envelope had to
                  go and inquire as to the address.
Mrs. St. Claire: How can you tell?
Holmes: The name, you see, is in perfectly black ink, which has
                  dried itself. The rest is of the grayish color which shows
                  that blotting paper has been used. If it had been written

> straight off, and then blotted, none would be the deep black shade. This man has written the name and there has then been a pause before he wrote the address, which can only mean that he was not familiar with it. (Doyle, 1891e, p. 89)

Holmes amazes not only Watson but also the missing man's wife with this observation. He notes confidently, perhaps arrogantly, that the letter is only a trifle, "but there is nothing so important as trifles" (Doyle, 1891e, p. 89).

The gift of Sherlock Holmes is his attention to detail. The physical scene, or the crime scene, is more than simply a site of an accumulation of evidence; a synergism arises from the interaction of offender, the victim, and the scene. A forensic anthropologist may be able to tell the height, weight, and even the race of an offender from a footprint, but a footprint says nothing of the offender's personality. It is imperative for the investigators to examine nonphysical evidence because it adds to the quality of the scene. From a profiling point of view, both physical and nonphysical evidence can provide clues to the offender's personality.

Holmes never reached the point at which he could be described as a psychological profiler. This is due in no small part to the influence of the school of criminology in vogue at the time. The classical school of criminology, which was quickly followed by the positive school, laid the theoretical groundwork for the assumption that humans are in complete control of their actions. Under positive school thinking, people were thought to become criminal because of the "savage genes" from their "savage ancestors" or other constitutional (or physical) factors (Ferrero-Lombroso, 1911). If the psychodynamic model had been better known and accepted at the time, Sherlock Holmes no doubt would have been more heavily involved in the psychological analysis of the criminals he investigated.

WILL GRAHAM AND *RED DRAGON*

Thomas Harris has written a terrifying novel about a serial murderer that is more than an explanation of the mind of a killer. Terrifying and strange, bizarre yet compelling, *Red Dragon* examines the psychological and mystical relationship between the killer, Francis Dolarhyde, and his profiler, Will Graham (Harris, 1981).

As the novel opens, Graham is a retired FBI agent living in Marathon Island, Florida, with his wife and stepson. Before his retirement, he was involved in a murder investigation so intense that it resulted in his leaving the Bureau. However, a friend and former coworker prevails on him to come out of retirement to undertake one last case, the case of the Red Dragon, a serial killer. Harris takes the reader inside the mind of the profiler as Graham goes to the crime scenes, one in Atlanta and the other in Birmingham, Alabama.

In Atlanta, the Leeds family has been killed, both parents and three children. The killer placed the children facing the bed, their backs to the wall. The parents were found in their own bed. Mr. Leeds was bound, tied to the headboard, and his throat was slashed.

After examining the Leeds home crime scene, Graham returns to his motel room, where he mentally reconstructs the crime. The eyes of the victims were open; Graham thinks, "Were they 'witnesses' to the killings? Were they an audience?" Recalling a lit candle in the bedroom, Graham thinks about how its glimmering light may have served as a visual facilitator of horror. "The flickering light would simulate expression in their faces" (Harris, 1981, p. 29). Carrying on a mental conversation with the unknown killer, Graham asks,

> Why did you move them [the children] again? Why didn't you leave them that way? There's something you don't want me to know about you. Why, there's something you're ashamed of. Or is it something you can't afford for me to know?
>
> Did you open their eyes?
>
> Mrs. Leeds was lovely, wasn't she? You turned on the light after you cut his throat so Mrs. Leeds could watch him flop, didn't you? It was maddening to have to wear gloves when you touched her, wasn't it? (Harris, 1981, p. 29)

Totally immersed in the multiple killings of the two families, Graham creates a profile of the killer that helps to narrow the scope of the investigation and provides a structure on which to base an understanding of the killer's personality. With sophisticated police technology, including techniques not currently in the repertoire in the real world of forensics, the Red Dragon is eventually brought to justice in a rather unusual way.

No other novel, in our opinion, gives the reader such vivid and realistic insight into the mind of the profiler, despite the retorts of former FBI agents. Although it is a work of fiction, it illustrates well the introspective nature, the art that the process of profiling requires. *Red Dragon* provides a fictional introduction to the real world of profiling and to the art involved in the profiler's immersion in a case. In this novel, there is little hard science to the profiling process; Graham proceeds for the most part based on his feelings, and these feelings almost destroy him.

Will Graham becomes personally involved in the Red Dragon case. He loses his objectivity. He becomes so intimately involved that he carries on conversations with the unknown and unseen perpetrator as well as with the victims. He believes in the need to go to the crime scene because there still lingers a "shadow" of the crime. Photographs, written reports, witness statements, and so on almost lead to fatal consequences, not only for Graham, but for his family as well.

CLARICE STARLING AND *THE SILENCE OF THE LAMBS*

In Harris's next book, *The Silence of the Lambs*, Will Graham has apparently returned to Marathon Island, just a few miles from Key West (Harris, 1988). The book opens at the FBI Academy at Quantico. Clarice Starling has been called to the section chief's office. Jack Crawford remembers her as a graduate student when he lectured at a criminology seminar at the University of Virginia. He has called this agent-in-training to aid him by interviewing Dr. Hannibal Lecter, the infamous cannibal and serial killer. A psychiatrist, Lecter is in prison and anticipates no release from his cell.

Starling and Lecter develop a strange relationship, and he offers her some information about a particular murder case. Meanwhile, her relationship with Crawford deepens and she learns some concepts and precepts of the profiling process from both. Another murder occurs in Potter, West Virginia. This killing has some similarities to other known killers already incarcerated.

Standing next to the body, Crawford asks Starling,

> "What do you see, Starling?"
> "Well, she's not a local—her ears are pierced three times each, and she wore glitter polish. She got maybe two weeks or so hair growth on her legs. And see how soft it's grown in. I think she got her legs waxed. Armpits too. Look how she bleached the fuzz on her upper lip. She was

pretty careful about herself, but she hasn't been able to take care of it for a while." (Harris, 1988, p. 76)

With these few observations gleaned from the physical evidence, the scope of the investigation narrows slightly. Starling is starting to learn her trade as a profiler and this assists her in tracking down Jame Gumb, aka Buffalo Bill. These traits dissipate in the next book, *Hannibal,* because of her emerging personal relationship with Lecter.

In this book, the reader is alerted to the role of physical evidence as it contributes to the psychological profile. Certainly, the FBI would not send an agent-in-training to interview a serial killer such as Lecter. This criticism is often aimed at Harris, but in his defense, and he is our personal friend, this is a work of fiction. Starling is viewed as a neophyte, with no real experience in law enforcement, although her dead father was a former sheriff in West Virginia who was killed in the line of duty. She quickly learns from two professionals: One is the section chief and the other is a psychiatrist and serial killer.

ZOE KOEHLER: A FEMALE SERIAL MURDERER

Lawrence Sanders's novel, *The Third Deadly Sin,* is the story of Zoe Koehler, a woman with a deep fantasy life that involves the killings of male strangers (Sanders, 1981). Zoe has never really come to terms with her female identity and there is a hidden part of her personality that no one but her victims has seen. She works in an office during the day, arrives at work daily on time, eats her lunch at her desk, and goes home to an empty apartment. She has felt rejection all her life. Her father psychologically isolated himself from her in her childhood and her husband deserted her after only a few years of marriage. Further, the millions of men in her city barely acknowledge her existence.

Zoe's painful menstrual periods announce a metamorphosis during which she changes from a nondescript entity to a killer. She changes from her drab work clothes to seductive clothing, transforming her appearance further with a wig, and travels across town to cocktail lounges at convention sites. (Because she works at a hotel, she is aware of the various conventions in town at any given time.) She allows herself to be picked up and accompanies the man to his room, where he anticipates a sexual encounter. In one such incident, after Zoe and her victim went to his room, she says, "I have to make wee-wee and then I'll come back to you.

I'll do anything you want. And I mean anything" (Sanders, 1981, p. 34).
After removing her clothes, she returns to the room holding a Swiss
Army Knife beneath the towel she is carrying. She plunges the knife into
the man's neck.

> [The victim] made a sound, a gargle, and his heavy body leaped con-
> vulsively from the bed. Blood spouted in streams, gobbets, a flood that
> sprayed the air with a crimson fog. It soaked the bed, dripped onto the
> floor.
> With bloodied, slippery hand, she drove the knife blade again and
> again into his genitals. No triumph or exultation in her face. Not grin-
> ning or yowling, but intent and businesslike. Saying aloud with each
> stab, "There. There." (Sanders, 1981, p. 34)

Edward X. Delaney, a central figure in several of Sanders's novels, is
a retired detective from New York's finest who serves as a special consultant to the police department. Delany, an amateur profiler, assumes an
unofficial posture in investigating the "Hotel Ripper Case" He tells his
wife that he suspects the killer is a woman. He says,

> All I'm trying to do is to put together a profile. Not a psychological
> profile—those things are usually pure bullshit. I'm trying to give the
> killer certain personal and emotional characteristics that give us a more
> accurate picture of the kind of woman she is. (Sanders, 1981, p. 200)

Despite his protests concerning the nature of profiling, Delaney
develops a psychological profile of the unknown suspect. He offers a picture of a woman, 5' 5" to 5' 7" tall, "probably a young woman, say in the
area of eighteen to forty" (Sanders, 1981, p. 200). How does he come up
with this age range? "She's strong enough to rip a man's throat and she's
young enough to have menstrual periods" (p. 200). Because the killings
occur monthly, 26 days apart, Delany connects the murders with a
woman's menstrual cycle. Using practical reasoning, Delany continues.
He decides she must be intelligent; she carefully plans each act, washes
the evidence away, and leaves no fingerprints. In addition, he believes the
killer dresses conservatively, acts in a conservative fashion, and is probably "mousy. Until she breaks out and kills" (p. 328).

Delaney's profile is accurate. It has led the police to narrow the investigation and finally to obtain an arrest warrant for the murderer. They are
too late, however; they find her dead alongside a lover.

DR. LASZLO KREIZLER:
THE ALIENIST AND *THE ANGEL OF DARKNESS*

Caleb Carr has written a fascinating novel about killing and psychological profiling (Carr, 1994). In *The Alienist*, a profile is developed of an unknown child killer. The character of Dr. Kreizler is trying to get inside the mind of the serial killer. He and his inner circle of friends brainstorm in their developing of a profile.

> "I don't understand," I said, "Why would the murderer cut their throats if he'd already strangled them?"
> "Blood lust," Marcus answered, very matter-of-factly, as he ate his soup.
> "Yes, blood lust," Lucius agreed. "He was probably concerned with keeping his clothes clean so that he wouldn't attract any attention during the escape. He needed to see the blood—or maybe smell it. Some murderers have said it's the smell rather than the sight that satisfies them." (Carr, 1994, p. 100)

The profile continues. The profilers believe the killer's mother was unloving, rejecting, and uncaring, and that the killer has some kind of deformity having to do with the eyes. The profile proves accurate and the killer is eventually brought to justice.

In his next book, *The Angel of Darkness*, the story is told from the perspective of Kreizler's young protégé (Carr, 1997). The doctor again offers a profile throughout the book that is changed as his friend, the detective, feeds him with more information. The profile leads the reader to a point where the killer is better understood as a murderous personality.

Although the stories are set in the late 1800s, psychodynamic information becomes a part of the profile. But the later developments that have made profiling more than simply an educated "guessing game" are missing from the considerations of Dr. Kreizler. But considering the time and the crimes, the profile in fiction is an enlightening and educational experience.

OTHER WORKS OF FICTION
AND PSYCHOLOGICAL PROFILING

Perhaps one of the most intriguing works of fiction concerning murder, mayhem, and profiling are the works of John Sandford. His *Prey* series is alive with the work of his protagonist, Lucas Davenport, a wealthy detective with the Minneapolis Police Department (Sandford, 1994, 1995, 1997, 1998, 1999, 2000, 2001). Earning his wealth from the development of software, Davenport uses his knowledge of the human condition and the hard sciences and applies them to homicide cases. Davenport offers various profiles of the killers. For example, in *Chosen Prey* (2001), Davenport examines the "cemetery" that the unknown serial killer has made. He knows the killer's "ideal victim type" and shares his thoughts with his police investigators and his girlfriend, Weather. The profile is not a written document but a working mental picture of the type of person they are looking for. *Secret Prey* and *Certain Prey* follow this same basic format. The detective is just as concerned with the physical evidence as well as the nonphysical evidence; they both blend and point to an offender, presently loose but soon to be captured.

Patricia Cornwell has invited us all to join in the fight to eradicate crime through the efforts of Dr. Kay Scarpetta, a medical examiner in Virginia. Dr. Scarpetta is both a physician and an attorney. In books such as *Post-Mortem, From Potter's Field, Black Notice,* and others, Scarpetta investigates crime along with her detective partner, Pete Marino (Cornwell, 1991, 1996, 1999). Looking at the physical evidence at the crime scene, the corpse, or what the evidence suggests, Scarpetta and Marino are able to look at crimes and make a profile of the unknown subject.

In *Roses Are Red*, psychologist and homicide detective Dr. Alex Cross takes on a new criminal, The Mastermind (Patterson, 2000). An antagonist, this criminal genius is responsible for bank robberies and murders. Pairing with a young FBI agent, Cross offers a profile.

> Here's what we know now. A single man placed the Citibank, First Union, First Virginia, and Chase robberies and murders. We know he's selecting crew members that are willing to kill. He's only interested in recruiting killers.
>
> Our profile tells us he's a white male between thirty-five and fifty. He's probably well-educated, with a thorough knowledge of banks and their security systems. He may have worked for a financial institution in the past, or even more than one, and might have a grudge against them. He robs banks for the money, but the murders are probably for revenge.

As the story develops, the "mini" profile proves fairly accurate. Although The Mastermind is not apprehended, his identity becomes known to the reader as one of the FBI agents.

PROFILING IN FACT

In a novel, the successful resolution of a murder is usually neatly reached. Too often, the reader notes that the crime is cleanly solved in the last page or two. Unfortunately, profiling in fact does not always yield the same result. Let us examine two cases that illustrate this phenomenon: Adolf Hitler and the Mad Bomber, George Metesky.

Profile of Adolf Hitler

In 1943, the Office of Strategic Services (OSS) sought the help of Dr. Walter C. Langer, a psychiatrist. Dr. Langer, commissioned by Colonel William "Wild Bill" Donovan, was given the task of providing the OSS with "a realistic appraisal of the German situation. If Hitler is running the show, what kind of person is he? What are his ambitions? We want to know about his psychological make-up—the things that make him tick. In addition, we ought to know what he might do if things begin to go against him" (Langer, 1972, p. 19).

Langer hired three research assistants who were all familiar with the psychodynamic model. The researchers scoured the New York City Library and their own reading lists, and solicited personal interviews with people who had intimate knowledge of Hitler. Langer's goal was to provide the OSS and Donovan with an objective psychological profile of Hitler that "might serve as a common basis for decisions in the future" (Langer, 1972, p. 31).

As the tide of battle turns against Hitler, it may be well to consider very briefly the possibilities of Hitler's future behavior and the effect that each would have on the German people as well as on ourselves.

1. Hitler may die of natural causes.   This is only a remote possibility because, as far as we know, he is in fairly good health except for his stomach ailment which, in all probability, is a psychosomatic disturbance. The effect such an event would have on the German people would depend on the nature of the illness that brought about his death. If he would die from whooping cough, mumps, or some other ridiculous disease, it would be the physical proof needed to break the myth of his supernatural origins.

2. Hitler might seek refuge in a neutral country.   This is extremely unlikely in view of his great concern about his immortality. Nothing would break the myth more effectively than to have the leader run away at the critical moment. Hitler knows this and has frequently condemned the kaiser for his flight to Holland at the close of World War I. Hitler might want to escape as he has escaped from other unpleasant situations, but it seems almost certain that he would restrain himself.

3. Hitler might get killed in battle. This is a real possibility. When he is convinced that he cannot win, he may lead his troops into battle and expose himself as the fearless and fanatical leader. This would be most undesirable from our point of view because his death would serve as an example to his followers to fight on with fanatical, death-defying determination to the bitter end. This would be what Hitler would want for he has predicted that

> We shall not capitulate . . . no, never. We may be destroyed, but if we are, we shall drag a world with us . . . a world in flames. . . . But even if we could not conquer them, we should drag half the world into destruction with us and leave no one to triumph over Germany. There will not be another 1918. (Langer, 1972)

At a certain point he could do more toward the achievement of this goal by dying heroically than he could by living. Furthermore, death of this kind would do more to bind the German people to the Hitler legend and ensure his immortality than any other course he could pursue.

4. Hitler might be assassinated. Although Hitler is extremely well-protected, there is a possibility that someone might assassinate him. Hitler is afraid of this possibility and has expressed the opinion that

> His own friends would one day stab him mortally in the back. . . . . And it would be just before the last and greatest victory, at the moment of supreme tension. Once more Hagen would slay Siegfried. Once more Hermann the Liberator would be murdered by his own kinsmen. The eternal destiny of the German nation must be fulfilled yet again, for the last time. (Langer, 1972)

This possibility, too, would be undesirable from our point of view inasmuch as it would make a martyr of Hitler and strengthen his legend. It would be even more undesirable if the assassin were a Jew for this would convince the German people of Hitler's infallibility and strengthen the fanaticism of the German troops and people. Needless to say, it would be followed by the complete extermination of all Jews in Germany and the occupied countries.

5. Hitler may go insane.   Hitler has many characteristics that border on the schizophrenic. It is possible that when faced with defeat his psychological structure may collapse and leave him at the mercy of his unconscious forces. The possibilities of such an outcome diminish as he becomes older, but they should not be entirely excluded. This would not be an undesirable eventuality from our point of view because it would do much to undermine the Hitler legend in the minds of the German people.

6. German military might revolt and seize him.   This seems unlikely in view of the unique position Hitler holds in the minds of the German people. From all the evidence it would seem that Hitler alone is able to rouse the troops as well as the people to greater efforts. As the road becomes more difficult, this should be an important factor. One could imagine, however, that as defeat approaches, Hitler's behavior may become more and more neurotic and reach a point where it would be well for the military to confine him. In this case, however, the German people would probably never know about it.

If his neurosis were discovered, it would be a desirable end from our point of view because it would puncture the myth of the loved and invincible leader.

The only other possibility in this connection would be that the German military should decide, in the face of defeat, that it might be wiser to dethrone Hitler and set up a puppet government to sue for peace. This would probably cause great internal strife in Germany. What the ultimate outcome might be would depend largely on the manner in which it was handled and what was done with Hitler. At the present time this possibility seems extremely remote.

7. Hitler may fall into his enemies' hands.   This is the most unlikely possibility of all. Knowing his fear of being placed in the role of the vanquished, we can imagine that he would do his utmost to avoid such a fate. From our point of view it would not be undesirable.

8. Hitler might commit suicide.   This is the most plausible outcome. Not only has he frequently threatened to commit suicide but from what we know of his psychology, it is the most likely possibility. It is probably true that he has an inordinate fear of death, but being a hysteric he could undoubtedly screw himself up into the super-man character and perform the deed. In all probability, however, it would not be a simple suicide. He has too much sense of the dramatic for that, and because immortality is one of his dominant motives, we can imagine that he would stage the most dramatic and effective death scene he could possibly think of. He knows how to bind people to him and, if he cannot maintain the bond in life, he will certainly do his utmost to achieve it in death. He might even engage some other fanatic to do the final killing at his orders. Hitler has already envisaged a death of this kind, for he has said to Rauschning, "Yes, in the hour of supreme peril I must sacrifice myself for the people" (Langer, 1972).

This would be extremely undesirable from our point of view because if it is cleverly done it would establish the Hitler legend so firmly in the minds of the German people that it might take generations to eradicate it. Whatever else happens, we may be reasonably sure that as Germany suffers successive defeats Hitler will become more and more neurotic. Each defeat will shake his confidence still further and limit his opportunities for proving his own greatness to himself. In consequence he will feel himself more and more vulnerable to attack from his associates and his rages will increase in frequency. He will probably try to compensate for his vulnerability on this side by continually stressing his brutality and ruthlessness.

His public appearances will become less and less, for, as we have seen, he is unable to face a critical audience. He will probably seek solace in his Eagle's Nest on the Kehlstein near Berchtesgaden. There among the ice-capped peaks he will wait for his "inner voice" to guide him. Meanwhile, his nightmares will probably increase in frequency and intensity and drive him closer to a nervous collapse. It is not wholly improbable that in the end he might lock himself into this symbolic womb and defy the world to get him.

In any case, his mental condition will continue to deteriorate. He will fight as long as he can with any weapon or technique that can be conjured up to meet the emergency. The course he will follow will almost certainly be the one which seems to him to be the surest road to immortality and will, at the same time, drag the world down in flames.

This profile stems from a psychodynamic perspective of Hitler's personality and the world as it existed at the time of Hitler's final situation. The psychological profile of Hitler himself included the following elements:

- Hitler's parents influenced him tremendously.
- Hitler's father was cold, distant, and domineering.
- Hitler's mother was judged to be considerate, long-suffering, and overly affectionate to Hitler.
- Hitler felt some rejection from his mother's refusal to leave his abusive father and husband to care and protect young Adolf.
- Because of the influence of his parents, Hitler in his adult years was unable to establish and maintain strong personal relationships with others.

From this perspective, Langer and his associates were able to predict the behavior of Hitler in the possible ending of World War II. A picture emerges of Hitler as infallible and omnipotent. His sole vision would be the responsible agent for the advancement of Germany into a superpower status. Langer believed that because of the relationship with his parents, Hitler thought he could prove his worth to his parents by leading Germany once again to the status it so rightly deserved.

Thus Hitler saw himself as an intellectual, a man of the world, and the savior of the German people. He was a patron of the arts, despite his failure in his youth to be admitted to an art school; an outstanding legal scholar despite no formal training in that area; and, when he was in his 20s, he grew a Christ-like beard and wanted to be a Catholic priest. During World War II, he likened himself to Christ for the German people.

Benefits of the Profile

Langer's profile was intended to offer insights into Hitler's personality so that if he was captured at the end of the war, an interrogation strategy would be in place that would help authorities elicit information from him.

To help the OSS plan for several eventualities, the profile offered several possibilities as already mentioned. Despite its strong Freudian psychoanalytic orientation, Langer's profile proved to be amazingly accurate as far as the scenarios for the war's end were concerned. Hitler did commit suicide in a bunker with Eva Braun. He never married, perhaps because he never found anyone he felt was enough like his mother. Hitler's writings from the time near the end of the war indicate that he appeared to be on the fringe of mental illness. He also left many documents that pointed toward some unusual sexual leanings: coprolagnia, urolagnia (sexual excitement gained from eating feces and drinking urine), and others. Langer's work was not in vain. It proved to be a worthy attempt to use profiling as a tool to understand an aberrant personality.

The Mad Bomber and Dr. Brussel

In the 1950s, New York City was alerted to a series of bombings that paralyzed the city with fear. George Metesky was finally arrested, in some part because of the profile developed by psychiatrist Dr. Brussel. Living with his two unmarried sisters in a suburb of New York City, Metesky made trips often to the downtown area. One explanation that he used was to attend mass at St. Patrick's Cathedral. Later in the investigation it was determined that the visits to the city aligned themselves with the bombings.

Dr. Brussel was approached by a detective from the New York City Police Department and asked to develop a profile. The profile included the following:

- The bomber was middle-aged—probably around 50.
- The bomber was neat, meticulous, and skilled at his work. Everything from the carefully constructed bombs, to the neat lettering, to the careful planning of the bombs indicated his neatness.
- The bomber was overly sensitive to criticism.
- The bomber was foreign or spent the majority of his time with foreign people.
- The bomber had at least a high school education but probably no college.
- The bomber was a Slav and probably Roman Catholic.
- The bomber lived in Connecticut, not New York.
- The bomber suffered from an Oedipal complex.

With the information passed along, and reasons for the elements mentioned, the police went to the home of the Mad Bomber and were amazed when he went to his bedroom to change clothing for his "visit" to police headquarters. He was dressed in a double-breasted suit, mentioned in the profile with the following statement:

When you catch him he'll be wearing a double-breasted suit.

This is perhaps the first case of psychological profiling on a local level that gained a sense of professionalism and lent credence to psychological profiling. The statement of the double-breasted suit seemed to legitimize the total effort by Brussel. In addition, the profile itself was instrumental in the total investigative effort by the law enforcement agency. It was successful in a real world series of criminal activities.

PROFILE OF A RAPE CASE

Police departments often seek the help of profilers, usually when they have exhausted all of their leads. Recently, a suspected serial rapist was apprehended in a southern state. In the trunk of his car was found videos of more than 20 of the women he had raped. The police wondered why someone would carry such incriminating evidence in his car. The alleged rapist was visible in the tapes along with the protesting victims. When it was explained that the man had a sexual paraphilia called triolism, and that by seeing the videos he was once again reliving the acts of rape, this led to a better understanding of the person and suggested a plan of interrogation.

In another state, a rapist was involved in multiple rapes. Posing as a repair technician, he would be invited into the victim's home. After gaining control of the situation, he would ask each victim a simple question: Did she have a sewing kit in the home? Each victim admitted that she did. He would then rape each in their beds. Remarkably, each bed was a four-poster bed. This suggests that some stalking occurred before selecting a victim. After the rape, the women were forced to stand by the foot poster, placing the wooden poster between her breasts. He would then take the needle and thread and sew the nipples together, in effect attaching her to the poster as he made his getaway. Where would one learn of such a horrific act? Did this have something to do with an earlier experience in his life? Did he learn it in a movie? This is a type of case for which profiling potentially is especially fruitful.

Another serial rapist terrorized women in a southern city. When the investigators became convinced that they were dealing with a serial rapist, they sought the help of an outside agency that studied the crimes and produced "a criminal personality profile." These profilers believed that actually two rapists were involved in the total of 34 rapes that had been under investigation: One was responsible for 29 rapes and the other for the remaining 5.

The first author of this book was asked to provide a profile in this case. According to the profile, all 34 rapes were committed by one offender who was white (as described by the victims), married, a Roman Catholic, and employed. He probably lived near where most of the rapes had taken place and had likely been raised in a sexually repressive home atmosphere. Given that he was Catholic, it was probable that he was not the product of a broken home; that is, it was unlikely that his parents had divorced. He probably now lived in his own home with his wife and children, maybe two or three children, and drove his well-maintained car to the scenes of his rapes.

This profile proved to be remarkably accurate. When the suspect was apprehended, it was found that he was indeed responsible for all the rapes. He was Catholic and lived in his own home with his wife and two children. His parents lived not far from his home and he was employed as a skilled worker for a manufacturing company. He stalked his victims and drove his pickup truck, which was in excellent condition, to the sites of attacks.

It would be impressive evidence of the usefulness of profiling if this profile had lead directly to the apprehension of this rapist, but this did not prove the case. Rather, one of the man's victims happened to recognize him when she saw him later at a shopping center; she followed him to the parking lot and copied down his truck's license number. He was soon arrested and the case was quickly resolved.

This rapist received 666 years in prison. In prison, he is a model prisoner, and is now eligible for parole. However, when released on parole, a neighboring state is waiting to prosecute him on an additional rape charge.

AN ACTUAL PROFILE: MRS. CHARLENE L. MILLER

The following represents an actual case profiled and is taken from the authors' files:

> Dear Detective Rivers:
>   Thank you for the opportunity to review this case. I have reviewed the two-page fact sheet, the pathologic diagnoses of the body document, the forensic anthropologist report, the map of the county and surrounding area, the photos, and the video. I have not talked with you or anyone else about a potential suspect and am offering the following as my general impressions of the type of person you may be looking for as a viable suspect in this case.

Age.   The age of this suspect would in the cohort of 32 to 36. Perhaps the age could be a couple of years older. There are several reasons for this belief. First of all, I don't see this as the first time this person has done this type of murder. What I am saying is that he has fantasized about killing a woman in this manner for several years. His fantasies have to become real, and for him to perpetrate the involved acts that he did to this victim takes a long time to finally act out as well as perhaps committing a murder or two before this particular murder. There are other items that would indicate that he would be about this age: the age of the those who "hang out" in the bars in this community as well as the energy taken in the commission of this crime.

Sex. The sex of the offender is male.

Race. I would believe that this suspect is white. There are several reasons for this. First of all, most murders are committed by persons who are of the same race as the victim. There was not reported any evidence that would indicate that the race of the offender is of any other race than white.

Intelligence.   I would think that this person is of average to less-than-average intelligence. I would not believe that this person is a "rocket scientist," but one who would blend in well with the other people he associates with and probably has the ability to work in jobs with little supervision. I would also think that he is not viewed as mentally retarded but as one who is a loner and one who is viewed by others who know him as being of average ability but a little strange or weird.

Education.   This suspect has a high school education or less. Also, while in school he adjusted well and presented no behavioral problems of any significance. He attended a local school in the area of your part of the state. He did not attend college for any significant part of time, and if indeed he did attend college, he stayed less than a semester. His mental ability would not stop him from enrolling into college, but his mental status and personal disorganization would prohibit him from finishing. In the school situation, he would have been an average student, probably not a behavioral problem.

Family.   This person is either an only child or one from a small family with one other sibling. His father was a passive person while the suspect was growing up and may have been deceased or absent from the family.

The mother was a domineering person, aggressive, and was the center of power within the family. She was the chief judge, jury, and executioner. What she said was law for the family. I would also believe that she has only recently died, perhaps within the last six months. In the family, the child lived under her control and the mother verbally abused the offender constantly.

Residence.   At the time of the present murder, the suspect lived in this local area and still does. There is something of a comfort zone in the manner in which he brings the dying victim back to the area where he is most familiar and most comfortable. There appear to be four dump sites here. The first one is the place in your jurisdiction where the torso was found; the other three sites are less comfortable for him and the dumping occurred at a later date. He lives closer to the first dump site than to the others.

The place where the torso was dumped is interesting for consideration. The residence of this offender is within a close driving distance and perhaps even within walking distance. The house itself would be nondescript and would blend in with the other homes in the area. This person is a longtime resident of this community. He would be a person who is well known and probably lived with his mother for a long period, perhaps to the time of her death.

Vehicle.   This person drives a car that is in poor cosmetic condition. The car is 8 to 10 years old, a domestic car, Ford, Chevrolet, or something similar, and is also one that is dirty, unkempt, and also in relatively poor mechanical condition. The trunk of the car would also be littered and there would be blood in it that would match the blood of the victim.

Employment.   This person is involved in a steady work situation. He is working in some type of construction work and something that demands physical labor. He may also be a truck driver. He is not, however, in a white-collar position. He shows some knowledge of the various jurisdictions and the manner in which the parts were dumped showed some knowledge that police do not always share information. He may at one time have been or presently be a volunteer, an auxiliary police officer, deputy sheriff, medical technician, foreman, and so on.

Psychosexual Development.   This killer is a seriously disturbed individual. The savagery of the dismemberment depicts someone who has anger directed toward women, manifesting itself in the manner in which he disfigured the face of the victim, that is, the "smile" on her face. The manner in which he cuts the parts of the body shows determination and anger plus making the victim less than a human being: "Not only are you nothing, now you are little bits of nothing."

The killer has placed the parts in a descending order of preference. First of all, the torso is found days before the other parts; this illustrates that he has a lower interest in the torso area and other parts are more important because they were kept longer. What is especially interesting is that the person has kept, or at least it has not been found, the skin from the neck to the waist. This is the most important part for him. I can see him skinning this body part and wearing it at night around the house where he lives alone.

This person may be a transsexual, perhaps a preoperative one, and may have tried to get counseling for sexual problems. I must stress here that I do not believe he is a homosexual. I think he has a tremendous problem with his sexuality. On the one hand he admires women for who they are, he wants to be like them, and that is the reason he keeps the breasts and looks inside the body cavity and the reproductive organs. But on the other hand, he hates women for the manner in which they (the mother?) have treated him. He also demonstrates this in the manner in which he selects his victims. The victimology shows that this victim was sexually active and frequented lower-class bars, drank excessively, and "ran around on her family." That the "victim was deserving" may have been a theme in the fantasy of the killer.

Interrogation. I would be happy to talk with you concerning interrogation strategies when you have effected an arrest.

CONCLUSION

The profile developed by Delaney in *The Third Deadly Sin* illustrates a point we will emphasize again later in this book: The daily activities of police officers provide them with learning experiences they can use in profiling cases. This point is also made by Captain Marino in Patricia Cornwell's novels. The knowledge base needed for psychological profiling is formed by an understanding of what both physical and nonphysical evidence can reveal as well as an understanding of basic precepts and principles of the social and behavioral sciences.

The attention in Sherlock Holmes's investigations offers a plain and simple message to investigators: the details, the trifles, are not to be ignored—answers are in the crime scene if one pays attention to them. "There is nothing so important as trifles" (Doyle, 1891e, p. 89).

During an interview, serial killer Ted Bundy stated that police officers take their cases too personally. Because of the total personal immersion in their cases, they lose their objectivity. In *Red Dragon*, Will Graham loses his objectivity, and his total immersion in the crime and into the mind of the killer lead him to emotional and health problems, early retirement, and almost fatal consequences (Harris, 1981). Of course, profiling in reality is not as neat and precise as it appears in fiction, and sometimes the profiles go unused. As we have shown, the profile of Hitler developed by Langer was never actually used and the profiles developed in the serial rape case discussed above did not lead directly to apprehension. Some profiles do lead to arrests, however, and we will discuss some of these at length later in this book.

Chapter 3

THE RATIONALE FOR PSYCHOLOGICAL PROFILING

When a particularly bizarre and sadistic crime has been discovered, an immediate question comes to mind: What kind of a person would commit such an act? Most crimes of this nature defy understanding and leave us with a sense of bewilderment and astonishment.

The appropriate questions are: What makes someone do something like this? What comprises a personality who enjoys mutilation, necrophilia, rape, or other forms of perversion and pain? To address such questions, profiling reconstructs a personality sketch for evaluation.

PERSONALITY AND CRIME

Some understanding must come to the forefront to meet the challenge of apprehending and prosecuting those perpetrators who commit crimes such as sadistic torture, rape, child molestation, and so on. What actually should be called for is personality profiling. The profile endeavors to shed some understanding on the type of person who would rape, pillage, mutilate, and kill.

A personality is nothing more than the sum total of what a person is. It is that person's total set of values and attitudes: The way he or she views motherhood and fatherhood, law and order, Democrats and Republicans, and all the other social, cultural, religious, and personal experiences that have been a part of his or her life. Each person, criminal or not, has a unique personality. Regardless of past experiences, parental background, or biology, each person relates differently, behaves differently, and possesses a different set of values and attitudes. What accounts for this difference? It is the variety and blending of five personality components: biology, culture, environment, common experiences, and unique experiences.

Biology

There are no adamantine data that suggest that an individual's personality is determined solely by the biological inheritance from his or her parents, grandparents, or other ancestors. It does appear that truly intellectually superior people do have children who are, themselves, of superior intelligence. It is also true that tall people tend to have tall children and short people tend to have short children. The key words here are *tend to*. There are always exceptions.

As far as intelligence is concerned, it simply may be that intelligence is only a score on a test. Some children score higher on standardized tests because of social factors rather than simply biological inheritance. These factors include social class, educational experiences, life's rewards, personal relationships, and varied other experiences that shape and mold the personality of the individual.

Culture

The culture in which a person is reared provides rules and values, part of the normative system of the society. Culture provides society's normative structure with prevailing words, ideas, customs, and beliefs; usually the powerful people who live in a given society control the proper way to behave.

But within each culture there are subcultures: male, female, poor, rich, criminal, and noncriminal. These subcultures have certain distinguishable characteristics that set them apart from the overall, prevailing culture. Each subculture insists on certain patterns of behavior. Each also rewards its members in its own unique fashion.

In other words, a person brought up in one part of a society will be exposed to elements of that particular society, which will differ from other parts of that society and culture because of the unique exposure to a varied set of subcultures. These exposures will have an influence on personality development.

Environment

The total surroundings of a person affect the perception and behavior of that individual. A person from the upper class, for example, will be exposed to a far different set of life experiences than will a person from the lower class. It is not only these day-to-day experiences that become an integral part of the personality but also the social class of an individual places that person into an arena where he or she will come in contact with a far different set of experiences and opportunities that other people in other social classes could never experience.

Common Experiences

All of us encounter common daily occurrences: first grade, second grade, and so on. Most members of western society have been exposed to baseball, automobiles, marriages, divorces. These activities are part of our cultural identity. Not all of us, however, have been to the same school or have been taught by the same teacher. Not all of us have been reared by the same parents, and not all of our parents are happily married. Not all children are brought up by their biological parents. Some may have been reared by their grandparents, by foster parents, or others. But enough of us reared in the United States have developed a modal personality type. This personality contains ideal values: trustworthiness, loyalty, honesty, and reverence, among others that we have all learned to hold dear and true.

Unique Experiences

What separates each of us is not the common experiences but the unique ones. This is the element that explains our individual personalities. Consider identical twins. The biological inheritance is the same, but identical twin studies report marked personality differences (Bouchard & McGue, 1990; Eaves, Eysenck, & Martin, 1989; Keller, Bouchard, Arvey, Segal, & Dawis, 1992; Loehlin & Nichols, 1976; Tellegen et al., 1988; Vernon, Jang, Harris, & McCarthy, 1997).

The answer to the question of why the twins are not identical in their personalities must certainly rest with unique experiences. After all, the twins have the same set of parents. However, one twin is slightly older than the other. The daily happenings, feedings, diaper changings, and verbal exchanges are all performed in slightly different sequences. This accounts, at least in part, for the differences in personalities.

NEW WAYS OF VIEWING
THE PERSONALITY

The personality of a violent offender must be viewed as more than simply someone who has gone through life much the same way as others in the same society. This cannot be the case. The personality of the very violent is different in substance from the modal personality type of American society. Those people who commit the crimes suitable for profiling are substantially different from law-abiding citizens as are their personalities. Theories attempt to define these differences but no satisfactory explanation has been accepted. Because the very violent do not share in the modal personality, and because impersonal violence is so difficult to understand, it is assumed that such perpetration of violence reflects a pathological personality condition that is reflected in the perpetrator's crime scene or scenes.

This is really not an extraordinary assumption. This same comment could be made about the law-abiding but neurotic person. The social and behavioral sciences have been doing this for years. Take, for example, the obsessive-compulsive personality. These people are anal in all they do. This will be evident in their homes, cars, personal effects, and personal hygiene. This personality disorder will take over their daily life activities. So it is with the very violent. The traits of this personality will be reflected in the perpetration of his or her crime, much as it is with the obsessive-compulsive personality.

The crime scene of the very violent reflects the violent personality. If one accepts this premise, then viewing crime scenes will take on a totally fresh and unique perspective. This new perspective, however, will be evident only if the profiler knows what to look for and where to look for it.

ASSUMPTIONS OF THE PROFILING PROCESS

Several assumptions can be made regarding psychological profiling. These assumptions are important to consider because they deal directly with the reasons why profiles are important and the manner in which certain information can be obtained and used to formulate a creditable criminal investigation assessment. These assumptions are detailed next.

The Crime Scene Reflects the Personality

The basic assumption of psychological profiling is that the crime scene reflects the personality of the offender. After all, how effective would profiling be if the crime scene itself was not indicative of the pathology assessment? The assessment will aid in the direction and scope of the investigation of the crime.

Not only is the manner in which the victim was fatally dispatched important, but the physical and nonphysical evidence will also lend, to some degree, an assessment of the type of personality involved in a particular murder. The amount of chaos, for example, might indicate that a disorganized personality was involved in this crime. If this is true, then we can make certain assumptions about particular social core variables of the unknown perpetrator. On the other hand, if the crime scene is "neat and clean" or thoroughly chaotic, then other assumptions might lead us to an offender who possesses a different set of social core variables.

The focus of the attack may also indicate certain information that aids in the apprehension of an unknown offender. For example, in a midwestern state, an elderly woman was killed in her own home. She was stabbed repeatedly and suffered multiple deep wounds to the upper legs and genital area. For reasons that we will further detail in a later chapter, the profile offered an assessment of the crime itself that, in part, resulted in the arrest of a man who was not considered a suspect at the beginning stages of the law enforcement investigation.

In essence, the total picture of the crime scene must be viewed and evaluated to obtain a mental image of the personality of the offender. One sadistic offender reported to us in a personal communication:

> I had once read a pornography book in my father's garage. This book was about rape. I believe I memorized the whole book. There was one part of the book which described a rape of a young girl. I made all of the girls I raped repeat the words of the girl in the book. This was the only way I could enjoy the rapes. Eventually, it was not enough to rape. The girl in the book was killed, so I had to kill.

This killer learned from an experience with violent pornography. But because of the constellation of his other experiences, combined with his family background, social and biological inheritance, and common experiences comprising his personality, he found sexual pleasure and personal satisfaction from the rapes and killings of scores of women. This killer was unable to stop his raping and killing as long as he was physically free to do so. This urging develops similarly to an addiction.

There is no denying that once the cycle of violence is set into motion, violence itself becomes a habit, a need that must be satisfied repeatedly thereafter. And, in this general sense, we're sure it can be said that the offender is addicted to impersonal violence.

The urging, compulsion, or addiction became part of the killer's personality. The manifestation of the urging became part of the crime scene, which was part of each of his crimes. Again and again, he acted out the scenario found in his father's pornography.

The Method of Operation Remains Similar

The behavior of the perpetrator, as evidenced in the crime scene and not the offense per se, determines the degree of suitability of the case for profiling (Gerberth, 1983, p. 401). The crime scene contains clues that experienced profilers determine to be signatures of the criminals. Because no two offenders are exactly alike, it is equally true that no crime scenes are exactly alike. As certainly as a psychometric test reflects psychopathology, the crime scene reflects a personality with a pathology.

Many serial offenders themselves are very aware of the nonphysical evidence that is present at a crime scene. One murderer remarked,

> First of all, any investigative onlooker to my crime scene would have immediately deduced that the offender was extremely sadistic in nature. The visible markers of bondage, nature of the victims' wounds and evidence of unhurried, systematic abuse should have indicated that these sadistic acts were not new to me. And that I had committed such brutal crimes in the past and would likely do so again. (Authors' files)

The offender further stated that

> From these points, it could have then been correctly assumed that although brutally violent, the offender was nevertheless intelligent enough to attach method to his madness, cautious and aware enough of his surroundings to make sure he proceeded unseen in the commission of his deeds. Further, because such a brutal offense was unprecedented in this location, it could have been correctly

assumed that the offender was very new to the city; if he was a drifter, he was at least someone who very possibly could decide to leave town as suddenly as he arrived (which is exactly what he did). (Authors' files)

The remarks from this killer show the one dimension of personality— the conscious dimension—that profiling often neglects. This murderer and rapist illustrates by his remarks the elements within his crime scenes that truly reflect his personality. The method of operation, the M.O., was repeated many times in the course of his rapes and murders.

The Boston Strangler

From June 1961 until the following January, Boston was terrorized by the brutal murders and strangulations of 13 women. The crime scenes reflected hate, chaos, and other elements that serve as the impetus for profiling. For example, Mary Sullivan, the Boston Strangler's last victim, was found nude in her bed. A broom handle was found inserted into her vagina. Both breasts were exposed, and the Boston Strangler had ejaculated onto her face and into her mouth.

A profiling committee was established. Comprised of a psychiatrist, a gynecologist, an anthropologist, and others, a psychiatric profile was developed. There were two suspected offenders in the 13 killings. According to the profile, one killer, Mr. S., was raised by a domineering, seductive mother; unable to express hatred toward his mother and directing instead the anger toward other women, especially older women, he lived alone and, once he was able to conquer his domineering mother, he could love like normal people. The younger women were killed by the other suspect, a homosexual who was acquainted with the victims.

Albert DeSalvo was apprehended and convicted not as the Boston Strangler but on a burglary charge. DeSalvo, married and living with his wife, had an insatiable sexual appetite. A satyr, he demanded sex from his wife five or six times a day.

DeSalvo was sentenced to prison for life for crimes connected with eyewitness accounts of a suspect described as wearing a green jumpsuit (aka the Green Man). After being incarcerated for only a few days, DeSalvo escaped but was quickly recovered. For the next few years, he served his sentence without incident, but was stabbed to death in prison by another inmate (Frank, 1966, p. 379).

The Signature Will Remain the Same

A *signature* is the unique manner in which a certain offender will commit a crime. It may be the manner in which he will kill, certain words he will use in the rape, or a certain way in which he will leave something at the crime scene.

In a midwestern state, two elderly women were murdered. Neither was raped. They were left in a public park in full view. Their driver's licenses and their keys were placed on their stomachs. In another state, several hundred miles away, a female impersonator was killed in a similar fashion, strangled, and his driver's license and his car keys were also left on his stomach. At first blush, it would appear that there are two killers. The victims were different: two elderly females and one young man who was allegedly homosexual and liked to dress in women's clothes. The victimology would not suggest that they were committed by the same person. However, the placement of the drivers' licenses and the victims' keys should be considered "signatures" and indicators of the uniqueness of the crime. This signature should alert the investigators that the crimes were committed by the same person and some sense of cooperation should exist between the various jurisdictions.

Ray Hazelwood, the retired FBI agent who spent the latter part of his career with the FBI's Behavioral Science Unit, lectures to law enforcement across the United States about the importance of considering the signature and its influence on the profiling process (Hazelwood, 1994).

The Offender Will Not Change His Personality

As many people believe, the core of our personalities does not change fundamentally over time. We may change certain aspects of our personality, but the central core is set, and we make only minor alterations due to time, circumstance, pressure, and so on. We may want to make fundamental changes in our personalities but find it is difficult or impossible to do. So it is with the criminal personality. It has taken years to become the person he now is. He will not, over a short period, radically change. It is not simply a matter of not wanting to change. He is not able to change. This assumption has fundamental importance to the profiling process. The inability to change will result in the perpetrator committing a similar crime in a similar fashion. Not only will the criminal commit the same crime, but he may force the victim to act out a scenario that he has also forced previous victims to perform.

The Worth of the Psychological Profile

Perhaps the most accurate profile of all concerned the Mad Bomber, George Metesky. Dr. James Brussel, a psychiatrist, developed the profile for the Bomber case. He accurately predicted that when the Bomber was eventually caught, he would be wearing a double-breasted suit. Amazingly, this was true.

Despite the accuracy of this particular profile, it is believed that profiling has still not proven its worth. Godwin (1978) concludes that,

> Nine out of ten of the profiles are vapid. They play at blind man's bluff, groping in all directions in the hope of touching a sleeve. Occasionally they do, but not firmly enough to seize it, for the behaviorists producing them must necessarily deal in generalities and types. But policemen can't arrest a type. They require hard data: names, dates, none of which the psychiatrists can offer. (p. 2)

Even the Federal Bureau of Investigation's research on the reliability and validity of profiling shows less than a unanimous endorsement of the profiling process. In its study of 192 cases in which profiling was performed, 88 cases were solved. Of that 88, in only 17% did a profile help in the identification of a suspect (Teten, 1995). The Bureau does claim, however, that its profile in the Wayne Williams case helped break his composure on the witness stand (Porter, 1983). This claim is hotly contested by Chet Dettlinger, a member of the Wayne Williams defense team. His contention, supported by Dr. Robert E. Blackwelder, another member of the defense team, was that the defense attorney wanted the jurors to see the real Wayne Williams on the stand, a gamble that backfired (Blackwelder, personal communication, March 10, 1987; Dettlinger & Prugh, 1984).

Jenkins (1994) levels a scathing attack against the worth of the profiles offered by the FBI agents Douglas, Ressler, and Hazelwood (Jenkins, 1994, pp. 70–79). The latter agent, now retired, offered the most "inaccurate profile in the Bureau's history" in the Charlie Hatcher case (Ganey, 1989, p. 22) and another debacle was the Clayton Hartwig profile concerning the explosion aboard the U.S.S. Battleship Iowa (Jeffers, 1992, pp. 177–229). Paul Lindsey, a former special agent with the FBI, denounced the claims made by Ressler in his autobiography *Whoever Fights Monsters* (Jenkins, 1994, p. 71). In addition, Smith and Guillen (1990) cite a case in which Douglas was brought in to offer a profile and the case is still unsolved 10 years later.

Despite the claims of the FBI concerning the validity of the their profiles and huge resources available to the Bureau, there is less than agreement among those in law enforcement that profiles specifically from the Bureau or generally from others are key elements in the investigatory process. Regardless, profiles will continue to be a part of many such investigatory efforts.

CONCLUSION

The personality of the violent offender is a result of a special combination of factors that include biological inheritance, culture, and environment as well as common and unique experiences. Because of this unique combination, the violent personal offender will commit crimes as an outgrowth of existing pathological conditions.

The crime scene reflects the pathology in this personality and the personality is a part of the crime scene. The nonphysical evidence will have important ramifications for the psychological profiling process. Because the personalities of individuals, either noncriminal or criminal, remain relatively inflexible, the criminal personality will continue to commit the same or similar crimes using the same or similar M.O.

Inflexibility of personality and perpetration of crimes aid the profiler in the task of developing a character sketch. Chaos and order, sexual torture or a quick kill, mutilation or not—all indicate a personality that has evolved over the years. It is no easier for the violent personality to suddenly and completely change patterns of behavior than it is for the law-abiding citizen.

CRIMINAL THEORIES AND PSYCHOLOGICAL PROFILING

The questions of why some people commit crime and how to stop are ones that have perplexed people since the dawn of civilized society. Despite the fact that we can build a station in outer space, talk to others via a cell phone almost any place in the United States, and investigate the causes of a plane crash with utmost precision, humans still cannot answer this age-old question with any accuracy.

In our classes, students routinely ask us why a certain offender would commit a heinous and bizarre offense against another person. After all, we are the experts, we should know. However, more often than not, there is no straightforward explanation why some people behave the way they do. Despite our experience, education, and simply our best guesses, our explanations concerning the etiology of many criminal offenders are just theoretically grounded guesses and nothing more.

We suppose that many students may be caught off guard by this admission that even some of the most educated people—and professed experts—simply have no basic answer why many offenders behave the way they do. But to say otherwise—or to pretend that we or any other expert in this field knows with certainty what makes a violent offender tick—is a lie. And any firm educational experience mustn't base its foundation on lies, mistruths, or suggestive interpretations.

Thus, we intentionally choose to start this chapter and the rest of the book with the basic idea that most of the time theories concerning the etiology of deviant or criminal behavior are based on nothing more than a series of educated guesses. No, there is no crystal ball nor are there any people in the forensic sciences (that we know of) that see visions of the criminals committing their crimes when they come in contact with the victims' personal effects. Nonetheless, what we are left with is a series of theories about why some people behave the way they do and what motivates others to refrain from these types of personal indiscretions.

The collection of knowledge that helps us explain human behavior is often referred to as theories of criminal behavior, a series of propositions linking one concept to another. For instance, strain theory purports that persons of the lower economic classes commit crime because they feel the only way they can achieve their legitimate goals of wealth and capital accumulation is through illegitimate means (Cloward, 1959; Merton, 1968).

Other social theories have been presented that take not a sociological perspective but rather a biological one. For example, biological explanations of criminal behavior state that some people are born with a predisposition toward crime, aggression, and violent behavior (Goring, 1913; Lombroso, 1876, 1917). Goring and many other theorists of this genre believed that just as children inherit their parents' genes (eye color, body build, and susceptibility to diseases), they also inherit their parents' moral and mental sentiments. Thus, if the parent had a drinking problem, addictive personality, or a problem with aggression management, so will the child.

Although all of these theories are based on sound arguments and often statistical proof, none that we will discuss later are capable of explaining in an aggregate sense why all people commit crimes or egregious deeds. Thus, it should be apparent that there is no one answer for why people behave the way they do. It may be that the offender lacks attachment to the rest of society, was born with bad genes, has a problem with aggression management, or it might merely be that this offender is just nuts. There truly is no one answer that any of us can point to that explains the etiology of *all* violent criminal offenders.

Even Ainsworth (2001) makes the point that society is continually in search of a single cause concerning the etiology of these offenders. Unfortunately, a single cause does not exist. Thus, the well-grounded student is forced to be well schooled in the variety of theoretical explanations of criminal behavior and to be able to draw from this knowledge when the indicators in the offender's modus operandi, crime scene, or victim attributes present themselves.

Therein lies the purpose of this chapter: to introduce students to many of the traditional criminological theories concerning violent or criminal behavior. Students will be able to develop a background database to assist them in profiling actual cases or simply cases they hear or see on television or some other form of media.

What this chapter is not is a complete collection of these theories and thought. Whole books have been written on these topics and due to space constraints we are forced to summarize a selection of what we feel are the most pertinent criminological theories. Should students wish to gain a fuller and more detailed explanation of these theories, we suggest that they peruse a resource text like Vold and Bernard's *Theoretical Criminology* or Lilly, Cullen, and Ball's *Criminological Theory: Context and Consequences* (Lilly, Cullen, & Ball, 1996, 2001; Vold & Bernard, 1986).

THEORIES OF CRIME AND CRIMINALITY

In the past, sociologists, psychologists, and criminologists have all argued about the source and nature of crime. Some sociologists claim that the root cause of criminality lies in the relationship of people to the existing social structure. They state that people commit crimes to acquire the resources needed for survival, resources they do not believe they can get through legitimate means. Psychologists, on the other hand, have tended to agree that the root causes of crime lie within individuals and their personality formation. Contemporary criminologists are not so sure that the root causes of crime can be attributed solely to either of the two sources but rather a combination of these two and perhaps many more.

This simple segregation of beliefs regarding the root causes of criminality is by no means conclusive. Presently, most sociologists and psychologists recognize that there is no one factor that we can attribute to the root causes of criminality. During the past 30 years, most people interested in this study of crime and its causes have begun to adopt an interdisciplinary approach, accepting that crime has many dimensions. One person may be motivated by individual causative factors, another by sociostructural factors, and another by biological or hereditary factors such as an aggressive personality. Most now would agree, however, that a majority of criminals are motivated and seduced into a life of crime by a combination of these aforementioned elements.

For the sake of brevity, we will introduce students to the two major sources of theories about crime. The theories that comprise these traditions will be explained in a brief manner for the sole purpose of familiarizing students with these explanations so that they can recognize the many dimensions of crime. Thus, the rest of this chapter will focus on individual- level and sociostructural theories.

INDIVIDUAL THEORIES OF CRIME

Under the rubric of individual-level explanations of crime, many different types of explanations exist to explain why one would commit crime and participate in a criminal career. In the past, many believed that demons or evil spirits possessed those who had committed heinous crimes or barbaric acts. Although our research and knowledge of the human psyche has evolved quite a bit since those days, demonic possession is still considered an individual explanation of crime causation in many parts of the world. Today, many individual-level theorists are more sophisticated and point to factors like personality formation as one of the most formidable reasons why one engages in a life of crime.

In order to distinguish individual-level explanations more thoroughly, we will divide this section into three different subsections. First, we will look at psychological explanations; second, psychiatric explanations; and third, we will examine biological factors believed to contribute to the decision to engage in a life of crime.

Psychology and Crime

Contemporary theories detailing psychological explanations about criminal conduct tend to emphasize both individual and environmental influences on criminality. These theories purport that something in the environment has triggered an internal response in the individual's own personality and its development then allows the individual to engage in immoral behavior and criminal activity with relative impunity.

In fact, many psychological explanations tend to denote various personality attributes exhibited by offenders that, if identified early, could predict future criminal behavior (Vito & Holmes, 1994). Thus, the emphasis for these theories is the identification of aberrant behaviors or tendencies, and how these are acquired, evoked, maintained, or modified (Bartol & Bartol, 1999).

Crime and Personality Formation

As discussed above, many of the psychological theories of crime have focused on an individual's personality and its formation. It is believed that impulsivity, the lack of an ability to delay gratification, and an innate aggressiveness are all components within an indvidual's personality. As

Neitzel (1979) notes, it is maintained that "crime is the result of some personality attribute uniquely possessed, or possessed to a certain degree, by the potential criminal" (p. 350).

One of the most prominent theorists of the psychological school of criminality was Hans Eysenck. Eysenck professed that sociological theories offered little to the discussion of crime and antisocial tendencies. Instead, he remained convinced that psychological factors (more specifically inherited features of the central nervous system) in interaction with environmental influences were the key to unraveling the crime causation nexus (Eysenck, 1977).

Although many of the constructs and suppositions purported by Eysenck have failed to withstand empirical scrutiny when tested alongside other causative factors, other research has found that personality may indeed play a role in many serial offenders' behavior patterns (Cochrane, 1974; Farrington, Biron, & LeBlanc, 1982; Feldman, 1977). For instance, in one study, Holmes, Tewksbury, and Holmes (1999) claim that many serial murderers report a phenomenon in their past in which they developed a fractured or split identity. Although this split may not meet the clinical definition of a split personality, the offenders interviewed claimed that they developed a side that allowed them to operate in society without being noticed and another side (the dark side) in which they were all powerful and wanted to serve notice to others about who they were, demonstrating their power through the commission of violent acts or murder. This phenomenon is called "Fractured Identity Syndrome" (Holmes, Tewksbury, & Holmes, 1999). Although this theory has not been empirically validated, it is based on Freud's and Goffman's principal that behavior in adults is based on traumatic experiences in childhood that have left a lasting mark on individuals and their personalities (Freud, 1930; Goffman, 1986; Redl & Toch, 1979).

Personality Characteristics

Other theories of criminal or antisocial behavior have focused more specifically on personality characteristics instead of personality formation. Although these theories are difficult to test empirically, most law enforcement agents, homicide detectives, and profilers will all attest that, based on their experience, they can tell you some of the personal attributes exhibited by those who commit grisly and heinous crimes. These personality attributes are a critical part of any profile and are often contingent on evidence (either physical or nonphysical) left at a crime scene.

Typical crime scene profiles will indicate that the offender is *aggressive, withdrawn, argumentative, isolated, social, antisocial, organized, disorganized, suspicious, paranoid,* and so on. These personality characteristics of serial offenders have been used for ages. Some are based on firm theoretical grounding and others on the investigator's experience and intuition.

One of the first large scale studies completed to link personality attributes with criminal tendencies was conducted by Schuessler and Cressey. This study found that of all the studies published prior to 1950, 42% found differences between the personality attributes of criminals and noncriminals (Schuessler & Cressey, 1950). Although a 42% concordance rate is not overwhelming evidence, nor conclusive of a distinct personality difference, other studies have found that those who choose to live life in the criminal element may indeed share some personal attributes.

For instance, when the Gluecks (Glueck & Glueck, 1950) examined the behavior and personality patterns of 1,000 delinquent and nondelinquent boys, they found that the delinquents are more likely to be

> extroverted, vivacious, impulsive and less self-controlled than the nondelinquents. They are less fearful of failure or defeat than the other delinquents. They are less concerned about meeting conventional expectations, and are more ambivalent toward or far less submissive to authority. They are as a group, more socially assertive. To a greater extent than the control group, they express feelings of not being recognized or appreciated. (p. 275)

Based on the results of this study, these researchers and many others developed quantitative predictive instruments in order to determine which youth or even which adults may later choose a delinquent or criminal career. The Gluecks's developed three such predictive inventories: One based on a potential offenders social background, the second based on character traits, and the third based on personality attributes as determined through an in-depth psychological interview (Glueck & Glueck, 1950, pp. 257–271). They found that for those scoring the best, only 10% of youth could be expected to engage in delinquency. Moreover, these researchers concluded that among those scoring the lowest, up to 90% of youth would participate in a criminal career at some future time (Craig & Glueck, 1963).

Other classic research, such as the study conducted by Dollard, Doob, Miller, Mowrer, and Sears (1939), found similar results. Dollard and his colleagues at Yale University stated that "aggression is always a result of frustration" (Dollard et al., 1939, p. 1). The policy implications of this research finding were clear. The truly violent and aggressive criminals were those who were frustrated by their life chances and conditions. And if these frustrated people could be singled out, and provided counseling, then their aggressive behavior could be held in check. Although this theory was oversimplisitic, it did foster further rsearch.

Researchers, including Berkowitz (1962, 1969), began to revise this hypothesis and found that although frustration may be linked with aggression, each individual deals with frustration differently. Some individuals may behave aggressively whereas others may repress their emotional reactions to frustration and vent in other ways. Nonetheless, Berkowitz found that frustration in not an innate reaction to blocked goals but rather a learned reaction. The individual must acknowledge his or her goals and learn that someone or something prevented the acquisition of these goals (Berkowitz, 1962, 1969).

In our own conversations with serial killers and other violent offenders, we found evidence that many of these individuals do lack the ability to receive criticism and withstand frustration. This frustration often serves as a catalyst for action, which serves to validate the offender's sense of importance and being in control. As one offender told us:

> So when I murdered this first person, it was not to fulfill an inner craving, but only because this person frustrated my aims by being completely unresponsive to my brutality. As this victim was seemingly in a catatonic state, oblivious to my violence, I derived no gain or gratification from my acts, and this individual, therefore, was useless to me. (Authors' files)

Obviously, more research needs to be done in this area, but the data thus far do not support any strong indication that any particular combination of personality characteristics produces a criminal mind. Even the contemporary widespread use of such tests as the Minnesota Multiphasic Personality Inventory (MMPI) and the DSM-IV has shown inconsistent results as far as particular personality traits and the criminal mind are concerned (Fisher, 1962; Funtowicz & Widiger, 1999; Tracey & Chorpita, 1997). Although not downplaying the importance or utility of these tests, subjective inventories are simply not valid with all people at all times.

Mental Deficiency

Other psychological theories are related to but not directly linked to the idea of personality formation. For instance, many early forensic psychologists suggested that crime and delinquency are directly related to mental deficiency or lack of intellectual ability. Deficits in intelligence may have direct influence on social adjustment and may indeed "cause" certain individuals to adopt a criminal or delinquent lifestyle. Research like that conducted by Hirschi and Hindelang (1977) indicated that despite how politically correct it may be to ignore intelligence as a predictor of future criminality, the correlations across studies appear to hold. They found that previous studies suggested that young persons with relatively low IQs may be more prone to delinquency than those with at least an average IQ (Hirschi & Hindelang, 1977). However, they are quick to note that there may not be a direct relationship between the two. High IQ may lead to better test scores and school grades, which in turn may lead to more opportunities and ability to reach goals. Thus, just because some individuals have low intelligence scores does not mean that they are or will be delinquent; it simply means that chances are greater for them to experience later-life stress as a result of their inability to function as efficiently as others (Block, 1995; Fergusson & Horwood, 1995; Lynam & Moffitt, 1995).

There may be another side to the issue of whether or not IQ is a causal factor in criminal behavior. Individuals with higher intelligence may be more apt to elude capture. It may be that the person with limited mental capacity simply lacks the ability to recognize the opportunity to avoid detection and subsequent apprehension and thus offenders of lower intelligence may be more visible than more intelligent persons in the criminal justice enterprise. However, few empirical data are available to validate this possibility.

Criminal Thinking Patterns

Separate but related to the concept of mental deficiency is the notion that although criminals may be just as capable of processing information as others, they may just process information and stimuli from the environment in different ways. For example, Greenberg (1988) stated that human beings constantly scan their environment and organize information about their world around them. From this type of cognitive constructionist viewpoint, it may be that delinquents and other criminals are no different than law-abiding citizens in their personal makeup; they just store the meanings of external stimuli in their minds in different and often distorted ways (Greenberg, 1988). Other researchers tend to agree. For instance, Yochelson and Samenow (1976) interviewed scores of criminals in hospital settings and concluded that the personality of the criminal is not fundamentally different from that of the noncriminal. In fact, the only difference between the two lies in the criminal's manner of reasoning. Yochelson and Samenow place emphasis on the general irresponsibility of the criminal coupled with his or her erroneous thinking pattern (Yochelson & Samenow, 1976). Samenow (1984), however, goes further. He states that,"It is not the environment that turns a man into a criminal. Rather, it is a series of choices that he makes starting at a very early age" (p. 34). From this perspective, the solution to the problem of crime rests with changing criminals' thought patterns and making it beneficial for them to restructure their perceptions of their world. Only by changing the way criminals think can we change their behavior.

Character Defects

Psychologists have expended great energy on research into the antisocial personality. Cleckley's *The Mask of Sanity* (1982) was the first major work to describe the behavioral and personality characteristics of individuals with the character defect of psychopathy. According to Cleckley, the psychopath is charming, has no sense of remorse or guilt, is narcissistic, is a habitual liar, has an inadequate sex life, and continually gets into trouble with the law.

No single accepted theory regarding what causes psychopathy exists. It may be that psychopathic individuals have a form of brain damage and tend to come from homes in which they have suffered mild rejection. There is less-than-unanimous agreement that psychopathy actually exists. In his study of hospitalized patients, Cason (1943) found common agreement for only 2 of the 54 behavioral traits supposedly typical of psychopathy. Cason's data suggest that there are no real personality differences between those who exhibit psychopathic behavior and those who do not.

Another possibility posited by some is that psychopathy may indeed be a reality but that it disappears from the personality by the time a person reaches his or her 30s. This change is based on the argument that the psychopath matures at a much slower rate than most people, reaching maturity around the age of 30. An alternative theory is that the psychopath

FIGURE 4.1 Sigmund Freud

adjusts to society, and by his or her 30s is accomplished at masking his or her behavior and thus able to avoid identification.

Regardless of the various theories concerning the etiology of the criminal mind, psychology offers a perspective unlike any other discipline. Perhaps most important, methodological psychology offers statistical probabilities regarding demographics as well as propensity to commit criminal, and sometimes violent, behavior.

Psychiatry and Crime

A second common area of explanation for the involvement of individuals in criminal acts falls under the rubric of psychiatric explanations. Psychiatric models of criminality follow the traditional psychoanalytic perspective advanced by its founder, Sigmund Freud (see Figure 4.1). This perspective derives its impetus for explaining criminality through an exploration of the unconscious drives and motivations of individuals who participate in deviant, and sometimes criminal, deeds.

According to Freudian thought, the quest to understand the motivations or tendencies toward criminal behavior begins with the assumption that all people are born with innate drives to fulfill their wishes and

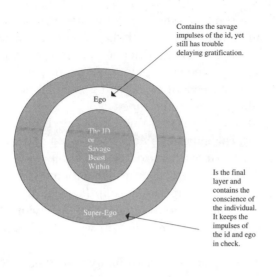

Contains the savage
impulses of the id, yet
still has trouble
delaying gratification.

Ego

The ID
or
Savage
Beast
Within

Is the final
layer and
contains the
conscience of
the individual.
It keeps the
impulses of
the id and ego
in check.

Super-Ego

FIGURE 4.2 Freud's Elements of the Human Psyche

whims. These drives include the motivation to eat, sleep, and engage in sexual behavior. According to Freud, these drives are a natural part of the evolution of humankind. They have allowed people to adapt to inclement weather and conquer the environment. However, these drives and innate motivations have also caused war, famine, and civil distress.

Freud's Building Blocks of Personality

The building block of psychoanalytic theory is based on the concept that the human psyche is comprised of three primary component parts. These parts—the id, ego, and super-ego—are the building blocks of an individual's personality (See Figure 4.2).

The first of these, and the core element of human behavior, is called the *id*. The id contains the unconscious instinctual part of the personality and the savage impulses of the individual that centers on instant gratification. Most of these impulses lie in the area of sex and aggression (Holmes, 1983; Redl & Toch, 1979).

The second part of the inner human psyche is called the *ego*. The ego is best conceptualized as an insulating layer that attempts to protect the individual from the savage impulses of the id. Although the ego still wants what it wants—when it wants it—the ego-dominated person understands that there is a time and a place for everything. It is the conscious part of the personality that is able to delay gratification of the savage impulses of the id. However, in this layer, no attempt is made on the part of the ego to measure the social cost and benefit of engaging in illicit activities. This activity is left to the third layer, or the *super-ego*.

The super-ego is the third and final building block of Freud's psychoanalytic theory. The super-ego acts as the mediator between the unconscious self and its external environment. This level of the individual's psyche tells the person what types of behavior are appropriate and which are not. Although the super-ego is influenced by the outside world, most lessons about the consequences of behavior stem from experience and not perceptions of how the self would look relative to its environment.

This pattern or building block of personality theory has set the stage for researchers in the 50 years following Freud's observations to begin exploring and testing his theories. Although we still do not have definitive proof that any of these three layers exist, our understanding of the human psyche is premised on their very existence. This is not to say that serious research has not been attempted. Aichorn (1935), for example, has related an underdeveloped super-ego to the criminal personality. Abrahamsen (1944) views the criminal as an id-dominated person. That is, the criminal responds to the basic aggressive and sexual urges of the id and fails to evaluate or appreciate the pain and suffering of the victim. As Abrahamsen notes, "The criminal rarely knows completely the reasons for his conduct" (1944, p. 137).

The criminal may have either an overdeveloped or an underdeveloped super-ego. Whichever is the case, this leads to a psychological state of guilt and anxiety, or *anomie*. Because of this feeling of anomie, the individual is in a constant state of desire for punishment—punishment that will remove the guilt and anxiety and restore the person to a state of psychological equilibrium.

Freud's View of the Source of Crime

According to Freudian tradition, the source of trauma to the super-ego originates in early childhood. The unregulated id is the direct link to crime, but, because of early conflict, the guilt is evident in youth. Freud (1930) was aware of this and stated

In many criminals, especially youthful ones, it is possible to detect a very powerful sense of guilt which existed before the crime, and is therefore not its result but its motive. It is as if it was a relief to be able to fasten the unconscious sense of guilt onto something real and immediate. (p. 52)

Psychoanalytic Treatment

With psychoanalytic treatment, the psychiatrist or other qualified mental health professional trys to reach deep inside the individual and uncover the base reason why a person behaves a particular way. Hypnotherapy is one type of treatment in which the focus is not on the conscious mind but rather the unconscious one. If Freud was right, then the target of traditional psychotherapy is the ego or even the id. And if a psychiatrist can delve into these levels, well below what the conscious mind is able to do by itself, the root causes of antisocial behavior will be uncovered and the individual can then make amends from the inside out.

Other types of treatment, like that received by the majority of inmates in prison facilities across the country, rely on appealing to the super-ego and attempting to redefine for the individual what behaviors are acceptable and those that are not. These traditional forms of treatment do little to remove the hedonistic drive, brought about by some type of pain or emotional scar, but rather try to apply a temporary fix or a Band-Aid to a gushing wound. For these reasons, it is easy to see that if we are indeed able to delve into the unconscious mind and discover the root causes of behavior, this type of treatment offers much more promise than the Band-Aid treatments that the criminal justice system has become so famous for. However, this is dependent on the actual presence of the id, ego, and super-ego.

The factor that many people believe psychiatrists ignore in their approach and interpretation of criminal and violent behavior is the environment. This simply is not true. Although the psychiatric model relinquishes the importance of the environment, it does not ignore it. Most theorists of this perspective believe that the source of most personality disorders is held within the individual and it is the individual who is in need of treatment, although the environment may trigger responses in an already wounded individual.

In summary, theories under this framework believe that violent offenders—at some point in their lives—have experienced a fissure in their personality and psychosocial development in which they do not truly understand why they desire or engage in socially, and often times legally, prohibited acts (Abrahamsen, 1952; Roche, 1958). This perspective's main contribution to criminal theory is the creation of an awareness of the unconscious and the role of guilt and anxiety as they relate to crime.

Constitutional Theories

In today's world, most would agree that a person's psyche and one's environment play an important role in the propensity to engage in a life of crime or even violent crime. We all have heard and have come to accept that the major correlates of criminal behavior are poverty, inadequate educational opportunities, alcohol and drug dependency, and being a product of a broken home. There have, however, been several criminological theorists in the past who have posited that one's decision to engage in a life of crime or even homicide is not so much a product of a lack of social bonding or a break or fissure in the personality of the individual but rather a function of genetic inheritance. In essence, most constitutional criminologists believe that a large proportion of criminals are thrust into a life of crime not because of the social environment in which they were raised but rather from the genes they inherited from their forebears.

Although very few theorists at present now believe that heredity is the sole cause of criminality, constitutional criminological theories still stand as plausible explanations for why some individuals choose to live life on the fringe and others do not. Although it may not be a strong predictive element compared to some of the contemporary social and structural models, researchers and students of the social sciences simply cannot discount genetic influence, either. One does not have to look too far to see proof of the effect of heredity.

One of the most famous studies in the biological school of criminality was the examination of the descendents of the Jukes. This study traced the descendants of Ada Jukes and found that most of her family members were either criminals, prostitutes, or welfare recipients (Dugdale, 1877). Other studies such as the one conducted by Goddard (1912) reached similar conclusions.

Perhaps the best test of constitutional criminality lies in the research that looked at the criminal propensity of biological twins raised since birth in separate homes. These studies have consistently found that twins sharing the exact same gene pool but raised isolated from each other are more likely than fraternal twins raised in identical surroundings to subscribe to similar life styles (Christiansen, 1977; Lange, 1929; Rowe, 1985; Wilson & Hernstein, 1985).

Despite consistent findings over the years confirming that crime and aggressive propensities may indeed have a biological root, social scientists have continued to argue about how strong of a predictor biology is and what parts of our DNA makeup contribute to our innate violent and aggressive tendencies. Because space constraints prohibit discussion of all the indicators that researchers have been able to discern that may predict a propensity to engage in violence, we will focus in this section on three: heredity, physical characteristics, and chemical and hormonal determinants of criminality.

Heredity and Atavists

Cesare Lombroso (1836–1890), the founder of the positivist school of criminology, was perhaps the most famous and well-known constitutional criminologist. Lombroso was an Italian physician and amateur criminal anthropologist who proposed that crime and heredity were intricately related. In his book *l'Uomo Delinquente* (Criminal Man), published in 1876, he stated that some men were born with strong innate propensities to engage in a life of crime. Borrowing from the works of Darwin, Lombroso felt that the criminal was a separate species of humanity who had not yet evolved as much as the rest of the population (Savitz, 1972). The traditions and ideas of Lombroso were solidified into what we currently call the *positive school* of criminology.

Under the positivists tradition, many theorists believed that crime was a "natural phenomenon" for those individuals who were biological throwbacks of an earlier time (Goring, 1913; Lombroso, 1876). Lombroso professed that criminals could be identified by a series of distinguishing physical characteristics, such as their large appendages, insensibility toward pain, an asymmetrical head, and many others.[1]

It is important to note that Lombroso retracted many earlier claims that these biological atavists were responsible for the majority of the crime problem. More than 20 years after he first published *l'Uomo Delinquente,* he acknowledged that it was possible that this theory could help explain the criminality of only 35% to 40% of habitually violent criminals (Lombroso, 1917). Furthermore, he even acknowledged that mental illness, psychological deficiencies, or even sociostructural

TABLE 4.1   Characteristics of Lombroso's Born Criminal Type

Physical Attributes of the Born Criminal	Ancillary Attributes of the Born Criminal
Asymmetrical face Unusually large or small ears A low, receding forehead Prominent eyebrows, jawbones, or cheekbones	Have more acute sense of touch on the left side of the body instead of the right Shows a greater insensibility toward pain Sharp vision but more often than not colorblind Less-than-average sense of hearing, smell, and taste Are extremely agile, even at advanced ages Ability to recover quickly from wounds Have little to no ability to distinguish between right and wrong Complete lack of shame, remorse, honor, or pity A passion for gambling and alcohol

SOURCE: From *Criminal Man, According to the Classification of Cesare Lombroso*, by G. Lombroso-Ferroro, 1911, New York: G.P. Putnam.

causes may better explain why the majority of individuals engage in violent crime.

Physical Characteristics and Crime

Other theorists claimed that different biological factors determined the likelihood that an individual would engage in a life of crime. In the 1940s, for instance, Sheldon and Stevens introduced their theory linking one's physical attributes and one's personality (Sheldon & Stevens, 1940). They called this process *somatotyping*. After collecting and coding data on the physical measurements of 200 university men, Sheldon and Stevens claimed the ability to delineate between three main body types: the *endomorph, ectomorph,* and the *mesomorph*. They then took these body types and correlated them to three clusters of temperament that were displayed by this sample. These temperament classifications were *viscerotonia* (a pleasure from eating and socializing), *somatotonia* (a tendency towards assertiveness and dominance, physical adventure, and exercise) and *cerebrotonia* (a tendency toward restraint in movement and emotional expression and a love of privacy) (Sheldon & Stevens, 1942).

The endomorph is a person who is fat and soft. In a relationship with others, he or she is gregarious, jolly, and easy to get along with. According to Sheldon, Hartl, and McDermott (1949), the endomorph is the least likely to get into trouble with the law because his body type determines his personality and disposition. The second body type that they described was the ectomorph. The ectomorphs are thin and fragile individuals. They are easily excitable, afraid of people, and introverted. Sheldon postulated that the ectomorph is less likely to engage in criminality because of a lack of self-confidence and inability to develop and maintain sustainable interpersonal relations with others (Sheldon, Hartl, & McDermott, 1949).

The final body type identified was mesomorph. According to this theory, the mesomorph represented the real problem. Described as athletic and muscular, mesomorphs craved adventure. Similar to Lombroso's biological atavist, Sheldon, Hartl, and McDermott (1949) described the mesomorph as being ruthless, psychopathic, and indifferent to pain.

Although innovative at the time, Sheldon and his colleagues never developed a full or complete classification system that could precisely identify offenders. In Sheldon's (with Hartl & McDermott, 1949) study, respondents were scored on 3 items (attributes of each body type) using a 7-point scale. Thus, any individual would receive only 3 scores ranging from 1 to 7 denoting whether they scored high or low on the attributes of that particular body type. Although not exactly clear, it is believed that if a person scored higher on one scale relative to the other two, that individual was categorized into that higher-scored group.

These primitive studies looking at personality and body type sparked a series of other research, each finding some link. For instance, Child (1950) found similar correlations between self-reported temperament and body type for a similar sample of 414 university students for mesomorphs and ectomorphs. And Cortes and Gatti (1965), studying adolescents, found significant correlations across all three measures. A comparison of the correlations between the works of Sheldon, Child, and Cortes and Gatti can be found in Table 4.2.

The results and findings of these somatotyping theories sparked interest in the study of body type as it relates to the development of personality,

TABLE 4.2 Correlations Between Physique and Temperament

Study	N	Endomorphy & Viscertonia	Mesomorphy & Somatotonia	Ectomorphy & Cerebrotonia
Sheldon (1942)	200	.79**	.82**	.83**
Child (1950)	414	.13	.38**	.27*
Cortes and Gatti (1965)	73	.32*	.42**	.31*

NOTE: *Significant at the .01 level **Significant at the .001 level
SOURCE: Men and Their Bodies: The Relationship Between Body Types and Behavior, by R. Montemayor, 1978, Journal of Social Issues, 34(1), 56. Reprinted with permission.

especially violent and aggressive personality types. So powerful was this influence that even the Gluecks alluded to their findings on delinquency and body types when they reported that delinquent boys were larger and stronger than nondelinquent youth (Glueck & Glueck, 1956). Even a follow-up study by Cortes and Gatti (1972) found that male delinquents in their sample were significantly more mesomorphic than their nondelinquent control sample.

Although Sheldon's somatotyping theory has recently lost favor in traditional criminological theory construction, biology and heredity does appear to play some role in the display of violence and aggression.

Chemical Imbalances and Hormonal Influences

Another perspective within individual level theories of crime is the biological school of criminology. This school of thought proposes that many children and adults engage in violent acts because of some type of chemical or hormonal imbalance within their bodies. Biological theories are now abundant in the extant literature. Some researchers have found that children who do not ingest the proper balance of vitamins and minerals have problems with their intellectual development, which then in turn may affect their choice to engage in later aggressive, violent, and abnormal sexual activity (Krassner, 1986; Neisser, 1996). The studies linking crime or aggressive behavior to biological factors or chemical imbalances run the gamut. For instance, one researcher was able to demonstrate a link between crime and insufficient ingestion of the vitamins C, B3, and B6 (Hippchen, 1981, 1978). And another found that for women, most crime was committed in the days leading up to or during a female's menstrual cycle (Dalton, 1971).

Due to the variety of research that has been done in this area and the consistent findings that hormonal or chemical imbalances may influence our bodies, this school of thought remains one that must be contended with and considered when attempting to explain the root causes of criminality. However, the ingestion of certain types of high protein or fatty foods should never be used as a defense. It may explain why some people feel more agitated and thus are less likely to inhibit their aggressive tendencies, but it does not explain how the motivation to commit crimes or other random acts of violence are placed in a potential offender's repertoire of behavior.

SOCIAL AND ECOLOGICAL THEORIES OF CRIME

The second generation of theories that we will discuss in this chapter have to do with social and structural theories. These theories are more concerned with social and environmental pushes and pulls into a life of crime than individual-level explanations. The primary focus of these explanations centers on how society is structured and how social stratification predisposes some groups of people to crime more so than others.

According to the structural-functionalist perspective, society attempts to function as a well-oiled, integrated, and orderly machine. Ideally, citizens would unanimously agree on society's values and goals, and social structures would function to implement these values and goals. Deviance and crime represent breakdowns of this mechanized system in which people stray outside the rules of expected conduct and exhibit self-expressive behavior to compensate for their inadequately attained social positions.

The structural-functionalist approach can be traced to the writings of Émile Durkheim (1965), who suggested that different interest groups have varied and conflicting views about types of behavior in civil society that are acceptable and those that are not. Durkheim's main contribution rests in his emphasis on the organization of social life rather than on psychological causes (Durkheim, 1965). He originated his theory of crime in the context of a movement toward modernization, the progression of a society from an organic to a mechanistic state.

Durkheim stated that the high rate of crime in mechanistic (modern industrialized) societies rests with the general feeling of anomie, a feeling of helplessness or normlessness that people develop because they lack attachment to society and others. He states that in primitive or organic societies, everyone performs all the work they need for subsistence and no one is dependent on others for their well-being or survival. However, when modern industrialized societies began to form, people began to divide labor and live separate and independent lives from the collective group. People in these societies began to lose touch with who they were, what they stood for, and instead began to identify themselves with their profession and biological family. According to Durkheim, this progression—away from the collective group to more divided, diverse, and segregated groups—left many in society suffering from anomie. In this condition, with no social bond attaching people to society and no collective sense of what was right or wrong, just or unjust, people got lost in the quest for personal and familial, rather than communal, betterment. Simply put, Durkheim felt that modern society, through the division of labor, caused significant amounts of strain to be placed on its constituents as they searched for who they were and how they fit in larger society.

Other sociologists have addressed the strain between society and the individual. Robert Merton (1968), for example, offers a theory that maintains that both social ends and the means to achieve those ends are learned. Some people in a society will have high aspirations; some will not. In U.S. society, economic rewards are deemed to be a socially approved goal. The socially approved ways of acquiring these goals are through hard work, education, and the delay of gratification. However, many in society are not able to reach these goals by employing these methods. Some are not able to go to school, cannot afford it, or simply do not have the requisite academic skills necessary to be admitted. These people can, however, achieve the goal of wealth and capital appreciation if they short-circuit the system. If they cheat, lie, or swindle others, or use some other illegitimate means, they find they can still achieve their goals. Thus, for many in the criminal element, the means are not as important as the ends, because the means in our society are not rewarded.

Social Ecological Approachs

Following the works of Durkheim and Merton in the 1930s, an important sociological perspective developed among a group of scholars at the University of Chicago. Important theoreticians such as Burgess, Reckless, Dinitz, Glaser, and Sutherland all became well-known names associated with this social ecological approach.

These theorists argued that crime and criminal proclivity was not something innate in the individual but was something that environmental stressors created. For instance, Park (1952), among others, felt that individuals in cities could be compared to animals in their natural habitat. Thus, humans in a collective space practiced the natural processes of invasion, dominance, and succession (Morris, 1966; Park, 1952; Warming, 1969). Crime, therefore, is a natural part of organized life and the more individuals of similar type inhabit an area, the more likely they are to invade the property and turf of others not belonging to their social group.

Crime as Learned Behavior

Scholars of the socioecological perspective broadened the discussion of the root causes of criminality. Durkheim taught us that crime was a normal and functional part of society and later authors found that crime was a natural evolutionary process. But that did not explain how people learned that criminal activity or the enactment of violence against others would bring them status or wealth. Those ideas were left to the theorists belonging to the social learning perspective.

One of the first theorists to adopt this perspective was Gabriel Tarde. Tarde and his colleagues (1903, 1969) believed that criminal behavior was not biologically determined as the positivists believed, but rather crime was learned in the interaction with others in a deviant social group (Tarde & Clark, 1969; Tarde & Parsons, 1903). According to Tarde's theory, people learned criminal proclivities in interaction with others and imitate each other in direct proportion to the amount of time they spend together. Although it was well known that people often mimic the behavior of others in peer groups, he went one step further. He stated that people of inferior social stature often imitated people of superior stature. The addition of this second clause meant that even normal, well-adjusted youth could be seduced into a life of crime simply by being in the company of a stronger, more aggressive individual or group. Thus, it was not likely that the good would rub off on the evil, but rather evil would always trump decency (Curtis, 1953).

Cultural Transmission Theories

Other theorists took this idea a step further. For instance, Edwin

Sutherland's (1937) theory of differential association began to examine this phenomenon as a theory of cultural transmission. According to Sutherland, criminal behavior is learned in primary group relationships, not through exposure to mass media, such as movies, radio, and comic books (Sutherland, 1937). This is not to say that some techniques for committing crimes may not be learned from these sources, but the inculcation of the necessary motives, drives, direction, and rationalization for the commission of crime takes place on a conscious level. The rearing of an individual with a criminal mind-set rests on the person's affiliation with those who favor violation of the law rather than those who favor obeying the law.

Social Bond Theories

Perhaps the most recent influential theory of deviance has been offered by Travis Hirschi (1969), who asserts that there is a bond between people and conventional society. Several basic elements in the theoretical construct of norms of a society are internalized. *Attachment* refers to a person's sensitivity to the way people think about him or her. *Commitment* is the extent to which a person's social rewards are connected to social conformity. Finally, *involvement* refers to the amount of time a person devotes to conventional activity. The higher the level of involvement, the lower the probability of criminal activity.

In essence, social theorists have taken the position that the criminal has learned to—or has been compelled to—commit crime through social situations often triggered by environmental influences. The core of the criminal commitment lies within the personality of the offender and the fiber of society. Society contains the goals, objectives, opportunities, and both legitimate and illegitimate means, as well as proscriptions concerning criminal behavior. Sociologists place little emphasis on the role of the unconscious in deviance or on mental deficiency as a causal determinant in crime.

COMBINING THE DISCIPLINES

Clearly, each of the types of theories of criminal and violent behavior are applicable in one way or another for each type of crime or violent behavior that you may investigate or hear about through media outlets. As stated in the beginning of this chapter, when trying to understand human behavior—especially behavior that is seen as vile and heinous—investigators must take a multidisciplinary approach. Exactly what makes an offender behave a certain way cannot simply be explained by individual factors but must also take into account the environment in which he or she was raised and how this environment transmitted a feeling of justification for his or her behavior.

The value of the various theories that come from these disciplines is found in the profiler's ability to blend them to reach an understanding of the personality of the perpetrator. There is nothing magical or mystical about this process; its success depends on the "truths" of the disciplines and how they add to the knowledge base of the law enforcement professional. Academic theories will never take the place of on-the-street police work and the psychological profile is not intended to bolster or refute academic theory; it is simply another tool available for use in the total investigative process.

KEY TERMS

- Anomie
- Atavist
- Attachment
- Cerebrontia
- Commitment
- Differential association
- Ectomorph
- Ego
- Endomorph
- Freud
- Goals
- Id
- Identity
- IQ
- The Jukes study
- Means
- Mesomorph
- Personality formation
- Positivist school of criminology
- Psychoanalysis

- Psychopathology
- Reasoning patterns
- Social bond
- Social learning
- Somatonia
- Somatotyping
- Strain theory
- Superego
- Viscerotonia

NOTE

1. For a complete list of these characteristics, see Table 4.1.

ANALYZING THE CRIME SCENE

Some crimes are more appropriate for profiling than others. Some of these were discussed in Chapter 1. Overall, we consider sadistic torture in sexual assault, evisceration, postmortem slashing and cutting, motiveless firesetting, lust and mutilation murder, and rape (stranger rape, not date or acquaintance rape) as crimes that qualify for profiling. Crimes such as check forgery, bank robbery, and kidnapping, in contrast, are usually not appropriate, nor are "smoking gun" or "dripping knife" murders. In this chapter we focus on those crimes to which the process of profiling is directly applicable.

BEYOND THE PHYSICAL EVIDENCE

Perhaps one of the most difficult things for investigators to accept is the need to look beyond the physical evidence. Homicide detectives are generally trained to reconstruct a crime based on the physical evidence found at the scene, such as blood spatters, fingerprints, and semen. This kind of evidence is often mistakenly thought to hold the key to the successful resolution of any criminal case.

While lecturing in classrooms and across the country on psychological profiling, we repeatedly tell our students that when they begin to profile a case, they should disregard the physical evidence and concentrate on nonphysical factors. Oftentimes, students and law enforcement officials are reluctant to do so. We have found that many people become too caught up in the physical evidence and this limits their ability to think "outside the box" to reconstruct the entire crime scene. However, once they are able to ignore the physical evidence, they can often deduce information about a suspect, including race, sex, employment status, residence, and so on. This interrelationship of physical evidence and nonphysical evidence is the key to the profiling process.

PSYCHOLOGICAL PROFILING TYPOLOGY

The Federal Bureau of Investigation has developed a typology of lust offenders that many profilers find particularly useful; it divides offenders into two categories—disorganized asocial offenders and organized nonsocial offenders. In their book *Sexual Homicide*, Ressler, Burgess, and Douglas (1988) delete the labels *asocial* and *nonsocial* in describing this typology. We believe this is unfortunate because the descriptive nature of these words is useful. There is a fundamental difference between nonsocial and asocial behaviors and these adjectives add valuable information that can help clarify the differences between organized and disorganized offenders. For the purposes of this text, we use the full original label to identify each type of offender.[1]

This typology can be useful when the crimes at issue involve sex as a primary motive. The offenders who commit such crimes as rape, sexual assault, mutilation, necrophilia, and picquerism are particularly suitable to categorization as organized nonsocial or disorganized asocial offenders.

The Disorganized Asocial Offender

Personal Characteristics

As the list of characteristics in Table 5.1 shows, the personality of this kind of offender is reflected in the label. The disorganized asocial offender, who is almost always male, is disorganized in his daily activities as well as in his general surroundings, including home, employment (if he is employed), car or truck, clothing, and demeanor. In other words, he is a totally disorganized person in all areas—appearance, lifestyle, and psychological state. We should note that this is a general description and it has not been empirically validated. Nonetheless, for the cases in which a "pure" personality has been found, these general characteristics have proven to be amazingly accurate.

According to the FBI's research data, the typical offender with a disorganized asocial personality tends to be a nonathletic, introverted white male. As children, many of these offenders have been victims of physical or emotional abuse. Their fathers were often absent; if the fathers were

TABLE 5.1   Profile Characteristics of Disorganized Asocial Offenders

Personal Characteristics	Postoffense Behavior	Interview Techniques
Below-average intelligence	Returns to crime scene	Show empathy
Socially inadequate	May attend victim's funeral/burial	Introduce information indirectly
Unskilled worker	May place "in memoriam" in newspaper	Use counselor approach
Low birth-order status	May turn to religion	Interview at night
Father's work unstable	May keep diary or news clippings	
Received harsh/ inconsistent discipline in childhood	May change residence	
Anxious mood during crime	May change job	
Minimal use of alcohol	May have a personality change	
Lives alone		
Lives/works near crime scene		
Minimal interest in news media		
Significant behavioral change		
Nocturnal		
Poor personal hygiene		
Secret hiding places		
Usually does not date		
High school dropout		

SOURCE: Scene and Profile Characteristics of Organized and Disorganized Murders. (1985). *FBI Law Enforcement Bulletin, 54,* 18–25. Reprinted with permission.

present and employed, their work was unstable. During their childhoods, these offenders had few real playmates; they tended to have solitary hobbies, to have imaginary and secret playmates, and to take part in few social activities. The disorganized asocial offender is a loner. The reason for this aloneness, however, is fundamentally different from that behind the aloneness of the organized nonsocial offender. The disorganized asocial offender is a loner because he is perceived by others to be "weird" or strange—his neighbors are often aware of his strangeness.

This perpetrator has usually experienced a great deal of difficulty in educational pursuits. While in high school, he participated little in extracurricular activities, and he probably dropped out of school as soon as legally possible. He is possibly below average in IQ (the FBI estimates the IQ of the typical disorganized asocial offender to be between 80 and 95), but this may be more a product of his social and cultural experiences than his native intelligence.

His status in his community is the product of several elements of his personality. Limited intelligence, involvement in unskilled work (often as a menial laborer), and few dates or other social contacts with women— all reflect a person who is alone not by choice but because of societal segregation.

Because of the combination of components described above, the disorganized asocial offender lacks the ability to plan out his crimes efficiently and the crimes tend to be spontaneous acts. This kind of offender does not feel comfortable venturing far from his home or work so he often commits crimes in his own neighborhood. He may walk or ride a bicycle to his crime sites ("Crime Scene," 1985). Generally, this kind of offender does not feel the need to follow his crimes in the news media.

The disorganized asocial offender normally lacks the initiative to practice good personal hygiene. This same characteristic carries over to his domicile as well as to any car or truck he may own. This trait, then, may theoretically carry over into the crime scene. Finally, as with all lust offenders, he will repeat his crimes.

Postoffense Behavior

According to the researchers at the Behavioral Science Unit (BSU) of the FBI, the disorganized asocial offender will tend to exhibit certain behavior patterns after he has committed a crime. First, he will need to return to the scene of the crime relatively soon afterward to envision and relive what has taken place. He may attend the funeral services of his victim, even the burial ceremony. It is not unheard of for such an offender to place an "in memoriam" message in the newspaper for his victim.

This offender may keep a diary in which he records his activities and victims. With the current widespread availability of instant photography and videotape equipment, it may be that soon this type of violent personal offender will commonly keep pictorial representations of his crimes. A part of this type of offender's diary, in addition to accounts of his acts, may be devoted to stories of his fantasies. One serial rapist related the following fantasy:

> My preference is for tight teenage girls—the tighter the better. [Talking with another rapist.] We've got to do this the right way.
>
> You really blew it but you were inexperienced. The first thing is to get a house with a windowless, underground basement. Equip it with steel cages [for holding victims], and make sure to soundproof it. Only then will we go out and hunt.
>
> But not just for anyone. Take your time, and find exactly what you want—you don't want to be attracting attention by snatching up a new one every little while. Find one that's perfect. Then we'll keep her locked up before you kill her and grab another. But if we torture, we'd best grab two so that we will always have one recovering while we're busy on the other. (authors' files)

After an offense, the disorganized asocial offender may change his address but it would be unusual for him to move to a far different environment because he feels comfortable only with the familiar. If he moves to an area that is drastically different, he may suffer great feelings of anomie. He may therefore move to a similar domicile in a similar area. Ironically, the disorganized offender may often change jobs frequently. Although this element is not consistent with his own personality attributes, one must keep in mind that this change is often not of his own choice. Some may try to enlist in the military but this is usually unsuccessful because they either cannot pass the physical or psychological tests or, once enlisted, receive a general discharge.

Interviewing Techniques

Once in custody, the disorganized asocial offender may respond differently to questioning than might the organized nonsocial offender. This perpetrator may be more likely to respond to an interrogator who uses a relationship-motivated strategy. It may be a good idea for the interrogator to appear to "empathize" with him. For example, if an offender says that he has seen a demon and that the demon demanded that he kill, it might be wise for his questioner to tell him that although the questioner has not personally seen this demon, if the killer says it exists, it does indeed exist.

Because this kind of offender is not accustomed to lengthy personal contacts with others, it may be beneficial for interrogators to keep up a constant stream of conversation, perhaps introducing something into the conversation that has to do with the crime scene. The establishment of a positive personal relationship may also prove beneficial in securing some statement concerning the involvement of the suspect in the case.

Another characteristic of the disorganized asocial offender that may be useful for interrogators to know is that the offender tends to be a night person. Considering this, the interviewer might take the opportunity to interview this person when he is "at his best"—at night.

The Organized Nonsocial Offender

Personal Characteristics

The organized nonsocial offender is the disorganized asocial offender's opposite. He has an organized personality that is reflected in his lifestyle, home, vehicle, and personal appearance.[2] This kind of offender may be called an anal personality type; in his life, there is a place for everything and everything must be in its place.

Ted Bundy exemplifies such an offender. Because of his personality, Bundy would have found it very difficult to deviate from his accustomed way of doing things. As a result, he was connected with at least four murders because he charged his gasoline and signed receipts for his purchases. He was placed in Golden, Colorado, on the day Suzy Cooley was abducted and killed; in Dillon, Colorado, when Julie Cunningham was murdered; and in Grand Junction, Colorado, when Denise Oliverson was reported missing. Michael Fisher was able to secure a murder indictment against Bundy in the Caryn Campbell case when Fisher was able to place Bundy in the immediate vicinity of the Snowmass Ski Lodge because of his gasoline purchases.

As Table 5.2 shows, organized nonsocial offenders are basically organized in everything they do. They are nonsocial because they choose to be so. These offenders' solitariness is different from that of disorganized asocial offenders, who, as noted above, are loners because they appear to be strange. Organized nonsocial offenders are loners because they often feel that no one else is good enough to be around them.

In addition, there are precipitating factors involved in the crimes of the organized nonsocial personality ("Crime Scene," 1985, p. 19). These precipitating factors may be either real or imagined. As one serial killer told us:

> One night I finally got a date with a young woman I had been trying
> to date for 6 months. We went out for a drink before dinner. We were
> sitting at the bar when a guy walked by. She watched him as he
> walked down the bar. I felt that she should not look at him while she
> was with me. So, what could I do? I killed her. (authors' files)

The young woman who was this killer's victim had challenged his
sense of self-importance. The killer believed he "had no choice"—he
had to kill to regain his rightful position. Although the injury this
offender perceived the woman had done him was only imagined, it was
real for him.

Other attributes of the organized offender include average intelligence; some such offenders may have done well in school, and many are

---

TABLE 5.2 Profile Characteristics of the Organized Nonsocial
Offender

Personal Characteristics	Postoffense Behavior	Interview Techniques
High intelligence	Returns to crime scene	Use direct strategy
Socially adequate	Volunteers information	Be certain of details
Sexually competent	Police groupie	Be aware that offender will admit only to what he must
Lives with partner	Anticipates questioning	
High birth-order status	May move body	
Harsh discipline in childhood	May dispose of body to advertise crime	
Controlled mood		
Masculine image		
Charming		
Situational cause		
Geographically mobile		
Occupationally mobile		
Follows media		
Model prisoner		

SOURCE: Scene and Profile Characteristics of Organized and Disorganized Murders.
(1985). *FBI Law Enforcement Bulletin, 54,* 18–25. Reprinted with permission.

at least high school graduates. (Ted Bundy was a college graduate and a law school student.) These offenders are socially competent and have sex partners. Some are married and most are intimate with someone. Many come from middle-class families and are high in the birth order. Their fathers held stable jobs and were often inconsistent about discipline. For many such offenders there is a history of some drug use, especially alcohol and marijuana. Bundy, again as an example, was a heavy user of alcohol and marijuana during his crimes.

The organized nonsocial offender feels comfortable venturing away from his home. He is able to work and carry on personal, although superficial, relationships. He also is psychologically able to widen his network of relationships and can travel farther and farther away from his home and work to cruise for victims, which, more important for the profiler, hinders his apprehension.

Because of his personality, this type of offender has no trouble making friends. He is also able to change employment as often as he chooses because he makes such a good impression and appears to have qualifications that he may in reality not possess. Many have good jobs. John Wayne Gacy owned a construction company. Chris Wilder was a race car driver. Ken Bianchi was a "psychologist" and security officer.

The organized nonsocial offender has a masculine personality. He often dresses in a flashy manner and drives a car that reflects his personality. As mentioned above, unlike the disorganized asocial personality offender, he feels comfortable in widening his range when cruising for victims or when trying to avoid detection. Using Bundy again as a prime example, he was suspected of abducting Roberta Kathy Parks from the campus of Oregon State University. He drove her (apparently still alive) almost 300 miles back to Seattle. This was not an isolated incident. He also was alleged to have driven from Seattle to Ellensburg, Washington, for the abduction and murder of Susan Rancourt. The disorganized asocial offender, in contrast, ranges only within his immediate neighborhood because this is the only place he feels comfortable.

With a positive self-image bordering on egomania, the organized nonsocial offender may be said to have a character disorder. Commonly, he is termed a full-blown sociopath. He believes that he knows best, not only for himself but for everyone else as well. Because he is always right, he is reluctant to accept criticism even when it is meant constructively; this offender perceives any kind of criticism to be destructive.

Postoffense Behavior

For the organized nonsocial offender, the crime becomes—at least partially—a game. Such an offender will often return to the scene of the crime for the purpose of reliving the sensations he felt there. Some, like Edmund Kemper, will be tempted to return to the scene but will not because they have "seen one too many stories of one too many people" who have been caught by the police when they did so—a piece of information Kemper picked up from watching television. The organized nonsocial offender often learns many details of police work from television and other sources. He may even associate with police or other law enforcement agencies because the police talk about the cases that are special to them. As Kemper said of his relationships with police, "I became a friendly nuisance" (Home Box Office, 1984).

When interviewing one serial killer, we asked him about another case where the killer was suspected of killing scores of young women, although only a few of the bodies had ever been found. The killer's reaction was, "You only find the bodies they [the serial killers] want you to find." When asked why a killer would want some bodies to be found and not others, he said, "To let you know he's still there."

Because of his charm and charismatic personality, this type of person may be the last to be suspected of a crime. Even if suspected, because he often possesses intelligence and social graces, he may be able to anticipate investigators' questions and prepare responses to suit his own situation.

Interviewing Techniques

The BSU recommends that this kind of offender be confronted directly during the interviewing session. Offenders of this type respect competence, even when it may lead to their arrest and conviction. However, when using such confrontation in the interrogation, the interviewer must be absolutely confident about his or her information. If the interviewer presents "the facts," he or she must be certain that they are true and accurate. This type of offender will know immediately when he is being conned and he will understand immediately if false "evidence" is presented to him that the police actually have no case. This can close the door on successful resolution of a case because the offender will never volunteer any information that can be taken as any kind of admission of guilt. This type of offender will admit to only what he must. The interrogator should not hope that once he is confronted with all the known facts the floodgates of information will open.

Some believe that a single-interviewer strategy is best. In the Ted Bundy case, Donald Patchen and Steven Bodiford (personal communication, June 10, 2000) interrogated Bundy frequently during a short period. The interviews took place mostly at night. Finally, after several sessions, Bundy admitted, "There's something deep inside me, something I can't control." However, after he had the chance to sleep and psychologically regroup, Bundy denied having admitted even that.

CRIME SCENE DIFFERENCES

It has been theorized that the crime scenes of organized nonsocial offenders and disorganized asocial offenders will differ along the same lines as the differences in their personalities (see Table 5.3). That is, those who are organized in their lives in general will also be organized in the perpetration of their crimes and those who are disorganized in their everyday lives will be disorganized in the perpetration of their crimes; as such, differing degrees of organization and disorganization should be evident in crime scenes.

The organized nonsocial offender takes great care in the perpetration of his violence. This offender makes certain that the evidence will be destroyed. Also, in the case of homicide, he will often kill at one site and dispose of the body at another site. The disorganized asocial offender, on the other hand, attacks his victims suddenly, in unplanned or barely planned violence. The surprise, or blitz, attack results in a crime scene that holds a great deal of physical evidence. The following case, taken from the authors' files, provides an example.

Case Study

A 75-year-old widow had lived in the same housing project since 1937 and had been living alone since the mid-1960s. On July 4, when her son came to pick her up to spend the holiday with his family, he found his mother's body in her bed. She had been stabbed repeatedly and decapitated. The weapon was a butcher knife that had belonged to the victim. Blood spatter was found on the walls by her bed as well as on the ceiling, showing that the attack had been carried out in a frenzy. The woman had been sexually assaulted, and semen was found in her vaginal vault as well as on the bedspread and in the bedclothes.

TABLE 5.3 Comparison of Crime Scenes of Organized Nonsocial and Disorganized Asocial Lust Killers

Organized Nonsocial Killer	Disorganized Asocial Killer
Planned offense	Spontaneous event
Targeted stranger	Victim unknown
Personalizes victim	Depersonalizes victim
Controlled conversation	Minimal conversation
Controlled crime scene	Chaotic crime scene
Submissive victim	Sudden violence
Restraints used	No restraints
Aggressive acts	Sex after death
Body moved	Body not moved
Weapon taken	Weapon left
Little evidence	Physical evidence

SOURCE: Crime Scene and Profile Characteristics of Organized and Disorganized Murders. (1985). *FBI Law Enforcement Bulletin, 54,* 18–25. Reprinted with permission.

There was a great deal of physical evidence at the scene. No other murders similar to this one were known, and a profile was requested. The profile suggested that the offender was a black male, early 20s, single, living within the immediate neighborhood, and living with his mother or alone. He probably had a history of mental illness and probably had been hospitalized or institutionalized for his mental condition. In addition, the profile suggested that once the offender was apprehended, the interrogators might try to establish a personal relationship with him.

Within six weeks, three other elderly women were attacked. All had lived within a one-mile radius of the original attack. Of these three women, the first was 70 years old. She was stabbed 21 times in the neck with such force and rage that a half-inch of the scissors was left lodged in her neck. The next victim, who was also attacked in her home, was stabbed in the neck 11 times. The last victim succeeded in warding off the attacker and called the police. A suspect was apprehended.

In the course of the interrogation, the suspect admitted that he had been in the homes of the victims. In the case of the decapitated victim, he denied stabbing her but did say that he had "killed a demon" that had been chasing him. Elaborating on his story, he stated that the only time he was safe from the demon that had been after him was when he was on a city bus or in jail. On the evening of the first attack he got off a bus and the demon was there waiting for him. He ran and entered the house at the first door he came to. The demon ran past him and then into the victim's bedroom. The killer grabbed a butcher knife from the kitchen, ran into the bedroom, and repeatedly stabbed the demon.

The profile in this case was accurate. The amount of evidence, the chaos evident in the crime scene, the weapon belonging to the victim as well as its being left at the crime scene, the violence done to the victim, the lack of restraints, the body left at the death scene—all suggested a profile that did indeed narrow the scope of the investigation.

Relationship to Victims

Organized nonsocial offenders and disorganized asocial offenders also tend to have different relationships to their victims. Both types select "strangers" as victims but the character of the strangers is different. The disorganized asocial offender may be aware before the crime of the existence of his victim but he has no personal relationship with that person. In the case related above, for example, the killer lived in the neighborhood and may have been familiar with the locations of the apartments and knew the victims who lived there before the murders occurred. For the organized nonsocial offender, however, the victim is a targeted stranger. One offender told us in an interview about his typical choice for a victim.

> If I had made a composite of my "typical" victim, it would read like this: The individual would be white, female, between the ages of 13 and 19, given the adolescent dress and manner. I would say that perhaps 75% of my victims fell under this general description. Obviously there is a pattern of selectivity here, else this large percentage figure would not so closely fit the description I've laid forth. Just as obviously, it wasn't a matter of my victims' "just being there."
>
> But just how conscious was this selectivity and why did roughly three quarters of my victims fit this mold? In answer to the first question, I would have to say that it was not entirely conscious in that I didn't hold a general picture of an 18-year-old adolescent, white female in my mind. Certainly more and more often than not, I was roaming the streets in search of females in general, but with no specific age group in mind. Yet 75% of the time the person who

"clicked" and "registered" in my mind was the girl I described above. More accurately, I was reacting to the "click" in my gut, more so than to predetermined, sought-after characteristics. Yet the predisposition toward victims of that general description, subconscious or not, was there.

This violent personal offender seemed to have some understanding of the reason for his selection of young white females. He went on to discuss how very popular female students rejected him in high school. Of another nationality, he was averse to dating young women of his own ethnic group and he provided some insight into this reluctance, citing some shame about his own background. The slightest resistance to his social overtures met with rage.

Usually, minimal conversation takes place between the disorganized asocial offender and his victim. It is a blitz attack and the establishment of any relationship is not a requirement. In contrast, conversation between the organized offender and his victim is a language of intimidation once the victim is within the offender's "comfort zone." The vehicle for the initial contact now becomes the vehicle for control. The organized nonsocial offender appears able to assay the vulnerability of his stalked victim. One serial killer remarked, "I can tell by the way they walk, the way they tilt their heads. I can tell by the look in their eyes" (Authors' files).

Victims of organized nonsocial offenders often suffer vicious attacks prior to death. Sometimes these offenders use restraints to render their victims helpless and to heighten victims' fear, which the offenders may need to see in order to gain full satisfaction. Disorganized asocial offenders, in contrast, usually have no need for restraints because their purpose is not to intimidate or to instill fear. One organized nonsocial offender described to the first author his reaction to one victim's failure to show the fear he wanted to see.

When I sighted the women [his two victims] they meant absolutely nothing to me as human beings. Indicative of the worthlessness they held in my eyes was my extreme rage toward the first woman, who I felt was defying me through her "unwillingness" to "suffer well." Undoubtedly she was instead paralyzed by cold and fear, but, in my own distorted mind, her silence and lack of struggling was a defiant sign against being reduced to brokenness and worthlessness, and therefore, the contempt I felt for her defiance was such that I killed her right away, forgetting her almost instantly as I went to the second woman.

In an organized nonsocial crime scene, normally the weapon not only belongs to the offender but is taken from the crime scene. This is not true of the disorganized asocial offender. This violent personal offender does not think through what he is about to do; the act is spontaneous. Bringing a weapon to a crime scene shows at least some form of rudimentary planning and this offender does not think ahead.

The moving of a body from the crime scene may be an indication that the unknown suspect is an organized nonsocial type. The disorganized type has no desire or need to move the body. Once the killing has been accomplished, his mission is over.

CONCLUSION

In this chapter we have discussed a typology of offenders that has important implications for law enforcement profiling of lust killers. We have addressed the typical personal characteristics and postoffense behaviors of disorganized asocial and organized nonsocial offenders as well as the interviewing techniques recommended for use with each type of suspect. We have also discussed the differences that may be found in the crime scenes associated with the two types of offenders.

Investigators will find the guidelines laid out in the typology discussed here to be useful in their profiling of violent crimes as they take into account the chaos or lack of chaos in a crime scene, the presence or absence of a weapon, the presence or absence of mutilation of the victim, and other details. Of course, not all crimes are lust killings. In the next chapter we will address the use of profiling in suspected serial murder cases.

NOTES

1. The FBI also has dropped the words *nonsocial* and *asocial* from the labels in its typology but, as explained, we retain both terms here because we believe they have important meanings.

2. See Chapter 7 for a discussion of staging, signatures, and other elements of crime scene assessment as they pertain to organized and disorganized offenders.

ARSON AND PSYCHOLOGICAL PROFILING

The deliberate setting of fires has a long history, as varied as the fires themselves. There is no reason to believe that the motivations for all firesetters are the same or even similar (Forehand, Wierson, Frame, Kempton, & Aristead, 1991; Holt, 1994; Orr, 1989; Sakeheim & Osborn, 1986; Webb, Sakeheim, Towns-Miranda, & Wagner, 1990). To the contrary, arsonists are as diverse as their motivations and anticipated gains and are different from other types offenders (Kolko & Kazdin, 1992; Sakeheim, Vigdor, Gordon, & Helprin, 1985). This may seem strange at first blush, but the motivating factors as well as the planned gains may be known only to a few. The purposeful firesetter, for example, may be an arsonist for property gain or a pyromaniac who sets fires for erotic pleasure (Law, 1991). However, the exact role of sex as a motivating factor may have been grossly exaggerated (Quinsey, Chaplin, & Uphold, 1990; Rice & Harris, 1991).

Although the analysis of sex as a basic motive is one of the main foci of this chapter, we also examine the crime scenes themselves to gain insight into social and demographic information, information that may be gleaned from the crime scenes themselves.

WHAT IS ARSON?

Arson is the willful and malicious burning of property (Douglas, Burgess Burgess, & Ressler, 1992, p. 165). This, however, is one simple definition; there is more to arson than this rudimentary denotation. Three components, which are listed in Table 6.1, comprise the crime of arson.

TABLE 6.1   The Components of the Crime of Arson

Burning of property	Must be shown to be actual destruction, at least in part, not just scorching (although some states include any physical or visible impairment of any surface).
Incendiary in origin	Proof of the existence of any effective incendiary device, no matter how simple it may be, is adequate. Proof must come from considering and ruling out other possibilities.
Malice involved	Burning is shown to be started with malice; that is, with the specific intent of destroying property.

SOURCE: From *Kirk's Fire Investigation* (3rd ed., p. 103), by D. DeHaan, 1991, Englewood Cliffs, NJ: Prentice Hall. Reprinted with permission.

Arson is a combination of both a legal component and a behavioral dimension. These forms may come in the construct of types of arson.

Forms and Types of Arson

In an early study, Macy (1979) classified the crime of arson and placed it into five forms:

- Organized crime (loan sharking, extortion, and other crime concealment)
- Insurance and housing fraud (overinsurance, blockbusting, parcel clearance, gentrification, stop loss, and tax shelters)
- Commercial (inventory depletion, modernation, and stop loss)
- Residential (relocation, redecoration, public housing, and automobile)
- Psychological (children and juveniles, pyromania and political) (p. i).

A better strategy to understand the phenomenon of arson is to examine the various types of arson, and as later explored in this chapter, the personality and the behavior of the firesetter.

Gilbert (1986) reports five different types or classifications of fires (see Table 6.2). Recognizing that the types, forms, and motivations vary from one type of fire to another—even those that are not considered to be crimes of arson—it is also important to consider other factors involved in

TABLE 6.2	Different Types of Classifications of Fires
Natural fire	This type of fire results from a work of nature, such as lightning. There is no sure way to prevent a natural fire.
Accidental fire	An accidental fire can result from faulty equipment within a structure, when a person smokes in bed, and so on.
Unknown fire	This type of fire results when an investigation fails to yield the exact cause of a fire.
Suspicious fire	This type of fire is often investigated, but the investigators find no clues why the fire started. Arson may be suspected, but an investigator is unable to prove it with the available evidence.
Incendiary fire	In this type of fire, the investigator finds accelerants on the floor, attesting to the fact that this fire was intentionally set.

SOURCE: From *Criminal Investigation* (p. 444), by J. Gilbert, 1986, Columbus, OH: Charles M. Merrill. Reprinted with permission.

the crime; the personality, the extent of the arson problem, and the assessment of crime scenes that involve arson.

STATISTICS ON ARSON

Data concerning arson is collected nationally by two federal agencies: the National Fire Protection Association (NFPA) and the Federal Bureau of Investigation. The former agency collects data on structural fires that have occurred as well as nonstructural and "suspicious" fires. The FBI's statistics are gathered from reports that identify fires termed and identified as arson by the reporting local agencies. However, as Douglas, Burgess, Burgess, and Ressler (1992) report, "the statistics compiled by both the NFPA and the FBI closely agree" (p. 164).

The U.S. Department of Justice (1993) reports that almost 20,000 crimes of arson were reported in 1992 (p. 418). Interesting to note, the arrest rate for arson is lower than any other Part I or Part II offenses—only 7.6 per 100,000 incidents. Other interesting statistical data regarding arson

TABLE 6.3 Arson in the United States: Arrests in 1992

Age	Total Cases	Under 15	Under 18	18 and Older	
Number	16,322	5,210	7,968	8,354	
Percent		32	49	51	
Sex	Total Cases	Male	Female		
Number	16,322	14,139	2,183		
Percent		87	13		
Race	Total Cases	White	Black	American Indian or Native Alaskan	Asian or Pacific Islander
Number	16,275[a]	12,430	3,572	135	138
Percent		76	22	.8	.8[b]

SOURCE: From *Uniform Crime Reports: Crime in the United States, 1992* (pp. 428–432), by U.S. Department of Justice, Bureau of Justice Statistics, 1993, Washington, DC: Government Printing Office.
a. Because of unreported data, this number does not agree with previous reported total arrests.
b. Because of rounding, these figures do not total 100%.

and arrests is reported in Table 6.3. One problem with the accumulation of data is that it obviously depends on the method by which the data are collected. One would expect that all of the numbers match; however, this does not always appear to be true. The Department of Justice's Bureau of Alcohol, Tobacco, and Firearm's report (as seen in Table 6.4) offers data from reporting agencies depicting various arson statistics.

Regardless of the relative agreement of gathered data, it is apparent that arson is indeed a very serious personal and financial problem: Millions of dollars are expended in this crime. This does not, obviously, include the immeasurable cost of human lives lost because of the firesetter. In the 5-year period from 1988 to 1992, more than 400 people were murdered in arson fires—some intentionally, some accidentally. There is no way to measure the financial impact of lost lives. And of course, what is intended here is to look not only at the fires themselves (which is actually secondary in this discourse) but to look at the arsonist as an individual. We will try to develop a mental image, the psychological profile, of the type of person who intentionally sets fires for varied reasons. The motivations vary from one firesetter to another, as do the social core variables, the motivations, and the anticipated gains.

TABLE 6.4 Arson Statistics

	1988	1989	1990	1991	1992	5 Year Total
Number of incidents	538	489	571	724	567	2,889
Number killed	55	49	143	124	52	423
Number injured	194	167	218	426	254	1,259
Property damage (in millions)	499.9	437.8	317.5	544.7	257.2	2,057.1
Insurance dollars saved (in millions)	27.8	29.7	29.4	31.7	41.3	159.9
Cases submitted	169	165	181	220	288	1,023
Defendants recommended for prosecution	389	347	354	423	478	1,991
Convicted or pled guilty	19	57	41	67	53	237

SOURCE: U.S. Department of the Treasury; Bureau of Alcohol, Tobacco, and Firearms. (1992). *1992 Explosive Incidents Report.* Washington, DC: Government Printing Office (p. 66).

A VIEW OF THE FIRESETTER

Among all age groups, arson is almost equally split between adults and juveniles. Juveniles commit 49% of all reported arsons. However, among these juveniles, 26% of all reported arsons are committed by children between the ages of 10 to 14. In the adult years, 17% of the arsons are committed by adults in the cohort of 25 to 34 years of age. After the age of 35, there is a slow and gradual decrease in the number of arsons committed.

Arson is also seen as a male crime: More than nine of ten arsons are committed by males. Regarding race, it seems that blacks are slightly over-represented; blacks account for more than one in five reported one-time arsonists but less than 10% of serial arsonists. Whites account for slightly more than three of four arsons. Native Americans, Native Alaskans, Asians, Hispanics, and Pacific Islanders account for the remainder. Table 6.5 offers additional statistics about arsonists' backgrounds.

These statistics are important to consider when one starts the profiling process. By combining what is typically known regarding the statistics

---

TABLE 6.5 Portrait of an Arsonist

Prior Arrest History

87% had a felony arrest
63% had multiple felony arrests
24% had a prior arrest for arson

Location of Residence in Relation to Arson Scene

21% lived within 5 blocks
30% lived ½ to 1 mile away
20% lived within 1 to 2 miles
16% lived more than 2 miles away
 7% lived in a home or institution

Motivation for Crime

41% revenge
30% excitement
 7% vandalism
 5% profit
 5% concealment of another crime

SOURCE: One Man, More Than 100 Fires: Seattle Area's Wave of Terror, by L. Sharn & D. Glamser, 1994, March 24, *USA Today*, p. 9A. Reprinted with permission.

---

of arson, the various typologies, the principles of profiling, and so on, a psychological assessment of the arsonist may develop.

Other basic characteristics are common to many serial arsonists. Sapp et al. report basic data that include social core variables such as marital status, education, and so forth. Table 6.6 contains this information.

TYPOLOGIES OF FIRESETTERS

Certain typologies indicate various differences among firesetters. Rider (1980b), in reviewing the work of Lewis and Yarnell, suggests several types (Lewis & Yarnell, 1951; Rider, 1980b).

First, consider the jealousy-motivated adult male, who does this as a reaction against an incident that he has perceived to affect his vanity and personality. The next is the would-be hero. This firesetter rushes into a fire scene, saves a life, and so on, and is the apparent hero because of his swift and decisive action. This would include firefighters, police officers, and others who respond to calls, as well as the passerby who just "happens" on the scene. Another type reported is the volunteer fireman

(Text continues on page 95)

TABLE 6.6   Attributes of Serial Arsonsists

Occupation	*Percent*
Menial laborer	28.2
Retail sales	2.6
Service worker	5.1
Maintenance worker	7.7
Police-security	7.7
Fire service	2.6
Office-clerical	10.3
Food service	5.1
Homemaker	2.6
Medical service	5.1
Marital Status	*Percent*
Single	65.9
Significant other	8.5
Married	6.1
Separated	3.7
Divorced	14.6
Widowed	1.2
Gender	*Percent*
Male	94.0
Female	6.0
Childhood Family Status	*Percent*
Both parents	57.5
Father only	3.8
Mother only	12.5
Father, stepmother	1.3
Mother, stepfather	10.3
Foster home	8.8
Other relatives	6.3
Ethnicity	*Percent*
White	81.9
African American	9.6
Hispanic	7.2
Native American	1.2
Marital History	*Percent*
Never married	53.7
Married once	36.6
Multiple marriages	9.7

(Continued)

TABLE 6.6   (Continued)

Highest Grade Completed	Percent
3	1.3
4	2.7
5	2.7
6	6.7
7	1.3
8	5.3
9	13.3
11	16.0
12	26.7
13	1.3
14	4.0
15	1.3
16	2.7

Institutional History

Type of Institution	Mean Times in Institution
Orphanage	1.3
Foster home	1.6
Juvenile detention	4.1
State juvenile home	1.7
County jail	4.9
State prison	2.0
Federal prison	1.3
Mental health	3.2
Other institution	1.3

Sexual Orientation	Percent
Heterosexual	75.4
Homosexual	8.7
Bisexual	15.9

Psychological History	Percent
Depression	3.8
Dyslexia	3.8
Stress related	3.8
Multiple diagnosis	34.6
Alcoholism	11.5
Hyperactive child	7.7
Brain damage	3.8
Suicidal	19.2
Borderline personality	3.8

(Continued)

TABLE 6.6 *(Continued)*	
Unspecified problem	3.8
Psychotic outburst	3.8
Felony Arrest Record	*Percent*
Multiple arrests	63.4
Arson	23.9
Aggravated assault	1.4
Burglary	2.8
Grand theft auto	1.4
DWI	1.4
Robbery	1.4
Attempted arson	1.4
Child molestation	2.8
Method of Apprehension	*Percent*
Turned self in or confessed	21.1
Informant	7.0
Witness	12.7
Key evidence recovered	4.2
Law enforcement investigation	38.0
Caught in act	9.9
Arson while in Jail	4.2
Caught fleeing the scene	1.4
Multiple events	1.4
Plea Offered	*Percent*
Guilty	52.6
Not guilty	28.9
Changed to guilty	10.5
Combination	7.9
Area of Arsons	*Percent*
Work/school	2.5
To/From work/school	7.5
After work hours	42.5
Days off/weekends	10.0
Multiple locations	12.5
Home or other	25.0
Distance From Home to Arson Site	*Percent*
0 – 1 block	2.7
1 – 2 blocks	5.4
2 – 5 blocks	12.2
½ to 1 mile	29.7

(Continued)

TABLE 6.6 (Continued)

1 – 2 miles	20.3
2 – 5 miles	4.1
5 – 10 miles	5.4
10 – 20 miles	2.7
20 – 40 miles	2.7
Varied distances	6.8
Home/institution	6.8
Mode of Transportation to Scene	*Percent*
Walked	60.8
Bicycle	5.1
Motorcycle	2.5
Automobile	16.5
Truck	1.3
Already at scene	7.6
Mixed modes	6.3
Living Arrangements at Time of Arson	*Percent*
Parents	23.3
Alone	16.3
Female roommate	4.7
Male Roommate	7.0
Both sex roommates	2.3
Spouse	2.3
Spouse and children	4.7
Grandparents	7.0
Institution	14.0
Mixed	18.5
Type of Residence	*Percent*
Rooming house	18.1
Hotel/motel	2.4
Apartment	23.8
Single-family house	42.9
Institution	11.9
Method of Victim/Site Selection	*Percent*
Knew the people	2.9
Worked there	5.9
Random selection	17.6
Walking distance	5.9

(Continued)

TABLE 6.6 (Continued)	
Means of Gaining Access	*Percent*
Open entry	37.8
Broke in	18.9
Had a key	2.7
Lived there	10.8
Set outside	13.5
Multiple means	16.2
Ignition Device	*Percent*
Wooden matches	7.9
Book matches	57.9
Cigarette lighter	17.1
Combination	6.6
Molotov cocktail	2.6
Cigarette	2.6
Road flare	1.3
Candle	1.3
Gunpowder	1.3
Items Left at Scene	*Percent*
Gas can	13.9
Matches	47.2
Other devices	11.1
Cigarette lighter	5.6
Multiple items	25.0

SOURCE: From *A Report of Essential Findings From a Study of Serial Arsonists*, by A. Sapp, T. Huff, G. Gary, D. Icove, & P. Horbert, unpublished manuscript. Reprinted with permission.

who joins the department to fight fires, many of which he will set himself. The fire buff is similar to the police groupie in that he wants to associate with professional firefighters, frequents the fire station, and many times is an active person in the community who has a special interest in the work of the fire department. The "excitement" firesetter ignites the fires because of his need for personal excitement, but it does not include a sexual component or a sexual fantasy. The following section details more thoroughly the pyromaniac's firesetting experience. These individuals have an irresistible urge to start fires. Table 6.7 provides some elements of a pyromaniac's profile.

(Text continues on page 98)

TABLE 6.7 Additional Elements in the Profile of the Typical Pyromaniac

Age	*Heaviest concentration between ages of 16 to 28; highest frequency at age 17.*
Gender	Male
Race	Predominantly white
Intelligence	Ranged from mentally defective to genius (approximately 22% of those with no explanation for their firesetting were low-grade defectives).
Physical Defects	Found to be frequently present
Enuresis	Present in some
Mental Disorders	Psychopathy, as well as psychotic disorders, were identified within the category; the compulsive urge also appears to reflect a neurotic obsessive-compulsive pattern of behavior.
Academic Adjustment	Poor educational adjustment, although some pyromaniacs were intellectually bright. Their academic performance was marginal or they were scholastically retarded underachievers.
Rearing Environment	Pathological, broken, and harsh rearing environment with inconsistent discipline and parental neglect. Pyromaniacs noted an unhappy home life.
Social Class Structure	Some pyromaniacs emerged from middle- or even upper-socioeconomic levels, whereas others were products of lower-class environments.
Social Adjustment	Socially maladjusted, severe problems in developing and maintaining interpersonal relationships
Marital Adjustment	Although some pyromaniacs were married, their marital adjustments were poor.
Sexual Adjustment	Sexually maladjusted and inadequate; limited contact with women.
Occupational/ Employment History	Most frequently unskilled laborers, if employed. They accepted subservient positions and became resentful when they realized that their work was degrading.
Personality	The pyromaniac has been described as a misfit and feeble person, a physical coward with feelings of inadequacy, inferiority, insufficiency, and

(Continued)

TABLE 6.7   *(Continued)*

---

	self-consciousness. They are introverted, seclusive, aloof, frustrated, and lonely people. They have unconscious fears of being unwanted and unloved and suffer from a wounded self-esteem and a lack of pride and prestige. They often project an image of calmness and indifference (anxiety and tension are present nonetheless). They have vague feelings, however, that their defenses will fail them and that these repressed impulses will emerge. They tend to be defensive and obstinate in attitude and ambivalent toward authority. Although they have an inner dependency on authority, they also have contempt for authority. In fact, they have repressed their rage and hatred toward society and authority figures. They lack ambition and aggressiveness. Some stated that they did not want to really hurt anyone. They are apologetic but ashamed for being apologetic. They seek expression through excitement. Some pyromaniacs have been found to be quite intelligent, neat, and methodical in their behavior. They have a need to be recognized and have a sense of worth. They have a craving for power and prestige. They fail to express remorse or to accept responsibility for their firesetting behavior.
Criminal History	Many had histories of delinquency and criminal behavior, including runaway, burglary, theft, and other property offenses.
Use of Alcohol	Alcohol was frequently used as a method of social escape and a way to remove social inhibitions, but they did not set fires because they drank.
Suicide	Some attempted suicide after arrest and incarceration.
Motives	The exact motivation in each case was unknown, however, the following motives were identified: (a) Desire to be a hero and center of attention

---

(Continued)

TABLE 6.7 (Continued)

	(craving for excitement and prestige), play detective at the fire, render first-aid, help rescue victims, assist firefighters; (b) Desire to show themselves sufficiently clever to cause the "experts" (firefighters and detectives) problems and to render them helpless. They have grandiose ambitions to be the executive who directs the firefighting activity and puts the firefighters into action; (c) Enjoy destruction of property (vagrants exhibiting pyromania receive sadistic pleasure in watching the destruction of buildings); (d) Irresistible impulse (could not offer an explanation except driven by unexplainable force or impulse to set fires); (e) Revenge, although not consciously present was also considered to be a possible factor; (f) Sexual satisfaction (this was noted in only 40 cases).
Irresistible Impulse	No single precipitating factor produced this impulse. It was believed to be the result of an accumulation of problems that caused stress, frustration, and tension. Examples included: thwarted sexual desires, loss of employment, refusal of employment, death of parent or loved one, threats to personal security and masculinity, explosive protest over imagined immorality or promiscuousness of mother or spouse, fear of impotency, and so on.

THE PYROMANIAC'S FIRESETTING EXPERIENCE

Types of fires. Their fires were generally made in haste and in a disorganized fashion; often set in rubbish, basements, and in and around inhabited dwellings, office buildings, schools, hotels, and other structures in thickly populated sections of cities. Frequently, they were made in rapid succession. Matches, newspapers, and other available materials were used in starting the fires.

Number of fires. Frequently they started numerous fires, sometimes hundreds, until they were caught.

False alarms. They were also known to set false alarms.

Time of day. Their fires were often nocturnal.

Selection of target. Firesetting targets were often randomly selected for no apparent reason.

Regard for life. There was no regard for life. Fires were frequently set in and around occupied buildings.

Type of firesetter. Solitary (an insignificant number set in groups or with a partner).

Emotional state and behavior *just prior* to firesetting. Pyromaniacs frequently expressed the following symptoms preceding their firesetting: Mounting tension and anxiety; restlessness—an urge for motion; conversion symptoms, such as headaches, pressure in the head, dizziness, ringing in the ears, and palpitations; a sense that the personality was merging into a state of unreality; and an uncontrollable urge or irresistible impulse to set fires.

Emotional state and behavior *during* firesetting. While setting the fire, pyromaniacs felt that the act was minimally their own; they described the emergence of a sort of dissociative state (a transient sensation of being controlled by an external force, a feeling of being automated). They recognized that the firesetting was senseless but they did not have the control to prevent it. To a casual observer, they would appear normal.

Emotional state and behavior *after* setting firesetting. Pyromaniacs expressed a sense of relief and even exaltation. After setting the fires, their tensions subsided. Few expressed sexual satisfaction in setting fires. They often stayed at or near the fire as a spectator or to assist the responding firefighters by rendering first aid or rescuing victims from the fire. Some enjoyed playing detective at the fire scene. Some pyromaniacs, after setting the fires and ensuring that the firemen would respond, went home to a restful sleep.

Arrest. Some pyromaniacs ensured that they would be identified and arrested; some even turned themselves into the police. Many continued set fires till apprehended. The arrest seemed to release the magical hold the irresistible impulse had on them. It was a relief for them to be stopped from setting fires.

Confession. Pyromaniacs often readily confessed or admitted guilt, although they expressed no remorse or regret for their behavior; neither did they generality accept responsibility for their firesetting activity. They were most often quiet and cooperative under arrest.

TYPES OF ARSONISTS

Douglas et al. (1992) report several types of arsonists. In addition to terrorist or extremist groups, these types include those who commit arson for vandalism, excitement, revenge, profit, and crime concealment.

Vandalism

The arsonist of this ilk tends to be younger and oftentimes he will act in a group. The typical target is an educational facility but residential, as well as vegetative, areas can also be selected. The young person will often come from a lower-class background, live close to where the crime occurs (usually within one mile), and live at home with his parents. This person does not, at least at this time of his life, abuse drugs or alcohol. In addition, sexual gratification is not a motivating factor in his crime or his target selection. He will usually act in the afternoon and during the week. Some obvious reasons for this include his age. For example, this person may still be in school and attend classes during the day. Because of this, setting fires will occur after the school day. From the information regarding the typical firesetter according to age, we saw that the 49% of all arsons are committed by young people and most of them are between the ages of 10 and 14.

After the fire is set, the vandal will flee the scene and tend not to return. However, if the arsonist does return, he will watch the scene from a safe distance.

Excitement

Douglas et al. (1992) report subtypes of the excitement arsonist: the thrill seeker, the attention seeker, the recognition seeker, and, finally, the sexual perversion type.

This excitement arsonist craves attention and finds that setting fires is one way to gain such needed attention. He will set fires and watch the activity from a guarded distance. If the firesetter does remain at the scene, he will try to blend in with the other bystanders.

Targets for the firesetting include vegetation, dumpsters, construction sites, and residential areas. This firesetter will use incendiary materials that are rather simple; however, Douglas et al. (1992) suggest that the older the perpetrator, the more complex the firesetting device. For example, if the individual is close to 30 years old, there may be a time-delayed mechanism involved. There appears to be some type of learning involved with the setting of multiple fires. The younger excitement arsonist is more likely to use matches, cigarettes, and the like; that is, simple methods to set a fire. Unlike the vandal firesetter, this arsonist tends to come from a middle-class family in which he lives with both parents.

This type of offender will often have an arrest record, and the older the offender the longer the arrest history. The arsonist will typically commit his crime alone but may on occasion commit arson in the company of others. Again, sex does not play an important motivation role unless a particular firesetter has attached a sexual component. In this case, the alert investigator will look for sexual paraphernalia (e.g., semen at the scene, pornography, etc).

Revenge

The revenge firesetter operates from a perspective of trying to right a real or imagined injury. This arsonist may be quite different from other arsonists, especially those who could be termed as serial arsonists. This firesetting may be a one-time occurrence because it may be centered on the destruction of a particular dwelling, business, or facility of someone who has done this offender an injustice. The focus of the attack may be directed toward an individual, a business (e.g., a former employer's business structure), a government structure, or an action directed toward a group of persons such as a rival gang.

This arsonist usually comes from a lower-class background but is more educated than either the vandalism or excitement arsonist, usually completing more than 10 years of formal education.

Women are often of the revenge arsonist type: She will burn personal items of her former lover or husband. These items would include such things as clothing, bedding, or other intimate items. The typical targets for the revenger arsonist, if a male, are residential and personal property units.

This firesetter will often commit crimes on the weekends, and in the afternoon, evening, or early morning hours. The location of the attacks usually are within a one-mile radius of the home of the offender. He or she will flee the crime scene, trying to personally distance himself or herself from the fire, and, moreover, will seldom return to the scene of the crime. Also, unlike the other two previously discussed arsonists, this firesetter will often use alcohol to lower inhibitions.

Sex is not usually a motivating factor. The precipitating factor in this form of arson is something that the arsonist believes was a personal affront. This affront may be real or imagined. However, it is sufficient that it will result in the firesetter setting a fire, sometimes several, to the personal property of the victim. It must be also remembered that this affront may have occurred several months or even years before the arson.

Crime Concealment Arson

With this form of firesetting, the arson is usually secondary to the commission of another crime. The purpose of the fire is to conceal or hide the more primary crime. For example, a husband kills his wife, decapitates her, buries her head in the backyard, and then burns her corpse inside the house. The fire department then finds the headless body, notifies the police, and then the police find the head buried in the backyard. The purpose of this fire was to hide the original crime of homicide.

Many of these crimes of arson are set with an abundance of liquid accelerant, but because of the naivete of the firesetter, evidence of the original crime might not be totally destroyed. Ressler, Burgess, and Douglas (1988) stated that this form of crime scene tends to be more of the disorganized variety. Consequently, there is apt to be more physical evidence at this type of crime scene if for no other reason than the disorganized offender is more likely to leave physical evidence.

Concerning some of the social variables and personality traits of this arsonist, the offender is likely to be an adult male from a lower-class background who commits his crime in the evening or in the early morning hours, lives alone, lives slightly farther away from the crime scene than the other types we have mentioned thus far, will often commit the crime in the company of another person, and will flee the crime scene once the fire has started.

As with most firesetters we have mentioned so far in this section, sex is not a primary motivating factor. The goal here is simple and utilitarian: to eliminate evidence from a crime that has already occurred (e.g., a homicide, a burglary, a motor theft, etc.). If the primary crime is murder, then this arsonist is usually not a serial arsonist because predominantly, with this type of person, the crime of homicide is a one-time occurrence. When this is the case, the firesetter usually acts alone. However, if the fire is set to hide crimes like burglaries, robberies, and so on, this may be the work of a serial arsonist who will usually be accompanied by another person when the fire is set.

Alcohol plays an important role in the commission of this crime. Here, the alcohol lessens the inhibitions of the firesetter and enables the perpetration of the crime. Drugs may also play a role here.

Nothing is mentioned by Douglas et al. (1992) concerning the education, employment, and arrest record of this type of firesetter. It may be inferred that he, too, is limited in his educational pursuit. If employed, it is in menial jobs that require little education and he may have a long history of involvement with the criminal justice system because crimes such as burglaries and robberies are common serial crimes. In addition, almost four of five are single.

Profit Arsonist

The least passionate arsonist is the adult male who sets fires for material gain. Sometimes, this firesetter is hired by a failing business owner who wishes to collect insurance monies, deplete an inventory, and the like because the business is not succeeding as expected. The times of the fires are typically after business hours, in the evening, or the early morning hours. There is no motivation to cover a crime, no sexual motive, nor one induced by revenge. The motivation here is to set a fire because of material gain. This person hired by others to commit this crime may indeed be a serial arsonist. The anticipated gain may be in the form of money or goods.

This type of firesetter tends to be single and lives alone. He lives usually more than a mile away from the location of the fire and travels by vehicle to the scene of the crime. Often, by the time the fire or explosion occurs, he may already be far away from the scene. He may have an accomplice, one who will assist him in setting up the fire itself, and this second person may be in the position of an apprentice.

His experience with the criminal justice system may be quite extensive. He may have an arrest record in robbery, burglary, public disorderly conduct, and public drunkenness. In addition, because we have noted that this man may be a serial arsonist, he also may have an arrest record as an arsonist.

Douglas et al. (1992) report this firesetter is usually 25 to 40 years old and has less than a high school education, usually about a 10th-grade level. This type of arson is a crime of premeditation, which suggests that the arsonist is at least of average intelligence. The reason for his lack of academic performance might rest with social forces rather than intellectual abilities. In addition, the crime scene itself would be organized.

Of course, each crime should be approached as if the perpetrator is a unique individual. Even while recognizing the singularity of the offender, we can make certain assumptions about the personality of the offender that ideally can lead to the apprehension of a suspect. This is the goal of psychological profiling. (For a synopsis of all the types discussed in this section, see Table 6.8.) As a profiler, certain physical elements, as shown in Table 6.9, are particular to the five types of arsonists reviewed above.

ORGANIZED VERSUS DISORGANIZED PERSONALITY

As might be surmised from reading previous chapters, some of the concepts we have already discussed have important implications regarding organization (or the lack of organization) at the crime scene. As with other types of offenders, some arsonists may be better organized than others. Therefore, the same concepts that apply to other organized offenders may also be true of the arsonist who also possesses the organized personality.

We might also look for social and personal items that send this person into "the fall," especially if the crime is committed for motives that are intrinsic to the personality of the offender. A negative social happening or breakup of an intimate relationship, for instance, may cause the offender to resort to arson as a means of resolution.

TABLE 6.8   Types of Arsonists and Social and Behavioral Traits

Characteristics	Vandalism	Excitement	Revenge	Crime Concealment	Profit
Age	Juvenile	Juvenile	Adult	Adult	Adult
Social class	Lower to middle class	Middle	Lower class	Lower class	Working class
Time of crime	Afternoon	Afternoon, evening	Afternoon, evening early morning	Evening, early morning	Evening, morning
Day of crime	Weekdays	Varies	Weekends	Varies	Weekdays
Lives with	Parents	Alone	Alone	Alone	Alone
Alcohol or drug use	No	No	Yes	Yes	Yes
Proximity to crime	< 1 mile	< 1 mile	< 1 mile	> 1 mile	> 1 mile
Committed crime alone	No	Yes	Yes	No	No
Stays at crime scene	Yes	Yes	No	No	No
Sexual motivation	No	No	No	No	No
Education	Grades 6–8	Grade 10	Grades 10+	< High school	< High school
Employment	No	No	Yes	Yes	No
Arrest record	Juvenile	Yes	Yes	Yes	Yes
Marital status	Single	Single	Single	Single	Single

SOURCE: Material for this chart was compiled from *Crime Classification Manual*, by J. Douglas, A. W. Burgess, A. G. Burgess, & R. Ressler, 1992, Lexington, MA: Lexington; *A Report of Essential Findings From a Study of Serial Arsonists*, by A. Sapp, T. Huff, G. Gary, D. Icove, & P. Horbert, (1992), Unpublished manuscript.

Douglas et al. (1992) report that the organized arsonist will display certain elements at the crime scene. These elements are shown in Table 6.10.

Of course, these components would be expected if we consider the type of personality and their implications on the crime and as reflected

(Text continues on page 107)

TABLE 6.9   Search Warrant Suggestions for Five Types of Arsonists

Vandalism

Spray paint can
Items from the scene, especially if a school was the target
Explosive devices: fireworks, firecrackers, packaging, or cartons
Flammable liquids
Clothing: evidence of flammable liquid, evidence of glass particles,
   for witness identification
Shoes: footprints, flammable liquid traces

Excitement

Material similar to incendiary devices used: fireworks, containers that
   components were shipped in; packaging, wires, and so forth
Floor mats, trunk padding, carpeting: residue from accelerants
   (not conclusive evidence but indicative)
Beer cans, matchbooks, cigarettes: to match any brands found at the
   scene

House

Material similar to incendiary devices used: fireworks, containers that
   components were shipped in, packages, wires, and so forth
Clothing, shoes: accelerant and soil samples if vegetation fire
Cigarette lighter, especially if subject does not smoke
Diaries, journals, notes, logs, recordings, and maps documenting fires
Newspapers, articles reporting fires
Souvenirs from the crime scene

Revenge

If accelerants used: shoes, socks, clothing, glass particles in clothing
   (if break-in)
Discarded, concealed clothing
Bottles, flammable liquids, matchbooks
Cloth (fiber comparison), tape (if device used)
Clothing, shoes if liquid accelerant used (or homicide victim's blood,
   glass fragments of windows broken during burglary attempt)

Crime Concealment

Refer to category dealing with primary motive
Gasoline containers
Clothing, shoes if liquid accelerant used (or homicide victim's blood)
Glass fragments if windows broken during burglary attempt
Burned paper documents

(Continued)

TABLE 6.9 (Continued)

Profit

Check financial records

If evidence of fuel/air explosion at the scene, check emergency room
for patients with burn injuries

Determine condition of utilities (gas, electric) as soon as possible
(rule out gas, the common accidental cause of fires)

SOURCE: This material was adapted from *Crime Classification Manual*, by J. Douglas, A. W. Burgess, A. G. Burgess, & R. Ressler, 1992, Lexington, MA: Lexington. Adapted with permission.

TABLE 6.10 Crime Scene Elements Common for Arsonists

Organized Arsonists:

Elaborate incendiary devices (electronic timing mechanisms,
initiators, etc.)

Less physical evidence; if forced entry, more skillful (footprints,
fingerprints, etc.)

Methodical approach (trailers, multiple fire sets, excessive
accelerant use, etc.)

Disorganized Arsonists:

Materials on hand

Matches, cigarettes, more common accelerants (lighter fluid, gasoline)

More physical evidence left (handwriting, footprints, fingerprints, etc.)

SOURCE: This material was adapted from *Crime Classification Manual* (p. 166), by J. Douglas, A. W. Burgess, A. G. Burgess, & R. Ressler, 1992, Lexington, MA: Lexington. Adapted with permission.

---

in the crime scene. The more disorganized the personality, the more disorganized the crime scene. (These points are well illustrated in the writings of Douglas & Burgess, 1986; Douglas et al., 1992; Rider, 1980a, 1980b; and others).

CONCLUSION

The crime of arson exacts a high price—in millions of dollars a year as well as the incalculable loss of human lives. An initial step toward the successful resolution of this very serious crime is to understand the person who would commit arson. Recognizing different types of arson allows us to understand that there are also different kinds of personalities who set these fires.

PROFILING SERIAL MURDERERS

The motives, gains, and etiology of serial murder differ from those of other forms of homicide (Fox & Levin, 2001; Godwin, 1999; Holmes & Holmes, 1998). Fundamentally different from conventional homicide, serial murder claims more than 5,000 victims a year by an estimated *35* serial murderers currently at large in the United States (Holmes & Deburger, 1985b; Norris & Birnes, 1988; Rule, personal communication, May 21, 1985). Some researchers assert that as many as one third of all yearly homicides are attributable to serial killers (Linedecker & Burt, 1990, p. ix). It has been suggested that serial murder is on the rise (Gammage, 1991), and this epidemic of such homicides is reflected in a statement made by Robert Ressler, a retired FBI agent who was instrumental in the formation of the Bureau's Behavioral Science Unit.

> Serial killing—I think it's at epidemic proportion. The type of crime we're seeing today did *not* really occur with any known frequency prior to the fifties. An individual taking ten, twelve, fifteen, twenty-five, thirty-five lives is a relatively new phenomenon in the crime picture of the U.S. (Jenkins, 1994, p. 67)

Some scholars have expressed the fear that such statements may cause some members of the public to become unduly alarmed, and some believe that authors in this field are deliberately creating their own monster (Jenkins, 1994; Sears, 1991). In actual terms, there is no real measurement to ascertain if serial murder is increasing or not. According to Eric Hickey (personal communication, June 20, 2001), it is a tricky game to make a statement of infallibility in one direction or another.

It would be an error to assume that we are all potential victims of serial killers or that there is a serial killer around every corner. However, from our own experiences with police departments across the United

States, we believe that current estimates concerning numbers of victims may be too high but estimates of numbers of killers may actually be too low. In lecturing across the country, the first author seldom comes away from a lecture site without a police officer telling him about a serial murderer he had previously not known about. We estimate that there are at least 100 serial murderers currently active in the United States.

Estimates of the numbers of victims have been questioned by many experts, including Egger, Jenkins, and Hickey (Egger, 1990; Hickey, 1991; Jenkins, 1994). Keep in mind that some serial killers may kill no more than one victim a year or none at all during particular periods (perhaps because they are prevented from doing so by illness or incarceration). But no doubt a substantial number of the victims who fall prey to serial predators, including killers, each year are not recognized as serialists' victims because of lack of communication between law enforcement agencies (also known as "linkage blindness"; see Egger, 1990, 1998), law enforcement turf issues, and some law enforcement personnel's simple refusal to identify or accept some cases as instances of serial murder.

The number of victims any given murderer has is a defining characteristic for applying the label of *serial killer*. The most common number given is a minimum of three victims (Holmes & Holmes, 1998); however, some researchers, such as Jenkins (1994), prefer to reserve the label for killers of four or more persons and others believe the number should be as low as two, as Egger states in his book, *The Killers Among Us* (Egger, 1998, p. 5). If two were to be adopted by authorities and those within the criminal justice system as the defining number, clearly the number of offenders defined as serial killers would increase drastically. On the other hand, if a larger number is used, then the number of known serial killers would diminish accordingly.

TYPOLOGY OF SERIAL MURDERERS

Despite the similar motivations of all humans, individuals behave differently from each other (Drukteinis, 1992; Holmes & Holmes, 2001). These differences derive from a variety of factors. As stated earlier, social and behavioral scientists have formulated models to explain the behavior of various categories of people. The typology of serial murderers presented below has been developed based on interviews with and case studies of serial murderers, many of whom are currently incarcerated in U.S. prisons (Holmes & Deburger, 1985a, 1985b).

TABLE 7.1 Spatial Mobility and Serial Murderers	
Geographically Stable	*Geographically Transient*
Lives in same area for some time	Travels continually
Kills in same or nearby area	Travels to confuse law enforcement
Disposes of bodies in same	Disposes of bodies in far-flung areas
or nearby area	

SPATIAL MOBILITY OF SERIAL KILLERS

The initial distinction that may be made among serial murderers is in their degree of spatial mobility (see Table 7.1). Some serial murderers live in one area and kill in that same area or a nearby area. These offenders are termed *geographically stable* killers. There are many examples of this type of killer: John Wayne Gacy (Chicago), Wayne Williams (Atlanta), Ed Gem (Plainfield, Wisconsin), and many more. *Geographically transient* serial murderers, in contrast, travel a great deal in their killings. These offenders will cruise, not necessarily to look for victims but, more important, to avoid detection. As several serial killers have told us in personal interviews, if you are looking for victims, you can find them down the block. Geographically transient offenders log thousands of miles a year in their cars in pursuit of murder. They travel to avoid detection and to confuse law enforcement. Henry Lucas, Ted Bundy, Larry Eyler (Kolarik, 1992), and Chris Wilder (Gibney, 1990) are all examples of transient serial killers. (See also the work of Hickey, 2001, who adds a "place specific" trait to the typology predicated on mobility.) This place specific category is on a micro level (e.g., bathroom, bedroom, etc.). In our manner of thinking concerning the profiling process, this may have more to do with a "signature" than a "place." Regardless, Hickey has many valid points to make and the disagreement is only minor.

The Visionary Serial Killer

Most serial murderers are not psychotic; they are definitely in touch with reality and respond to that reality. Such nonpsychotic killers tend to be psychopathic; that is, they possess a character disorder (Carlisle, personal communication, June 18, 1998; Hale, 1998; Holmes & Deburger, 1988;

Holmes & Holmes, 1998). By contrast, visionary serial killers are propelled to kill by voices they hear or visions they see. These breaks from reality demand that they kill certain kinds of people. This type of killer is "outer directed" by these voices, sometimes from an apparition of the devil or a demon. Harvey Carignan was convinced that God spoke to him, demanding he kill young women. He judged women to be "evil" and he believed he was God's instrument in killing them (authors' files).

The visions and the voices experienced by the visionary serial killer may be perceived to be from God or the devil. The visions and voices legitimate for the offender violence against others, who are usually strangers. This kind of offender is truly out of touch with reality. In psychiatric terms, he or she is psychotic. A competent defense attorney for this kind of killer will typically encounter little difficulty in having the client declared "insane" or "incompetent" in court.

The visionary serial killer does not engage in any crime-scene "staging" or deliberate altering of the crime scene to disguise the manifest purpose in the commission of the crime (Douglas, Burgess, Burgess, & Ressler, 1992).

There are other psychotic killers who are not serial murderers. Some are mass killers; others are solitary-in-number killers. We must also bear in mind that usually a psychotic person is not under the control of a vision or a voice every hour of the day. Sometimes this person is lucid and aware but other times reality becomes distorted and demanding.

The Mission Serial Killer

The mission serial killer feels a need on a conscious level to eradicate a certain group of people. This type of offender is not psychotic; he or she does not hear voices or see visions. He or she is very much in touch with reality, lives in the real world, and interacts with that world on a daily basis. However, this person acts on a self-imposed duty to rid the world of a particular class of people: prostitutes, Catholics, Jews, young black males, or any other identifiable group. Such a killer may be either an organized nonsocial personality or a disorganized asocial type, but the former is more typical. Usually, when such an offender is arrested for the crimes, his or her neighbors are amazed at what was done, often saying such things as, "He was such a fine young man."

In one recent case, four young women were murdered in similar ways. One was a known prostitute and the others had alleged reputations for casual sexual encounters. The way they dressed appeared to convey their sexual availability and their willingness to participate in impersonal sex for money. The killer also mentioned that he stalked the women in the early morning hours after he got off from work. In his mind, their availability in the early morning hours signaled to him that they were prostitutes and thus deserving to die at his hands. The murderer of these women had a personal mission to rid his community of prostitutes. After he was arrested and during his interrogation he showed not only an awareness of his killings but a sense of pride based on the service he felt he had done for his community in eliminating such women who were, in his mind, responsible for the rise in the rate of sexually transmitted diseases. He also mentioned that he had sex with the women prior to killing them. The women were, in his statement, given a choice: to have sex with him or be shot. These victims chose to have sex rather than die. This judgment was fatal to them; this was a sign that they were prostitutes. Only a prostitute would consent to sex; "good" women would rather die than to have sex with a stranger, even at gunpoint.

The Hedonistic Serial Killer

The lust or thrill killer, a subtype of the category of hedonistic serial killer, has made a vital connection between personal violence and sexual gratification. This connection of sex with violence is firmly established and the offender realizes sexual gratification through the homicide. These offenders murder because they derive pleasure from the act; killing is for them an eroticized experience.

Because of the pleasure he gets from killing, this type of hedonistic killer's crimes are process focused, generally taking some time to complete, in contrast with the quick kill more characteristic of a visionary or a mission murderer, whose crimes may be described as act focused. The process-focused killing of the hedonistic murderer may include anthropophagy, dismemberment, necrophilia, torture, mutilation, domination, or other fear-instilling activities. Jerry Brudos, for example, cut off one foot from his first victim and dismembered the breasts of two other victims. He made epoxy molds from the breasts and mounted the molds on his fireplace mantle (Stack, 1983). Ken Bianchi and Angelo Buono took young women to Buono's home for the purpose of torture and murder. Often they covered their victims' heads with plastic bags until they passed out, reviving them later to continue their savage ritual (O'Brien, 1985). The hedonistic serial killer receives sexual pleasure from such interaction with a helpless victim. Other killers who may be classified as hedonistic include Robert Berdella (Jackman & Cole, 1992) and Jeffrey Dahmer (Bauman, 1991), as well as John Wayne Gacy (Cahill, 1986; Sullivan & Maiken, 1983).

Another type of serial killer who may also be classified as a hedonistic killer does not have sexual gratification as a prime motive. This is the *comfort-oriented* serial murderer who kills for personal gain. Professional assassins, for instance, kill because there is profit to be realized from their behavior. Other comfort killers may kill for profit people to whom they are related or with whom they have some kind of relationship; H. W. Mudgett, for instance, killed a variety of people—wives, fiancees, employees—to collect monies and properties. Usually, women who are serial killers are of this type; Aileen Wuornos (Kennedy & Nolin, 1992) and Dorothea Puente (Blackburn, 1990) are examples.

Apprehension of lust- or thrill-hedonistic serial murderers can be especially difficult if they are geographically transient. Their methods of killing make investigation of these crimes troublesome. Also, often this type of killer is intelligent, and if geographically mobile, his or her apprehension may be delayed for years.

The Power-Control Serial Killer

The power-control killer receives sexual gratification from the complete domination of his victim (Holmes & Holmes, 1998). As one serial murderer told the first author in an interview, "What more power can one have than over life and death?" Contrary to one description of the killing of a young woman that reported the serial killer's sexual pleasure connected with the act, the integral origin of pleasure for this kind of killer is not sexual; it is the killer's ability to control and exert power over his helpless victim (Michaud & Aynesworth, 1983). He derives his gratification from the belief that he has the power to make another human being do exactly what he wants. By dominating his victims completely, he experiences a sexual pleasure akin to the pleasure of the hedonistic serial murderer of the lust or thrill subtype.

This murderer is psychologically rooted in reality. Like the hedonistic killer, he does not suffer from a mental disease; however, a case may be made for a diagnosis of sociopathy or character disorder. This type of killer is aware of social and cultural rules and norms, but he chooses to ignore them. Like a true sociopath, he lives by his own personal rules and norms.

The killing by the power-control murderer is process focused; he will prolong the killing scene because of the psychological gain he gets from this process. Like the overwhelming number of serial killers, this type will kill with hands-on weapons; he especially has a tendency to strangle his victims.

SERIAL MURDERERS: GENERAL CHARACTERISTICS

A careful distinction should be drawn between the characteristics of serial murderers and the causes of serial murder. It is important to distinguish among the various types of serial killers as well as to inventory the characteristics of such murderers. In this context, *characteristics* are what appear to be commonalities among certain types of killers; *causes* are elements that may explain why certain behaviors occur (Holmes & Deburger, 1985b).

It is impossible to speak in absolute terms when dealing with aberrant personalities (Blair, 1993; Egger, 1998; Hickey, 2001; Holmes & Holmes, 1998), but the following generalizations may be asserted. The majority of serial killers appear to share certain characteristics. They tend to be,

- male
- white
- range in age from 25 to 34 years
- intelligent (or at least street smart), charming, and charismatic
- police groupies or interested in police work

Ken Bianchi exemplifies perfectly the embodiment of these characteristics: A white male, a private security officer, and an applicant for a police department, he was intelligent, charming, and young. Recall, however, that these characteristics are generalizations. Ottis Toole, for instance, was on the other end of the continuum. By no stretch of the imagination could he be called charming or intelligent and he was older than the average serial killer when he committed his crimes. One serial killer on death row in the same prison as Toole told us that Toole has the "IQ of Cool Whip."

As a serial killer's crimes progress, there appears to be a general tendency toward personality degeneration. In other words, there is less and less planning and although the time between the killing episodes decreases, the episodes increase in violence. Again, witness the case of Jerry Brudos. Brudos's second murder occurred 11 months after his first and the third occurred 4 months after the second; his last killing occurred less than a month later. Brudos amputated the left foot of his first victim, the left breast of his second victim, and both breasts of the third victim; he sent electrical shocks throughout his last known victim's body.

A Serial Murderer's Perspective

From the minds and emotions of serial killers comes the "truth" of serial murder. Unfortunately, most killers are either unwilling to talk freely about their crimes or are working on court appeals and do not feel free to talk about their cases and their emotions. This has proven to be true for most of the serial murderers who have been interviewed. However, one convicted serial killer who felt the need to talk freely about what he had done consented to speak with the first author; the following material is drawn from the taped interview that resulted. The interview took place in a small interviewing room normally reserved for attorneys to talk with their imprisoned clients. The interviewee said that he had killed scores of people but would not elaborate on the details of those crimes because of the lack of legal confidentiality attached to such an interview. He did say, however, that he felt he was an authority on serial murder, if for no other reason than that he was a serial murderer himself. The complete interview lasted eight hours.

> My comments pertain to various inner workings of serial murderers, offered from the perspective of someone who has been just such a killer: myself. There are various types of serial killers, so it is obvious that my input here will not be directly applicable to each and every murderer who bears that appellation. But there are many of this fold who, while appearing intelligent and rational and essentially normal to the unsuspecting eye, are nonetheless driven by a secret, inner compulsion to seize upon other human beings, usually complete strangers, for the purpose of subjecting them to deliberate terror, systematic brutalization, and then death. This is the type of killer I was. This is the type of killer I've endeavored to understand through many years of introspection. And it is upon the inner workings of this form of murderer—the sadistic serial killer—that I hope to present some insights for those who might benefit from my own unique, albeit unenviable, perspective.

Victim Selection

Among the issues we have heard discussed is the victim selection process. The traditional school of thought contends that serial murderers, on the whole, select their victims on the basis of certain physical characteristics, personal characteristics, or some combination that the victims possess. This assertion presupposes that, within the mind of each individual serial killer, there evolves a synthesis of preferred characteristics and, ultimately, a clear, specific picture of his ideal victim—male or female, black or white, young or old, short or tall, large busted or small, shy or forward, and so on. Then, as the reasoning goes, when a typical serial killer begins an active search for human prey, he will go to great lengths to capture and victimize only those individuals who closely fit the mold of his preferred "ideal."

We are personally convinced that every serial killer does indeed nurture a rather clear mental picture of his own ideal victim. However restrained the outer demeanor of many a serial murderer may appear, each is without question a hyperactive and exacting thinker, this "thought life" obsessively preoccupied with the smallest details of how and what he will do to his future victims. For throughout each thought, he pays particular attention to the varied modes of restraint, abuse, and destruction that will later be his options when a victim is on hand, his mind all the while deciding which of these options provide him the most of self-gratification. And, just as he focuses so attentively on the methods of violence that gratify the most, so does he pay close attention to those physical details and personal characteristics that he has determined, through his imagination, to be the ones most gratifying to find and abuse as the objects of his later violence. The ideal methods and the ideal victim, then, are fairly well established in the mind of a serial killer long before he actually seeks out his prey.

Notwithstanding this point, however, we strongly believe that in the case of most serial killers, the physical and personal characteristics on their respective list of victims only infrequently coincide with the desired traits of their imagined "ideal." Regarding this, our interviewed convicted serial killer comments

> In my own case, a host of assorted factors contributed to what I finally deemed to be my ideal victim, this mental vision consisting of such specific traits: gender, sex, race, size, shape, age, length and color of hair, dress, and certain characteristics concerning my ideal

victim's bearing. Yet, despite this collection of "preferred" traits, none of my actual victims ever completely fit the mold of my "ideal," and only a very tiny fraction possessed slightly more than half of the desired characteristics. The remainder of my victims fit no discernible mold or pattern whatsoever, beyond their common trait of gender.

And such is the case, we believe, with most serial killers—their ideal victim, and those whom they actually victimize, seldom are one and the same.

Two basic, interrelated reasons account for this disparity. The first centers on the extreme caution exercised by a serial killer in his predatory search for a victim; the second, on the nature of the compulsion that drives him to violence.

Addressing the first reason, it can be said that a serial killer is among the most alert and cautious of all human beings; this results from his foremost concern to carry out his activities at the very lowest minimum of risk to himself. However, as much as he has inwardly justified his intentions, he nevertheless *does* have an unacknowledged sense or awareness of the heinous nature of the acts he will commit. He is aware of the stakes involved—that there is absolutely no room for error—and therefore will mark out no one for capture unless he perceives the odds to be overwhelmingly in his favor. His motto might well be, "Whom I cannot seize safely and with ease, I will not seize at all."

This unremitting sense of caution has direct ramifications on victim selection in that, during the course of his search for human prey, a serial killer is seldom apt to find his preferred ideal victim in a position of safe and easy capture. However obsessed he may be with capturing his "ideal," he is frequently thwarted by the simple fact that, in actual practice, the opportunity for this hardly ever presents itself under the requisite circumstances demanded by his extreme caution. In truth, it is a difficult and time-consuming task to locate any potential victim who can be readily seized without risk of detection. And it is a task made all the more difficult and time-consuming when the parameters of selectivity are narrowed by any focus on an "ideal." A serial killer could, of course, bide his time. He could reject all other easy prey until, at last, his ideal victim appeared in circumstances perfectly suited to his caution. In actual practice, however, he rarely will choose to wait very long.

Why is this so? Because of the second reason given earlier: The nature of a serial murderer's compulsion for violence is such that it precludes any prolonged or self-imposed delay in acting out his brutal urges. Initially, he may set out fully determined to succeed at capturing his ideal victim regardless of how long he might have to remain on the prowl. But, as time passes without him promptly accomplishing this specific end—a common occurrence within his many hunts—his ballooning compulsion for violence itself will swiftly overtake any initially held obsession for a particular mold of victim.

This speedy shift of a serial killer's priorities might be likened to the conduct of a lion who finds himself hungry for a meal. Stirred to the hunt by his initial pangs of hunger, the lion sets out in search of gazelle—that is, gazelle in particular—because he happens to favor the taste of gazelle meat over all other savanna fare. Early in his hunt, a hyena and then a zebra cross well within his killing range, but the lion lets them both pass unmolested and continues on with his search for the preferred gazelle. As time passes, however, he finds that the gazelles just won't cooperate; they smartly keep their distance each time he nears, remaining safely outside his killing range. His hunger and frustration mounting with every passing moment, the lion quickly decides that *any* meal will do, be it a skimpy long-eared hare or a sickly emaciated monkey. In the end, it's the *meal,* not the *type* of meal, that really counts.

So it is with a serial murderer. A serial killer just will not defer acting out his violent urges simply because his ideal victim adamantly refuses to materialize at his beck and call. Instead, his intense and mounting hunger for real-life violence against a real-life captive inevitably compels him to settle for any soonest-available victim of opportunity. And it is this, the increasingly mounting stresses of a serial killer's compulsivity, and not such concerns as preferred physical or personal characteristics, which ultimately determines the matter of victim selectivity.

Perception of Potential Victims

As a serial killer steps away from his home to begin a hunt for human prey, it is almost always true that he knows absolutely nothing about the person who is fated to become his next victim. And, in truth, he really doesn't care. He doesn't care whether the stranger he'll soon encounter is a person of hopes and fears, likes and dislikes, past disappointments and goals for the future. He doesn't care whether the person loves or is loved. Indeed, he doesn't even care whether the person has a name. All such personal characteristics fall within the sphere of real-life human beings. And, as far as he is concerned, his next victim is not at all a human being in the accepted sense of the term. So, well before he ever crosses paths with his next victim, he has already stripped that person of all human meaning and worth; he has unilaterally decreed, in absentia, that the person is deserving of no human consideration whatsoever.

This, then, is a serial killer's personal perception of all his future victims; each one is nothing more than a mere object, depersonalized in advance, with each existing only for himself and only to be seized and used as he sees fit. Moreover, he perceives his unseen prey not just as objects to be used, but as objects worthy of extreme contempt, vicious abuse, and certain destruction. In the mind of a serial killer, nothing is more worthless and no one is more contemptuous than the nameless, faceless stranger for whom he sets out to hunt.

Why does a serial killer hold such an extreme and irrational disregard for others? How can he so utterly despise and count worthless another human being whom he has even yet to meet? The answer to these questions is that, after years of nurturing and reinforcing his compulsion or violence within his imagination, each serial killer comes to a place where he finds it absolutely necessary to act out his brutal mind-images. And this, in turn, thrusts him into the position of needing to perceive living human beings—the only pool from which he can obtain real-life victims—as worthless objects deserving the violence he desires to mete out. So, he mentally transforms them into hateful creatures because, in the twisted morality of his own making, it is only against such that he can justifiably and joyfully inflict his manifestly hateful deeds of violence.

Naturally, this outlook does not arise spontaneously or overnight. A serial murderer does not just wake up one fine morning with the desire to hate and kill other human beings. Instead, the entire sum of his initial violent activity takes place only in his imagination, usually minus the presence of any outwardly directed feelings of hatred. At first, he is perhaps only intrigued by the mind-pictures he allows into his imagination. Then, gradually, these begin to provide him with a sense of pleasure and self-gratification, arising from the heady sense of control and power and accomplishment he feels as he places himself in the role of the aggressor within his make-believe arena of violence. He perhaps cannot identify or articulate these sensations for what they are but, to him, all that matters is that they feel *good* and so he continues mentally playing out the violence that causes them to surface. For the moment, however, his "victims" remain wholly imaginary and he is content enough with this arrangement.

Thus, at this early stage, he almost certainly gives no serious thought to the possibility of carrying out violence over to actual, living victims.

As he continues dwelling on such images, however, he becomes like the budding heroin addict who finds he requires a more powerful jolt, a more powerful means of self-gratification. And it is at some point during this stage that a future serial murderer begins taking the steps that will help transform his undeveloped appetite for mental violence into a full-bloom compulsion for the same. Gradually, he grows more and more dissatisfied with the limited collection of mind-pictures that his imagination has worn out to excess, so he begins to search out newer and more sophisticated imagery to play out in his mind. This imagery—which he obtains from books, magazines, movies, or any other sources depicting new examples and new methods of violence—is introduced and tried out on his still-imaginary victims. This further reinforces mental violence as his primary means of self-fulfillment.

The next step in the progression is that violence on imaginary victims, however refined this violence may be, begins to lose its gratifying effects on the future serial killer. Thus, he switches gears anew and starts practicing his mental violence on real, living people—people he sees or knows from his school, his neighborhood, or his workplace—these taking the place of what previously had always been fictional, imaginary victims. At the start of this new trend, he is probably convinced that, despite the fact that he might actually enjoy inflicting real violence on say, the librarian from his school, or on the girl who lives next door, he still would never consider doing such a thing to them, or to any other living human being, outside the space of his own imagination. As much as he might believe this lie, however, this imaginary brutalization of actual human beings has fateful ramifications on the course of future events. For in order to inflict injury on the librarian or the girl next door, even if meant to be done strictly within his mind, he first and necessarily learns techniques that will later be used to sanction actual and willful victimization. This is exactly what he does, and he continues reinforcing the development of these techniques as he plays out, in his mind-pictures, his new game of replacing imaginary victims with real people. But even this new practice soon loses its novelty and gratifying effects. And, in part because he is now equipped with some experience at depersonalizing others, his deterring inhibitions gradually begin to dissolve in the face of his need for a more effective stimulus. For the first time, he begins seriously considering the thought of real violence against live human beings.

Finally, then, the decisive moment of choice arrives and the inevitable occurs. He has practiced violence in his mind for so long and has derived such intense feelings of personal fulfillment from this imagery that his appetite for this, when it arises, is virtually insatiable. Imagery, however, no longer cuts the mustard. The future serial killer knows now that his brutal fantasies must be acted out, that only this real violence will give him the measure of relief that his compulsion craves. And, just as he never denied himself relief in the past, so will he not deny himself relief in the present. Indeed, by this time, he finds it psychologically impossible to deny himself the relief that now can come only through literal violence.

And so he crosses over the line and begins to look on other human beings as potential victims and as the mere props they must later become on the stage of his acted-out violence. And as he continues thinking about them, he grows to despise them, even if for no other reason than they are walking free somewhere, as yet uncaptured, thereby denying him the relief he craves and is convinced he deserves. They are "denying" him and he "deserves" them. By these and other such twisted rationalizations, he provides for himself all the reasons he needs to justify hunting people down as if they were vermin.

All such self-serving justifications, of course, are nothing but willful self-delusion and deliberate lies. To a serial killer, however, such lies are entirely necessary. For deep inside of himself, each serial murderer does have an unacknowledged awareness of the fact that his future victims are innocent human beings deserving nothing of his wrath. Yet to admit to this fact directly, he would also have to openly admit that he—and the violence he intends to inflict—is altogether unjust and wrong. And, for a man grown accustomed to the goodness and the pleasure it provides, any such admission of actual wrong is intolerable. Not only intolerable, but impossible.

Perceptions During Violence

Once a serial killer is in possession of a live victim, the acts he carries out on this person are very often done as if on autopilot, these deeds almost always being a close reenactment of what he previously did only in his imagination. The reason for this is that he already knows from the countless mental scenarios of his past the degree of self-gratification he can obtain through certain specific acts and specific methods of violence. So, from among all these violent fantasies, he picks and chooses the individual cruelties that he feels will assure the most in the way of self-fulfillment.

These selections, then, comprise the process from start to finish that he carries out on the victim he has on hand.

Yet, if the serial killer places this kind of special emphasis on the careful and systematic acting out of his favorite mind-pictures, it is only because of the tremendous meaning and pleasure he derives from watching the degrading, dehumanizing effects they have on his victims as he methodically carries them out. To him, nothing is more important than to see his victim reduced to the very lowest depths of misery and despair. For if there is any single reason for why a serial killer does what he does, it is so he may feel enlarged and magnified in his own eyes through the willful and violent degradation of another human being.

This need for self-magnification is always, we believe, a mandatory prerequisite to any episode of violence. Just prior to his every decision to victimize, a serial killer always first experiences a sudden and precipitous psychological fall, an extreme low, which he can neither tolerate nor deal with in any rational fashion. Throughout his day-to-day existence, all of his meaning is derived from the fact that he thinks himself profoundly special, unique, and perfect over all other human beings on the face of the earth. So, with the sudden onset of this mental low, he finds it virtually impossible to respond to it—especially to the crushing sense of anomie it gives rise to—with anything else but unbridled inner rage. And it is this very same boiling rage that, in turn, fires up and triggers his preestablished compulsion for violence. The acting out of his cherished fantasies, he knows, will elevate him from his intolerable and infuriating psychological low; they will make things "all right" and cause him to feel good about himself; they will "prove," without any shadow of doubt, that he is really *somebody.*

This, then, aids in understanding the motivations and perceptions of a serial killer as he performs his actual deeds of violence. For when he finally has a live and helpless victim on hand, the violence he inflicts is not carried out just for the sake of violence alone, but, more so, for the purpose of reestablishing and reaffirming his own great worth via the brutal degradation of his victim. The long experience of his imaginary violence has already reinforced and "proved" the notion that, to become a *real somebody,* he needs only to display his power to debase, his power to break, and his power to destroy whomever he succeeds at capturing. So, in the twisted logic of a serial killer, he "proves" his own personal power and superiority by "proving" his victim's "worthlessness" through the demeaning violence he metes out.

The specific methods of violence he chooses to act out, then, are perceived as "good" and "righteous," perfectly appropriate for the present, as they have already been tried and tested in the imagination for their ability to restore his feelings of supremacy. And, once he actually begins, he is so intensely focused on the careful performance of this script-like process and on the restorative sensations they give rise to, that he leaves virtually no room whatsoever for perceiving his victim as anything other than a mere object, a lowly stage prop, a piece of meat necessary only for the literal acting out of his own self-serving drama.

The consequences of this outlook are that the struggles, the pain, and the outcries of a serial killer's victim inspire nothing in the way of pity; his victim is a worthless object, wholly depersonalized, and is therefore ineligible for a human expression such as pity. Rather than empathy, a serial killer feels a tremendous surge of excitement and euphoria at the sight of his victim's anguish, for this, to him, is what the whole violent episode is all about. His victim's misery is the elixir that thrills him beyond all measure, for it is his tangible assurance that all is proceeding according to his well-ordered plan; it is his visible "evidence" that he is the magnificent, all-powerful creature he always knew himself to be.

His real gratification comes from the subjugation, terrorization, and brutalization of his victim, and almost not at all from the actual murder of the victim. Thus, from a serial killer's viewpoint, his victim might be likened to a disposable paper cup, from which he takes a long and satisfying drink of water. Once the water is gone, his thirst quenched, the cup has served its purpose; it is useless and therefore can be crushed without thought and thrown away, as if it never existed. Similarly, once a serial killer's violence has run its course, providing the desired self-fulfillment, his battered victim is of no more use to him than a soggy, used-up paper cup. Because he no longer needs to terrorize or abuse, his victim is perceived as an object of inconvenience, a worn-out piece of luggage he no longer needs.

Analysis of the Psyche of a Serial Killer

Although it would be a mistake to say that all serial killers think alike, it would also be foolhardy to assume that there are not some similarities among them. These similarities have important implications for psychological profiling. The initiation of the "process" of violence must depend on some external force or forces. The external stimuli may be either real

Stage 1: Distorted Thinking

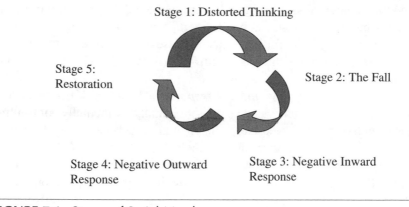

Stage 5:
Restoration

Stage 2: The Fall

Stage 4: Negative Outward
Response

Stage 3: Negative Inward
Response

FIGURE 7.1   Stages of Serial Murder

or imagined and the reality of the stimuli is important only to the violent offender.

As depicted in Figure 7.1, the usual psychological stage of the serial killer is *distorted thinking* (Stage 1). In this position, the killer is in a positive psychological equilibrium state. He is not in a position to ponder the repercussions of deviance because he has either blotted out the consequences or is at this time more interested in the intrinsic or extrinsic rewards of his behavior.

The serial killer will show many faces to society. Given that many (excluding visionary killers) are sociopaths, they use their charm to disarm others and to keep themselves in distorted thinking. No one, however, even the most charming, can remain in distorted thinking forever. Sooner or later, reality is going to challenge his position and he will tumble into *the fall* (Stage 2). It may be one thing or an accumulation of events, real or imaginary, that set in motion the serial killer's movement into this second stage. For example, if A, B, C, D, and E are incidents, and event E sets the killer into the motion of the fall, then A, B, C, and D helped to set the stage for the fall. Event E might be trivial, but for the violent offender it becomes all important. The stimulus may be personal or impersonal, but *the reaction is always personal.* The killer will store these incidents deep within his psyche because his ego is so large. The violent reaction that must follow is disproportional to the event.

This is not to say that each time the serial killer reaches this stage he will respond with personal violence. Sometimes his response may be symbolic (e.g., violent pornography accompanied by masturbation) but such a symbolic response can be only temporary and short term. At some time, the violent person finds physical release a necessity and the stalking process begins. There can be no return to distorted thinking once the fall occurs.

Stage 3 is the *negative inward response*. The serial killer must deal with feelings of inadequacy and he does so initially by mentally confronting these negative reality messages. His mental statement would be something like, "I'm too important and I don't have to take this!" He must validate his self-status and he will do this by the means he knows best, through the perpetration of violence. Now the mental preparation moves to Stage 4, *negative outward response*. This becomes a compulsive and necessary element in the serial killer's self-affirmation of personal superiority. At this time, the killer has no thought relating to possible consequences of his actions. Once he commences to validate and affirm his personal superiority, he is not in command. He chooses only vulnerable victims because he cannot risk a further negative reality message.

With his status once again reestablished, *restoration,* Stage 5, has been reached. Once he has entered this psychological state, the serial killer will think of the potential dangerous consequences of his behavior and realize that he must take care in the proper disposal of the victim. Such concerns, about victim disposal, recognition, and so on, are not vital to him until he reaches Stage 5. He must now take steps to minimize his personal risk. Once he has done what he needs to do, he returns to Stage 1, distorted thinking, and the cycle is complete.

PROFILING A SERIAL MURDER CASE

No act of violence can be executed without a fantasy (Douglas et al., 1992; Sears, 1991). The content and character of the fantasy will change from one person to another and from one type of serial killer to another. The fantasy of the visionary serial killer may center on a voice from God or a vision from hell. The sexual fantasy of the lust or thrill hedonistic serial killer may focus on a victim who is faceless.

The role and existence of the fantasy can lend some direction to the profiling process. An alert law enforcement professional investigating a case of serial murder, for example, can make use of the knowledge that a serial killer is unlikely to commit violence while in the distorted thinking phase of the cycle described above. If the murders "stop" in a case of suspected serial murder, the inference may be drawn that something positive is happening in the life of the unknown killer. Maybe he has married and a check on recently issued marriage licenses can turn up a possible lead. Whatever the exact events, something good may have occurred within the killer's life that has enabled him to remain—if only temporarily—in the distorted thinking phase. Only when something from reality challenges him and his self-perception will he tumble into the fall and start to kill again.

Elemental Traits in Crime Scene Evaluation

The crime scene characteristics common to organized nonsocial offenders and disorganized asocial offenders (Douglas et al., 1992), described in Chapter 5, can be combined with the typology of serial murderers. Take, for example, the visionary serial killer. This murderer modally reflects the disorganized asocial personality. The characteristics of this killer are reflected in the crime scene itself. There is ample physical evidence—overkill, the weapon belonged to the victim and is left at the scene, and so on. The personality characteristics are also similar. He is a loner, probably lives and works near the crime scene, and the victim is a victim of opportunity.

The mission serial killer is more likely to be of the organized non-social type. This serial killer selects one type of victim, stalks his victims, probably has an anal personality, and uses his own weapon, which will usually not be found at the controlled crime scene. For example, the manifest motive of the power-control serial killer is the ultimate possession of his victim. Sexual gratification can take many different forms, and this serial killer's satisfaction emanates from his complete domination of his victims. Ted Bundy is an excellent example of such a killer. For the power-control serial murderer, as for other types, there are five "windows" in the killing process (see Figure 7.2). For the killing to commence, a fantasy must set the process in motion. It is not the kill that terminates the process but the disposal of the body.

Table 7.2 lists the elements of crime scenes and their relations to the various types of serial killers. Combining the typology of serial murderers laid out above with the FBI's typology of violent offenders, especially when sexual gratification is one of the prime motives in a murder, allows the profiler to make the best use of both theoretical models.

The crime scene traits listed in Table 7.2 can be examined and matched with the different types of serial killers. For example, usually a

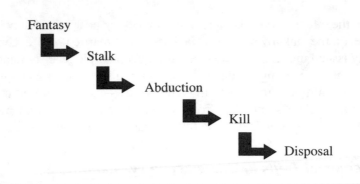

FIGURE 7.2 The Windows of Serial Murder

visionary, mission, or comfort serial killer will not move the body from the kill site. From a profiling point of view, the movement of the body denotes planning beforehand and after the kill itself. The physical evidence present in the kill site can be examined by the investigator. This is not to say that there is no evidence to be found in the dump site, but the movement of the body from the kill site to the dump site is in itself a valuable piece of information about the personality of the offender.

Only the visionary serial killer is not concerned with a specific victim type because he is outwardly motivated by his voices or visions. The hedonistic, power-control, or mission serial murderer carefully selects a victim who will fulfill a psychological need or whose death will result in material gain. Only the comfort serial killer, a *subtype* of the hedonistic type, will kill victims with whom he or she has a relationship of some kind; the others will murder strangers, usually with hands-on weapons in a violent fashion. Pills and poison are weapons that are usually associated with the comfort killer.

The kill scene is often obviously different from the disposal site. Visionary, mission, and comfort killers will usually not move the body from where the kill itself has occurred. Therefore, if the kill site is also the disposal site, then the perpetrator is probably one who lives close to the victim and shares many of the characteristics of the disorganized asocial personality type.

The weapon chosen; the owner of the weapon; evidence of necrophilia; evidence of penile or object penetration, or both; and other elements revealed by the crime scene can help the investigator narrow the scope of the investigation. If, for example, a series of prostitutes has been

TABLE 7.2   Crime Scene Analysis of Suspected Serial Murder Cases

Crime Scene Characteristics	Type of Serial Killer					
	Visionary	Mission	Comfort	Lust	Thrill	Power/ Control
Controlled crime scene	No	Yes	Yes	Yes	Yes	Yes
Overkill	Yes	No	No	Yes	No	No
Chaotic crime scene	Yes	No	No	No	No	No
Evidence of torture	No	No	No	Yes	Yes	Yes
Body moved	No	No	No	Yes	Yes	Yes
Specific victim	No	Yes	Yes	Yes	Yes	Yes
Weapon at the scene	Yes	No	Yes	No	No	No
Relational victim	No	No	Yes	No	No	No
Victim known	Yes	No	Yes	No	No	No
Aberrant sex	No	No	No	Yes	Yes	Yes
Weapon of torture	No	No	No	Yes	Yes	Yes
Strangles the victim	No	No	No	Yes	Yes	Yes
Penile penetration	?	Yes	Usually not	Yes	Yes	Yes
Object penetration	Yes	No	No	Yes	Yes	No
Necrophilia	Yes	No	No	Yes	No	Yes
Gender usually	Male	Male	Female	Male	Male	Male

murdered and necrophilia is involved, it may very well be that the killer believes he is receiving messages from God to rid the world of such "undesirables." This becomes more of a possibility if the crime scenes reflect a great deal of chaos with accompanying physical evidence. If necrophilia is not involved, the killer's motives may be more likely to have an inner source, a characteristic of the mission serial murderer.

The profiler can gain some basic information concerning the type of offender by matching the crime and disposal scene evidence with the type of serial murder category. Although computers may be of great help with such matching and their use may soon be quite widespread, the value of the profiler's personal involvement should never be underestimated.

Additional Profiling Elements

The information in this section concerning *crime* scenes and disposal scenes has been obtained through interviews with serial murderers. Interestingly, the murderers have told us some things that are incongruent with the theories of profilers and those who are psychodynamically oriented; the murderers themselves, however, are well versed in their own killing and what they did to their victims. This information was obtained from killers whose victims numbered from fewer than 10 to "scores and scores."

Blindfolds

One element in many killings is the presence of a blindfold. Blindfolds can take many forms: masks, rags, or other pieces of cloth may be used, or victims can simply be kept in total darkness. One obvious reason for a blindfold is to hide from the victim the identity of the killer. One killer said that he blindfolded his victims, none of whom he knew on a personal level or believed would recognize him, to confuse and terrorize them. There may be another dimension to the blindfolding process—it may be that it further depersonalizes and objectifies the victim. Hence, the fantasy of the serial killer is aided by the blindfold, which helps to block out the personal nature of the crime. One serial killer who was also a serial rapist described this phenomenon.

> After stripping off her clothes and tying her down to a cot, I prepared for the first part of my fantasy. [He wanted the woman to perform oral sex on him.] When I got on top of her, I felt very uncomfortable, nervous, and unsettled by the woman's wide-eyed facial expression. I couldn't understand why I felt that way, but I did know I couldn't begin to go on until I covered her eyes. (authors' files)

Only after he had blindfolded her did he feel comfortable enough to proceed with his attack.

So, contrary to some common assumptions, a blindfold found at the crime scene does not necessarily mean that there was a previous personal relationship between the killer and his victim. As one murderer said in an interview, "I blindfolded my victims because faces scream at you."

Attacks at the Face

Slapping at the face of a victim *depersonalizes the attack itself.* Remember the remarks Will Graham made to the Red Dragon killer: "Is there something you're ashamed of?" (Harris, 1981, p. 26). Regardless of how ruthless a violent offender may be, he is still a human being subject to the entire range of human emotions, shame included. When he is trolling for a victim, he more or less recognizes that his pseudocontempt for this eventual captive is but a shoddy excuse to justify the hunt. And when he finally does seize a stranger to victimize, his unacknowledged awareness of his victim's actual innocence gives rise to a creeping sense of shame—or some similar emotion—that he has to deal with in order to proceed with what he *knows is* wrong.

Of course, being an expert at glossing over this emotion, he will not let this deter him from his ultimate, selfish aim. One of his key means of eliminating the "shame factor" (such as when in possession of a complete stranger), however, is to blot out the eyes, mask the identity—to keep the person a *nonperson.* When there is no "real person" to face, only a prop with a rag over its eyes, there is no shame.

On a more pragmatic level, violence directed at the face of the victim is a device manifestly intended to control. An attack at the eyes is especially important because of the obvious reason that injury can result in blindness and therefore reduce the possibility of a personal identification. This is usually not a factor in a serial murder case because the killer has already made the decision that the victim will not survive a process-oriented murder event.

Oral sex can be viewed as a further attack upon the victim's face and a departure from the point of view that any such attack is an impersonal one. Of course, a utilitarian factor is involved in oral sex: The offender wants his victim to arouse him sexually. In this stance, oral sex is not perceived as an attack; rather, as one serialist stated, oral sex "was an acceptable usage of a nameless receptacle" (authors' files).

There is an inclination to believe that oral sex by itself can reveal little in terms of whether a crime has been perpetrated by a stranger or an acquaintance of the victim. Oral sex accompanied by blindfolding, however, would seem to point to a stranger-perpetrated offense. Oral sex with no evidence of blindfolding, especially when there has also been physical battering of the victim's face, tends to point to an acquaintance-perpetrated crime.

An attack in darkness combined with a blindfold is intended to terrorize as well as to depersonalize the victim. The blindfold, although reducing some of the personal element in the violence, renders the victim a nonentity and an object, but the attack at the face brings to the fantasy level of the perpetrator a personal but peculiar dimension.

Disposal of the Body

Lust, thrill, and power-control serial killers are the most likely kinds of serialists to dispose of the bodies of their victims. These types of killers share many of the personality attributes of the organized nonsocial personality type. The reasons they dispose of the bodies are varied, and whether the killer intends for a body to be found or not can be a factor. One serial killer, when questioned about why many victims had never been found, said, "You only find the bodies of the ones [the killer] wants you to find" (authors'files). He may have also been saying that the disposal of the body was a form of "advertisement" in his killing career. Of those interviewed, not one serial killer related any concern that the bodies should be found so that the victims' families could be relieved of doubt about their loved ones. The serial murderer is not concerned about his victims' families.

The disposal of the body is a signal that the killing process involving that particular victim is over. This completes the *windows* of serial murder, or the phases that serial killers go through in their killings. It is not a signal that the killing will start again. The murderer is now in a psychological state of euphoria, back in the distorted thinking stage of the cycle. He will remain in distorted thinking as long as reality does not challenge his position of self-importance.

For most serial murderers, learning how to dispose of bodies takes the same form as any other social learning process. In the same way one learns to do many everyday things, legal or not, the serial murderer learns the most personally beneficial manner of disposing of his victims. He will take care in the disposal because this is when he is most vulnerable. One serial murderer dumped many of his victims' bodies on a U-shaped curve in the road so that he could see both ways at the moment of his highest vulnerability.

A recent case provides an example of how a profiler's knowledge can be useful even for locating a missing body. The police in the case requested a profile from the first author after having first called in a psychic and an astrologer, both of whom believed that the killer had taken the body through town and dumped it in a large lake on the other side of the county. This profiler, in contrast, offered the opinion that the body would be found somewhere between the murder site, where the victim's purse was found, and a road where the suspected murderer was seen later the same day the victim was killed. A triangle was drawn on a map delineating the search area and the victim's body was eventually found within that triangle by hunters looking for game. The first author's reasoning was that a killer would not risk driving through a small town where everyone knew him to dump a body in an open area near a lake—nothing mysterious, nothing magical, just a hunch based in logic, accompanied by the luck of the two hunters' find.

Weapons

The weapon, as well as the torture used by the killer, moves the ritualist and the victim further apart from each other as human beings. Serial killers select their weapons of murder very carefully and usually kill with hands-on weapons for three reasons: (a) to touch the victim, (b) because the touch terrorizes the victim, and (c) because the touch degrades the victim. Hands-on weapons include straps (e.g., Jerry Brudos), women's hose (e.g., Ted Bundy), hands (e.g., Edmund Kemper), knives (e.g., Douglas Clark and Carol Bundy), hammers (e.g., Harvey Carignan), handguns (e.g., Beoria Simmons), and all other weapons that require or can be used in close contact. Fire is normally not a method preferred by serial murderers because serial killers are socialized into the use of other weapons to kill and terrorize. This is not to say that some serial murderers will not burn their victims with cigarettes, hot spatulas, or other objects, but the final means of murder requires physical contact.

When the abduction initially transpires, the killer and the victim are close together on a social yardstick. The killer needs to establish a distance between him and his victim immediately to prove his superiority. The dispatching of a helpless and vulnerable victim is the psychological agent needed to place him back into distorted thinking.

Dismemberment

Picquerism is the repeated stabbing and wounding of a person that results in sexual gratification. Accurately, dismemberment may be viewed as a form of picquerism, so the sexual dimension of that activity cannot be ignored. Dismemberment also demonstrates and validates the power and control the killer has over his helpless victim. He is "proving" that his victim is not only nothing, but, by the complete violation of the corpse, "the victim is now little pieces of nothing," as one serial murderer stated (authors' files). This unbridled violation of the body, now a corpse, generates some form of gratification for the serial killer, either sexual satisfaction or a psychological enhancement of the ego of the murderer.

Dismemberment, as might be expected, is most typical of the lust, thrill, and power-control types of serial killer. When visionary serial killers dismember, the sexual component is generally absent; such attacks are more likely to be the result of frenzied compliance with the demands of the killer's perceived demons. Knowledge of the dichotomy of organized nonsocial offenders and disorganized asocial offenders is useful to profilers who are confronted with dismemberment as an element of a crime.

Bondage

The more organized the kill, the more need for bondage. The blitz attack perpetrated by visionary and mission serial killers eliminates the need for bondage, which is used primarily to render the victim helpless and in the control of the serial killer. There are at least three additional motivations for bondage: (a) to hold the victim for torture, (b) to place the victim in a degrading situation, and (c) to hurt or injure the victim. The act of being bound is itself also a form of injury. Lust, thrill, and power-control serial killers, who connect sexual gratification with personal violence, have a need to see the distress of their struggling victims, and bondage serves this purpose.

Position of the Body

There is also a case to be made that the positioning of the victim's body can provide important information about the serial murderer, but some care must be taken in interpreting the meaning of any positioning.

The symbolic positioning of the body (e.g., in a degrading posture) may be a characteristic associated with the mission serial killer, or with the lust or thrill killer. The FBI notes that "if the [disorganized asocial] offender has mutilated the body, it may be positioned in a special way that has significance to the offender" ("Classifying Sexual Homicide Crime Scenes," 1985).

Duct Tape

Since the first edition of this book was published, we have made an interesting discovery regarding an apparent relationship between the use of duct tape and the background of an offender. We have talked with several offenders in prison who have used duct tape to bind their victims; they have learned about the efficiency of duct tape for this purpose during time spent inside prison walls. They stated that other offenders instructed them not only in the manner in which the tape should be applied but also the reason for using duct tape rather than another kind of tape or heavy twine. (This method is illustrated in the movie *A Few Good Men,* when a young Marine is forcibly removed from his barracks and bound with camouflage printed duct tape.) When duct tape is used on a murder victim, it may be an indication that the perpetrator has been in prison at some time or is a past or present member of a special services branch of the military.

Staging

As Douglas et al. (1992) define it, "Staging is when someone purposively alters the crime scene prior to the arrival of police" (p. 251). The deliberate staging of a crime scene may be indicative of someone who is an organized killer because it obviously takes some mental ability to realize that there is a need to change the crime scene to divert the investigation of the police. The organized nonsocial offender may realize that the police will be looking for certain nonphysical evidence that could indicate a certain type of offender with certain social core variables. The disorganized asocial offender may not have the mental ability to alter a crime scene deliberately. In addition, the disorganized asocial offender may truly not understand the investigatory process or the manner in which evidence is gathered and examined. If staging is evident in the crime scene, investigators would be wise to look for someone who fits the pattern of the organized nonsocial offender rather than the disorganized one.

Souvenirs

The immediate reason for a serial killer to take a souvenir from a crime scene is to have a reminder of what has transpired. The rational decision to take a souvenir involves the same mental process as might be used by someone collecting souvenirs while on a vacation. It reminds the killer not only of the event but of what has taken place during that event. The souvenir is also part of the psychological gain realized by the murderer during the kill. What is taken once belonged to the victim, and because of that, it reminds the serial killer of a personal aspect of the event.

Not all serial killers take souvenirs and those who do may not take souvenirs after every murder. The killer must make a decision to take a souvenir on a rational basis; in some cases, he may realize that there is little or no opportunity to take a part of the property of the victim without exposing himself to undue risk.

Sometimes when a serial killer takes property belonging to the victim it has less to do with the collection of souvenirs than with the prevention of identification of the victim—a way to hinder the investigation by law enforcement. If the body has been mutilated or somehow altered so that it is difficult to identify the victim, and there are no personal belongings of the victim at the scene, then the serial killer has indeed accomplished one of his purposes. The souvenir, on two levels, strips the victim of his or her identity.

Trophies

In the profiles we have submitted to police departments, we have always made a distinction between souvenirs and trophies. Trophies represent something a person has won, as a bowling trophy or a tennis trophy does. In the case of a serial murder, a trophy is something intrinsic in value; it not only represents something that has been done by the predator but also something that has value of itself. Thus, a trophy is something personal, such as a body part (e.g., a leg, a breast). A souvenir may be only a memento that recalls an experiential high point, whereas a trophy is not only a reminder of the experiential high but a visual reward that serves as an aphrodisiac.

CONCLUSION

The initial step for creating a profile in a serial murder case is the determination that the case under investigation is truly one of serial homicide. This may sound very rudimentary but as any investigator realizes, sometimes we all have tunnel vision, seeing only what we want to see. Once a homicide is "certified" as part of a serial murder case, the investigators must be prepared for the publicity and other ramifications that come with such a situation.

The methods, gains, and motives of serial murder are unique to each type of killer. If investigators are able to attain some understanding of the psychology of the serial killer and his propensity for violence, if they realize that the serial murderer feels that he is all-powerful and all-knowing, and that it is his birthright to feel this way, they may have a better understanding of the psychopathic serial killer. Knowledge about the nature of differing crime scenes can deepen this understanding. A chaotic or sadistic crime scene, or one in which overkill is apparent, can give investigators valuable information.

In this chapter we have attempted to fulfill two purposes for law enforcement investigators. First, we have introduced a unique typology of serial offenders that offers motives for action and evaluation of the serial killer's mind and a particular model for personal violence. Second, we have outlined some crime scene characteristics that investigators should consider. We will address these characteristics again later in this volume.

In closing, we want to emphasize again that a profile is no substitute for a comprehensive investigation; it is simply one more investigatory aid. A profile is rarely as accurate as depicted in fictional works such as *Red Dragon, Copycat,* and *The Silence of the Lambs.* Some authors have been very negative about the value of profiling. In a scathing criticism of the FBI's Behavioral Science Unit's operation, Jenkins (1994) charges that the profiles the FBI has offered in serial murder cases have been largely unproductive. One of the Bureau's own, Paul Lindsey, has been quoted as saying, "I mean, how many serial killer cases has the FBI solved—if any?" (Jenkins, 1994, p. 56). Jenkins even remarks that Ressler's claim that he coined the term *serial murder* is in error; Jenkins cites an earlier occurrence in the work of Lunde (1976). In the ongoing debate, our position is that profiling should be accepted as an *aid* to investigation. It will not by itself solve any crime despite the abilities of the profiler. In addition, no one profile will be 100% accurate; some errors in the profiling document will always exist. But if several profiles are secured, the investigator may be able to discover some commonalities and work with these so that the profile becomes the most reliable.

PSYCHOLOGICAL PROFILING AND RAPE

Rape is a crime that has certain cultural definitions. Brownmiller (1975) asserts that rape is "a conscious process of intimidation by which all men keep all women in a state of fear" (p. 115). She further adds that rape in time of war has long been considered the victor's prerogative; the vanquished surrender yet another form of "property." When women are viewed as chattel, rape confirms their inferior social position. Conversely, a study of rape in Pennsylvania conducted in the early 1970s espoused a position of victim precipitation (Amir, 1971). This stance "validated" many of the myths about rape, including that women secretly want to be raped, that the primary motive for rape is sex, and so on. In this chapter, we focus on the roles of sex and power in the repugnant crime of rape. Sadly, as reported by Edward and MacLeod (1999), these myths may have some impact on the commission of this most violent crime. Perhaps these myths as well as attitudes have contributed to the manner in which the rape rates are still extremely high (Ewolt, Monson, & Kanghinrichsen-Rohling, 2001). We do not have space available here to refute the above-mentioned myths about rape, but we want to stress that rape is a crime of *power* and *violence* in which sex is the weapon.

DEFINITIONS OF RAPE

Rape may be defined as the crime of having sexual intercourse with another person forcibly and against his or her will (Kenney & More, 1994, p. 33). Rape is often viewed, mistakenly, as a sexually motivated act; in reality, it is a violent crime. *Statutory rape* is sexual intercourse that is unlawful because it involves a person younger than the age prescribed by statute as the age of consent (Bennett & Hess, 1994, p. 361). *Forcible rape* is sexual penetration without a person's consent; this is the crime with which we are concerned in this chapter.

Although in this chapter we address primarily what may be called "stranger rape," it should be noted that in recent years the very character of what is viewed as rape has been changing because the phenomenon of "date rape" or "acquaintance rape" has received a great deal of attention (James, West, & Deters, 2000). In some ways, our cultural view of what constitutes rape may be shifting (Gibbs, 1991). Only with time will we gain improved perspective on this form of sexual crime (Dunham & Alpert, 1993, p. 91).

STATISTICS ON RAPE

According to FBI estimates (U.S. Department of Justice, 1993, p. 249), almost 150,000 rapes were reported in the United States in 1993. This figure does not include, of course, rapes that were unreported. The web site of Men Against Rape reports that there were 97,460 rapes in 1995; if the reporting rate is 16%, this would mean that there were 649,733 rapes in that same year (MASA, 2001). Johnson and Sigler (2000) report that almost 20% of all college women are forced to do something sexual that they do not wish to do. Many researchers believe that a great many rapes are not reported and for a number of reasons, including victims' feelings of shame, victims' beliefs that police will not believe them, victims' fear of reprisals, and victims' lack of faith in the criminal justice system (Palmiotto, 1994, pp. 253, 261). Bachman (1998) details that the likelihood of reporting a rape on the part of the female victim rests on whether the victim sustained physical injuries in addition to the rape and if the offender used a weapon (Bachman, 1998; Pino & Meier, 1999). On the other hand, women who are raped by their husbands, even though they typically suffer multiple assaults, tend to shun the police, social service agencies, and medical aid for their injuries (Bergen, 1998). Pino and Meier (1999) report that many men do not report being raped because it would be considered a personal affront to their masculinity. Whatever the reasons to report or not, victimization reports suggest higher rates of rape than the FBI data show (see U.S. Department of Justice, 1991, p. 6).

Men are raped at much lower rates than are women. One study suggests that males account for 1% of all reported rape victims (Groth & Burgess, 1980, p. 806) and Glick (1995, p. 207) notes that, of 141,000 rapes reported in 1992, males were victims in about 8% of the cases. (However, these statistics do not include men who are raped in prisons.)

The majority of rape victims are young, with those in the cohort of 16 to 24 years old being two to three times more likely than those in other age groups to become victims. Most rape victims are white, but black females are disproportionally represented among victims in comparison with their numbers in the general population. Rape victims also tend to be single and from the lower socioeconomic class (Schwendinger & Schwendinger, 1983; U.S. Department of Justice, 1988).

Marital rape, which we will not address further in this book because of the nature of psychological profiling, is undoubtedly underreported. Russell (1982) estimates that one husband in seven, on at least one occasion, sexually forces his wife to submit to coitus, oral sex, or anal sex.

Attempted but uncompleted stranger rape typically occurs on the street, in a park or playground, or in a parking lot or parking garage during daylight hours. Completed stranger rape most often occurs in the victim's home in the period from 6:00 p.m. to midnight (U.S. Department of Justice, 1988).

Rape statistics may be very misleading, given that some researchers believe that less than 10% of all rapes are reported. As noted above, there are many reasons for women's reluctance to report having been raped. Especially before rape "shield laws" were in place, women often feared that their own sexual backgrounds could be made an issue during the prosecution of a rape case. Indeed, many rape victims have been subjected to yet another vicious personal attack in the courtroom at the hands of defense attorneys. Perhaps the paramount reason many women are reluctant to report rape is the stigma that is still attached to the status of rape victim; in our society it is still common for members of the public to blame the victim, to believe that the victim somehow invited the attack or cooperated with the rapist.

Of course, every rape should be reported. In recent years, there have been some improvements in the rates of reporting, in part because of changes in the laws in many states that have effectively limited the right of accused rapists' defense attorneys to introduce in court the victims' sexual histories. Increased sensitivity within law enforcement and improved evidence gathering methods in cases of alleged rape, perhaps a side effect of the increase in the number of female police officers on many police forces, has also contributed to this trend.

There are those who believe that some women make false accusations of rape as a form of revenge against men they wish to punish, but it appears that although this occurs, it is very infrequent. One recent study found that only approximately 15% of all *accusations* of rape are unfounded (Palmiotto, 1994, p. 262). But that still leaves 85% that are not unfounded, a truly high and disturbing percentage. Of those who are raped, many victims suffer from posttraumatic stress disorder (PTSD) (Jenkins, Langlais, & Delis, 1998). This stress may become acute when the sexual assault occurs in a marriage in which the abuse is severe and accounts for great psychological and physical outcomes for the victim. Mahoney and Williams (1998) report that in homes where spousal rape occurs, a high degree of anxiety and distrust exists between the spouse and the abuser as well as between the spouses and the children. Thankfully, centers and shelters help those who suffer such abuse in the home. More women are taking advantage of these havens as well as the social services being provided (Moriarty & Earle, 1999).

SELECTED CHARACTERISTICS OF RAPISTS

A cursory examination of the research conducted on rapists in cases of stranger rape yields some general information. For example, rapists tend to be young, with 80% under the age of 30 and 75% under the age of 25 (Kelly, 1976; Queens Bench Foundation, 1976). Many come from lower-class backgrounds and are members of minority groups (often black); most choose victims of their own race (Hagan, 1986; Hazelwood & Warren, 1989). Many rapists' psychosexual backgrounds include histories of conflict and other trouble with women as well as marked inability to relate to women personally and sexually (Queens Bench Foundation, 1976, p. 189). Rapists are usually unarmed; in the one case in four when a rapist is armed, the weapon is usually a knife or other sharp instrument (Glick, 1995, p. 206; U.S. Department of Justice, 1988, pp. 16–18). Most stranger rapists plan their attacks (Amir, 1971) and most have histories of violence. One in three has a prior record for a violent crime and 25% have been before the court for rape (Queens Bench Foundation, 1976).

It should be emphasized that the above characteristics apply only to perpetrators of stranger rape. A growing amount of data suggest that date or acquaintance rape may be much more common than stranger rape, but that is a topic that is beyond the scope of this volume (Tewksbury, personal communication, March 28, 1995). We are concerned here with the violent personal crime of rape as perpetrated by rapists who have not had previous relationships with their victims.

PSYCHOLOGY AND RAPE

If we assume that rape is a crime of violence in which sex is the weapon, we can see that certain psychological elements may be expected to be present, elements similar to those found in other violent personal offenses. In addition to these elements, rapists appear to have three added dimensions to their pattern of violent behavior: power, anger, and sexuality (Groth, Burgess, & Holmstrom, 1977). Further, the following intrapersonal variables have been associated with the rapist personality: deficiencies in heterosocial skill development; the abuse of alcohol, other psychoactive substances, or both as biochemical lubricants; and exposure to violent pornography (Linz, 1989; Pallone & Hennessy, 1992).

The elements of power and anger in rape, combined with the crime's sexual component, lend themselves well to psychological profiling. The investigator will find many factors suitable to the examination and interpretation of a personality that insists on a violent personal attack—sometimes fatal—to find a release from tension and compulsion (Holmes & Holmes, 1996).

No simple way explains why anyone becomes a rapist. Certainly, not all rapists are alike and rapists' motives, anticipations, and expectations vary. A great deal of interest has been shown by researchers regarding the effects of early childhood interaction and later personality development of the rapist in which the relationship between the mother and the rapist has been the major focus. The rapist's relationship with his father has been considered to be less significant. The mother of the rapist is usually described as having been, in the rapist's childhood, rejecting, excessively controlling, dominant, punitive, overprotective, and seductive. The father is usually described as uninvolved, aloof, distant, absent, or passive, but occasionally punitive and cruel. Some researchers suggest that in the case of the sex offender, parental cruelty, inconsistency of discipline, envy, and sexual frustration as well as overstimulation or seduction are the principal factors that influence the rapist's sexual personality and criminal behavior (Holmes, 1983; Rada, 1978).

The rapist may have experienced parental seductiveness in childhood, usually from his mother; this may have ranged from covert seductive behaviors to actual sexual involvement. A history of early prolonged bed sharing with a sibling or parent may have sensitized the rapist unduly to sexual stimulation during childhood. In some cases, rapists have shared beds with their mothers into puberty. Many rapists also have a history of severe physical punishment by dominating, sadistic, and castrating mothers. Their fathers, if present, may not have lent needed support to their children when it was needed. Thus, a rapist's hostility toward women in general in adulthood may stem from the pain he suffered at the hands of a particular woman—his mother.

In summary, the professional literature suggests that parental rejection, domination, cruelty, and seductiveness are important factors in the early life of the rapist. During childhood, mild to moderate social maladjustments of the future rapist may be evidenced in fighting, temper tantrums, truancy, and stealing.

Regardless of their etiology, rapists are perceived somewhat differently by men and women in our society. Sanders (1983) points out that many men tend to look down on rapists as less than fully masculine.

> In effect, they "hit girls" and that is something only wimps and sissies do. This conceptualization of rapists is less flattering than that of their being truly "violent men"—men to be taken seriously, dangerous men not to be trifled with. It is also a good reputation for rapists since it scares the victims into submission. However, it is inaccurate. The greater the resistance of women in rapes, the more likely rapists will run off. In the world of violent men, rapists are considered punks and generally low life. . . . Thus, while rapists loom large as fiends and overpowering monsters to women, they loom small to men, more mice than men. (p. 73)

A study of violent rapists being treated at the Atascadero State Hospital in California reported the following (Queens Bench Foundation, 1976):

- The majority of the rapists demonstrated poor relations with women, lack of self-confidence, and negative self-concepts.
- Of the sample, 51% indicated they were seeking power or dominance over their victims.
- The majority had planned to have sex on the day they committed rape and 92% said rape was their intention.
- None of the 75 subjects indicated a lack of sexual outlet as a reason for his crime.

TYPOLOGY OF RAPISTS

Many researchers have attempted to classify various kinds of rapists (Amir, 1971; Becker & Abel, 1978; Cohen, Garofalo, Boucher, & Seghorn, 1971;

Douglas, Burgess, Burgess, & Ressler, 1992; Knight, Carter, & Prentky, 1989; Knight & Prentky, 1987). The FBI's Behavioral Science Unit has been somewhat successful in its attempt to offer a typology, and Groth, Burgess, and Holmstrom (1977) have designed a taxonomy predicated on the elements of power, rage, and sex. In an especially useful study for our purposes here, Knight and Prentky (1987) offer a typology that divides rapists into four categories: power reassurance, anger retaliation, power assertive, and sadistic (see also Bradway, 1990; Douglas et al., 1992).

Power Reassurance Rapist

Power reassurance rapists, also termed *compensatory rapists,* are the least violent and aggressive of the four types. They are also the least socially competent, suffering from extremely low self-esteem and feelings of inadequacy.

The backgrounds of such rapists vary. Knight and Prentky (1987) report that the overwhelming majority (88%) are from homes in which either mother or father was present. Many have had minor problems in school and their average education level is 10th grade. The compensatory rapist is most often single and lives with one or both of his parents. He is nonathletic, quiet, and passive; he has few friends and no sex partner. Often he lives in a home where he is dominated by an aggressive and possibly seductive mother. He may spend some time frequenting adult bookstores in his own neighborhood. Because of his limited education level, he is often employed in some type of menial occupation and is viewed as a steady, reliable worker (Knight & Prentky, 1987).

The power reassurance rapist may have a variety of sexual aberrations. He may be involved in transvestism, for example, or in promiscuous sexual behavior, exhibitionism, voyeurism, fetishism, or excessive masturbation (Shook, 1990). The possible voyeurism of such rapists is an important element for profilers to keep in mind, as it may lead these rapists to select victims in their own immediate neighborhoods (Kenney & More, 1994). For example, one such rapist with more than a score of victims reportedly stalked his victims by looking in their bedroom windows and then entering their houses through those windows when the opportunities arose (Barrett, personal communication, August 15, 1995).

Table 8.1 lists the social core variables of the power reassurance rapist. Of course, the variables shown in this table and the others in this

TABLE 8.1 Social Characteristics of the Power Reassurance Rapist	
Single	Menial occupation
Lives with parents	Frequents adult bookstores
No sex partner	Voyeur
Nonathletic	Exhibitionist
Quiet, passive	Transvestite
Social loner	Fetishist

chapter are meant as general guidelines; they will not fit perfectly every rapist who may be categorized as a particular type (Knight & Prentky, 1987).

Elements in the Rape Process

The basic purpose of rape for the power reassurance rapist is to elevate his own self-status. The primary aim is sexual, in contrast to the generally accepted notion that rape is not primarily a sexual behavior but a means of assault in which sex is secondary. For this rapist, the sex act validates his position of importance. He perceives himself as a loser and by controlling another human being he hopes to make himself believe that he is important, if only temporarily. For this reason, he uses only enough force to control his victim.

This kind of rapist's behavior during the commission of his crime is an expression of his sexual fantasies. For this reason, he is concerned with the physical welfare of his victim and will not usually harm her intentionally. He operates under the assumption that his victim actually enjoys the rape. He may request that his victim "talk dirty" to him but he will use little profanity himself in his verbal exchanges with his victim. He may politely ask his victim to remove her clothing and will often expose only the body parts necessary for the rape to occur (see Table 8.2).

The power reassurance rapist tends to choose victims from his own age cohort and within his own race, and he usually rapes within his own neighborhood or close to his place of employment because he travels on foot. He generally commits his rapes at night, in the period from midnight to 5:00 a.m. The time between rapes for this offender tends to be from 7 to 15 days. Although his rapes generally begin with relatively little violence, the violence may increase as an attack continues. He will choose

---

TABLE 8.2   Elements in the Power Reassurance Rape

Neighborhood attack	Rapist travels on foot
Rapist believes victim enjoys the rape	Rapist may be impotent
Little use of profanity	Use of weapons of opportunity
Rapist wants victim to "talk dirty"	Increasing violence during rape
Victim asked to remove clothing	Possible later contact with victims
Only body parts essential for the rape to occur are exposed	Possible covering of victim's face
Victim of rapist's age cohort	Rapes continue until rapist apprehended
Victim of rapist's race	Possible collection of souvenirs
Rape committed every 7 to 15 days	Possible keeping of diary by rapist

---

a weapon, if he needs one, from the home of his victim. He may also collect souvenirs from victim's home.

The power reassurance rapist is the only one of the four types of rapists described here who may later contact his victims to inquire about their health, as though he is concerned about the possible ill effects of the rape. This kind of rapist may also be so convinced that his victims enjoyed being raped that he may promise to return. In one case we know of, such a rapist promised to return the next day, and when he did, the police were waiting for him.

This kind of rapist may have some kind of sexual dysfunction, such as impotence. In addition, he may keep a diary in which he keeps track of the names of his victims and describes his rapes.

Interviewing Strategy

Like most kinds of rapists, the power reassurance rapist will continue raping until he is caught. Unfortunately, there is no clear-cut best strategy to use in interrogating this type of offender once he has been apprehended. The interviewer should be aware of the basic reason behind this offender's crimes: By raping, he seeks to resolve his self-doubts; he has no real intent to inflict harm on others. Because of this, one strategy that may be useful in interviewing is to appeal to his sense of masculinity. The interviewer

TABLE 8.3 Social Characteristics of the Anger Retaliation Rapist

Parents divorced	20% adopted
Ninth-grade education	Does not assault wife
Married	Athletic
Majority physically abused (56%)	Frequents bars
Socially competent	Likes contact sports
Hates women	Action-oriented occupations

might indicate to him that the woman who has been raped in the case under investigation has not suffered "undue" trauma and that the police realize the rapist had no desire to harm his victim; such a statement could set the stage for a "sympathetic" relationship that might result in the rapist's sharing information, not only about the rape currently under investigation but about other suspected connected rapes.

Because this kind of offender wants to be understood and not condemned, another possible strategy is for the interviewer to appear to empathize with the suspect, assuming the role of a "father confessor."

Anger Retaliation Rapist

Unlike the power reassurance rapist, the anger retaliation rapist has as his general overarching purpose is to hurt women. He wants to rape to get even with all women for the injustices, real or imaginary, he has suffered at the hands of other women in his life. As the list in Table 8.3 makes clear, this violent personal offender is usually very socially competent. Typically, the family situation from which he comes has been anything but pleasant or normal. More than half (56%) of the men in this category were physically abused during childhood by one or both of their parents. Approximately 80% come from families in which the parents are divorced; further, some 20% of the men in this group of rapists were adopted children and 53% have spent time in foster homes. Some 80% have been reared by a single female parent or other single female caregiver. Because of this rapist's experiences with his female significant others (e.g., mother, adoptive mother, foster mother), he has adopted a position of negative and hostile feelings toward women in general.

The self-perception of this offender is very important. He sees himself as athletic and masculine and for this reason he often seeks recreation that

TABLE 8.4 Elements in the Anger Retaliation Rape	
Neighborhood attack	Situation-precipitated attack
Blitz attack	Increasing aggression
Little planning	Rapes committed every 6 months to a year
Intent to harm the victim	Possible ejaculation onto the face of the victim
Use of weapons of opportunity	Anal and oral sex
Ripping off of victim's clothing	Victim of same age as or older than rapist
Use of excessive profanity	Possible retarded ejaculation

centers on contact sports and may also be involved in an action-oriented occupation, such as police work or race-car driving. He is likely to be married and, like many rapists, is not assaultive toward his mate. Supporting his macho image, he may also be involved in a variety of extramarital affairs.

This kind of rapist's friends will often report that he has a quick, violent temper. He seems to have an uncontrollable impulse to rape and his rapes tend to follow precipitating events involving his wife, mother, or some other significant woman in his life. This event can send him into a rage, and rape is the action that follows.

Elements in the Rape Process

As shown in Table 8.4, the anger retaliation rapist tends to rape close to his home. His attacks are sudden, or blitz attacks, which shows that there is little planning in his rapes. For this rapist the rape is not a sexual act; it is primarily an expression of anger. The aggression in the rape is intended to harm the victim.

The aggression manifested in the rape ranges from verbal assault to physical assault to possible murder. The rapist usually uses a great deal of profanity toward his victim and he will often rip off her clothing and assault her with weapons of opportunity, including his fists and feet.

The anger retaliation rapist has made a vital connection between sexual gratification and his expression of anger and rage. Once he secures his victim within his "comfort zone," he uses profanity for a dual purpose: to heighten his own sexual excitement and to instill fear and terror into the victim. He feels the need to express his anger and rage in many forms. For example, this rapist may rape his victim anally and then force her to perform oral sex on him immediately afterward. Following oral sex, he may ejaculate on her face in a further attempt to degrade her.

This type of rapist tends to seek women of his own race and in his own age group or slightly older. He stalks his victims close to his home and he tends to travel by car. Unlike the power reassurance rapist, after this rapist commits an attack he will make no further effort to contact his victim.

Interviewing Strategy

Keeping in mind this rapist's deep hatred of women, the interviewer should be male; this rapist believes that women in general have done him great injustices and he will not cooperate with any female officer in an interview. The interview should also be conducted in a very professional and businesslike manner. One ploy that might be used is for the initial approach to the suspect to be made by a team of officers in which one is male and the other female. Because this rapist will respond badly to the woman, the male officer can then suggest that the female officer leave the interviewing room. This symbolic move may convince the rapist that the male officer is the more experienced and powerful of the two and this may influence the rapist's level of cooperation. In reference to this strategy, we have even heard it suggested, at a presentation by the Behavioral Science Unit of the FBI delivered at the Southern Police Institute, that the male officer should speak in disparaging terms about the female officer after she has left the interviewing room. We find this a rather radical position; such a strategy may be considered by many to be unethical under any circumstances.

Power Assertive Rapist

For the power assertive, or exploitive, rapist, rape is an attempt to express virility and personal dominance. This kind of rapist has a sense of superiority simply because he is a man and he rapes because he believes he is entitled to—this is what men do to women.

For this offender, rape is not only a sex act, it is an impulsive act of predation. The aggression exhibited in the rape is intended to secure the compliance of the victim. The rapist is indifferent to the comfort or welfare of his victim; she is at his mercy and she must do what he desires.

TABLE 8.5   Social Characteristics of the Power Assertive Rapist

Raised in single-parent family (69%)	Frequents singles bars
Lived in foster homes (31%)	Macho occupation
Physically abused in childhood (74%)	Domestic problems
High school dropout	Property crime record
Serial marriages	Athletic
Image conscious	Dishonorable discharge from military

Some of the social core variables of the power assertive rapist are shown in Table 8.5.

Almost 70% of these rapists have been reared in single-parent families and a third of them have spent time in foster homes. Nearly 75% were victims of physical abuse during childhood (Knight & Prentky, 1987). This type of rapist generally has many domestic problems and has often been involved in a series of unhappy marriages. He is very image conscious and tends to be a flashy dresser. He is often a regular at singles bars and probably most of the other regulars know him as one who is always trying to pick up women, is loud and boisterous, and is continually trying to validate his image as a macho individual.

This type of offender may be involved in some kind of traditionally masculine occupation, such as construction work or police work. A uniform of some sort may be part of his masculine image. He often drives a flashy car, perhaps a sports car or a particular model that is a favorite among his social crowd.

Elements in the Rape Process

As Table 8.6 shows, the power assertive rapist often finds his prey in singles bars, where there is always an ample supply of females from which to select.

The attack of the power assertive rapist consists of a mixture of verbal and physical violence. If resisted, he will physically overpower his victim to get what he desires. This rapist will often rip or tear the clothing off his victim as a means to further intimidate and frighten her—after all, he believes, she will not need them in the future, so why take care in removing them?

TABLE 8.6 Elements in the Power Assertive Rape

Rapist cruises singles bars	Retarded ejaculation
Attacks occur from 7:00 pm to 1:00 am	Rapist has no further contact with victim
Victim's clothing likely to be torn	Victim conned or overpowered
20 to 25 days between rapes	No attempt by rapist to hide identity
Multiple assaults	Very brutal attack
Anal then oral assault	Victim of rapist's age group
Rapist selfish in behavior	Victim of rapist's race

This type of rapist may commit multiple assaults on a particular victim and his victims are usually of the rapist's age group. Not only will this rapist assault his victim vaginally, he will also often commit sodomy and then demand that she perform fellatio immediately after he withdraws. He may suffer retarded ejaculation, so he may force the victim to perform oral sex on him so that he can become physically aroused enough to rape. As noted above, for this rapist, sex is expressed as an impulsive act of predation.

The power assertive rapist tends to commit rapes in a 20- to 25-day cycle, a time span strangely similar to the length of a menstrual cycle. This contrasts with the tendency of power reassurance rapists to assault within 7- to 15-day cycles and that of anger retaliation rapists to commit new offenses approximately every six months to a year.

The power assertive rapist does not rape for sex but as an act of predation. He typically has a steady sex partner, a wife or lover. This rapist feels the need to rape and his aggression is intended to force the victim's compliance with his demands. The aggression of such rapists tends to escalate as they continue to rape. This kind of rapist may bring his own weapon to the rape situation, a behavior that shows forethought and planning.

The power assertive rapist does not hide his identity from his victims; masks, darkness, or blindfolds are not necessary. He has no intention of ever contacting his victims again.

This rapist will not apologize after the rape nor will he collect souvenirs or keep a diary. He generally makes a conscious determination to rape within his own race.

Interviewing Strategy

The power assertive rapist has little control over his impulses and thus may be considered to be close to the clinical evaluation of having a character disorder. Such persons are commonly termed *sociopaths* or *psychopaths.* This kind of rapist will not respond well to a police interview based on assumptions or guesses. He responds only to known facts and the interviewer must be certain to offer only those details of the crime that are known and verifiable. Investigators should know the details of the case and be certain of the suspect's involvement because the power assertive rapist will respond to a well-prepared case. If the questioning is not conducted effectively and professionally, any chance of gaining information from the rapist may be lost.

It is best for the interviewer to approach the interview session with all the facts in hand: the placement of the suspect at the scene, physical evidence that directly implicates him in the rape (or rapes), and other pertinent information that shows that the interviewer is a professional. What the police should communicate is, We know you did it, and this is how we are going to prove it. If the interviewer is in error about the facts, or if there is some other reason for the rapist to discount the interviewer's competence as a professional, it is unlikely that any cooperation will be gained from the rapist through any means, including intimidation, pleas for aid, and appeals based on the victim's welfare.

Sadistic Rapist

Of all the types of rapists discussed here, the sadistic rapist is the most dangerous. The aim of this offender in raping is primarily the expression of his sexual-aggressive fantasies. His purpose is to inflict physical and psychological pain on his victims. Many of the rapists who fall into this category have antisocial personalities and are quite aggressive in their everyday lives, especially when criticized or thwarted in their quests for personal satisfaction. This rapist has made a vital connection between aggression and sexual gratification—in other words, he has eroticized aggression and violence.

Table 8.7 displays the social characteristics associated with the sadistic rapist. As the table shows, some 60% have been reared in single-parent homes. The majority suffered childhood physical abuse and many come from homes in which there has been evidence of sexual deviance

TABLE 8.7 Social Characteristics of the Sadistic Rapist

Raised in single-parent home (60%)	Some college education
Parents divorced (60%)	Married
Lived in foster homes (13%)	No arrest record
Physically abused in childhood (63%)	Age range 30 to 39
Raised in sexually deviant home	Compulsive personality
Middle-class family man	White-collar occupation

(e.g., fathers who were rapists themselves). Many sadistic rapists have histories of such juvenile sexual pathologies as voyeurism, promiscuous sex, and excessive masturbation (Kenney & More, 1994, p. 96).

In his adult life, the typical sadistic rapist is married and is considered to be a "good family man." He often lives in a middle-class residential area in which crime rates are low, is viewed as an asset to his community, has a better-than-average education, and is in a white-collar occupation.

This kind of rapist exhibits a compulsive personality, a factor that can be particularly important in the profiling process. He demonstrates his compulsiveness in his personal appearance and in the vehicle he drives, which is neat, clean, and kept in good condition.

This offender is intelligent and probably does not have a police record. He has the ability to escape detection for his offenses, if for no other reason than because he carefully plans his rapes and carries them out within the parameters of his plans. His intelligence, knowledge of police work, antisocial personality, and care in the planning and implementation of his rapes make him especially difficult to apprehend.

Elements in the Rape Process

There is an expressive aim in the rapes of this kind of rapist. The aggression component of the rape is not simply for control; he intends to do personal harm to his victim. If this rapist is not apprehended, he will eventually begin to kill his victims (see Table 8.8).

The sadistic rapist uses his well-maintained automobile to stalk his victims. He takes great care in selecting victims, making certain that he is not seen and taking all precautions necessary to hinder the detection of his crimes and thus his apprehension. He generally takes his victims to a place where he controls the action, his "comfort zone" (Holmes &

TABLE 8.8   Elements in the Sadistic Rape

Victim stalked	Degrading language
Victim transported	Retarded ejaculation
Use of gags, bonds, handcuffs	Increasing violence
Possible use of blindfold	Rapist has rape kit
Possible triolism	Rapist may eventually kill
Victim's clothing cut	Periods between rapes vary
Elements of ritual	Victims' ages vary

Holmes, 1998, p. 120; Ressler & Shachtman, 1992). Warren, Reboussin, and Hazelwood (1998) suggest that distance plays an important role for the sadistic serial rapist. They report that serial rapists travel on average 3.14 miles to rape. Half of the rapists raped at least once within a half mile from their residence, which may place them at some risk for detection and arrest (Warren, Reboussin, & Hazelwood, 1998).

Less to control his victims than to instill terror in them, the sadistic rapist uses gags, duct tape, handcuffs, and other paraphernalia in the commission of his crimes. He may also blindfold his victims, also primarily to increase their fear. He may tell his victims what he plans to do to them, detail by detail, using excessive profanity and degrading language. As he is attacking his victim, he may call her by another name, perhaps his wife's or his mother's.

The sadistic rapist is very ritualistic. Each rape must go according to plan in order for him to experience the feelings he believes are necessary. He may need for his victims to say certain words to him for him to become aroused. Also, he may insist on oral sex as a prelude to coitus. Like the power assertive rapist, the sadistic rapist may suffer from retarded ejaculation. This rapist often carries in his vehicle a "rape kit" (Ressler & Shachtman, 1992); Ted Bundy, for example, carried a kit that included handcuffs, an ice pick, a ski mask, a mask made of panty hose, rope, black garbage bags, and a tire iron (see Figure 8.1).

As he continues his crimes, the sadistic rapist learns increasingly effective methods to stalk his victims and better ways of disposing of the bodies of those he has killed. For this rapist, murder is secondary. As Ted Bundy remarked to the first author during a 1985 interview while he was on death row at Florida State Prison, "A large number of serial killings [are] simply an attempt to silence the victims, a simple but effective means of elimination."

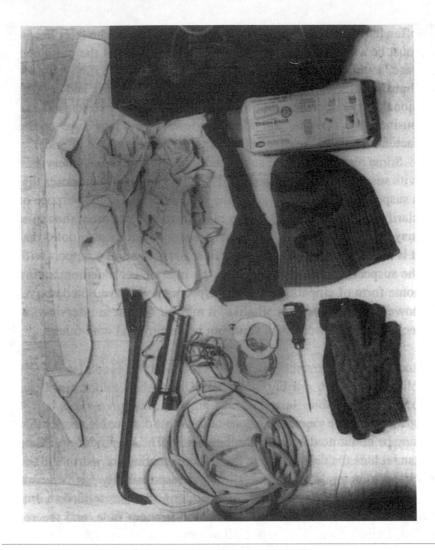

FIGURE 8.1 Ted Bundy's Rape Kit

The sadistic rapist is often mildly intoxicated and may be a recreational drug user. He feels no remorse for his crimes, and will continue to rape until he is caught. It is not unusual for this offender to escalate his violence to the point where the serial rapist becomes a serial killer.

Interviewing Strategy

Unfortunately, there appears to be no one interviewing strategy that is generally effective with this type of rapist. As the Behavioral Science Unit of the FBI notes, this type of offender requires eclectic interviewing techniques. The interviewer must be aware of the many variables and nuances of the particular case, as this offender is highly unlikely to cooperate if he believes that the interviewer is anything less than competent and professional. Any interview of the sadistic rapist should be conducted in a businesslike manner and the interviewer should be sure of the factual details of the case before presenting them to the offender.

Some researchers have suggested strategies for police interviews with suspected rapists in general. Hertica (1991, p. 39) proposes that a suspect be invited to come to the police station for the purpose of clarifying certain aspects of the case. In such a situation, the rapist may be anxious to give his side of the story. Hertica also notes that it is useful for the interviewing officer to try to build a rapport with the suspect; this may be aided by the interviewer's demonstrating some form of empathy with the suspect. As we have noted above, however, rapists are not all alike; it may be that these interviewing techniques will work with some but be detrimental with others.

CONCLUSION

Many people view rape as one of the most despicable crimes that may be committed against a human being. The by-products of rape can include the destruction of the victim's feelings of worth and the victim's internalization of feelings of responsibility for her own victimization. Although recent research on rape has tended to emphasize date or acquaintance rape over stranger rape, and the reported incidence of acquaintance rape has been increasing, the fact is that stranger rape still takes place. We believe that it is important to highlight this point, in part because many of the kinds of rapists described in this chapter continue to escalate their acts of rape and may move to murder. The investigation and resolution of cases of stranger rape, in which sex is the weapon used in crimes of personal violence, require the concentrated efforts of law enforcement.

PEDOPHILIA AND PSYCHOLOGICAL PROFILING

There is no doubt that the sexual abuse of children is considered a heinous act. This victimization of children is such an unexplainable phenomenon that its etiology and practice is most difficult to explain and understand. Consequently, we view those who prey on children to be truly "perverted" or dastardly ill. After all, what person could rape a child and not be ill? In addition, it may be that sexual child abuse is more common than originally thought. Even more disturbing is an assertion that child-sex is becoming more tolerated in American society (Leo, 1993, p. 37).

Unfortunately, there are those who regard children as sex objects and deserving in some way to be treated as exploited objects. In such a mind-set, there would be nothing wrong in sexually assaulting children. In fact, it may be that many child abusers believe the children chase the adult until the adult finally consents to sex. A most interesting attempt at neutralization, this mental manipulation of behavior and rationalization negates personal responsibility. The child is the cause, the prime mover; the molester is the victim. The predatory pattern of the molester will continue.

CHILD MOLESTER OR PEDOPHILE

Ambiguities are involved in the definition of child molesters and pedophiles. One definition classifies a child molester as "a slightly older individual who engages in any type of sexual activity with individuals legally defined as children." However, an accurate definition needs to include age, sex of victim, sex behaviors, and so on. The above definition, however, is very simple. It is devoid of any intricacies or refinements that aid in the understanding of the dynamics of the child offender or the behaviors that are manifested. Although a simple definition, it is also a starting point. This is not intended to be a criticism of the term or the definition. However, when investigating the child molester or pedophile, it is important to reach a better understanding. We take issue with the statement that, "For law enforcement purposes, a child molester is simply an individual who engages in illegal sexual activity with children" (Leo, 1993). This statement is so broad that it loses any implications for criminal psychological assessment.

For example, let us examine the word *pedophile*. The word pedophile means "a lover of children." It is that simple but it is also that complex. The pedophile has developed a sexual interest in children that ranges from fondling to mutilation and murder.

But of course, not all pedophiles wish to harm children. Some wish only to hold and fondle the child. To the other extreme, some sadistic pedophiles are only gratified with the death of their captive child. Because their range of behaviors is so diverse, and if we are to accept the definition of pedophilia to be the "loving of children," we can see how difficult—if not impossible—it is to rehabilitate pedophiles. And it is also true that child molesters, especially the preferential type, have no great love for children. Children are there to abuse and then discard. Because pedophiles or molesters are so varied, what implications does this hold for change? This is, however, not a book on treatment and rehabilitation; we shall leave that to others who are in the correctional enterprise and view sex offenders, including pedophiles, as amenable to treatment. The focus of this chapter, as is the focus of the book, is solely as an aid in investigation.

Accepting our definition of pedophilia as a perverse lover of children is the first step in the investigation process. Now we need to become more specific. The Diagnostic and Statistical Manual of Mental Disorders of the American Psychiatric Association defines pedophilia as "the acts or fantasy of engaging in sexual activity with prepubertal children as a repeatedly preferred or exclusive method of achieving sexual excitement." This is a classic definition that illustrates the action involved (sexual), the age of the child-victim (prepubertal), and an indication of duration (repeatedly or exclusive). But another group of pedophiles, termed *hebephiles*, prefers children who are already into puberty. Seldom is this term used. It is indicative of a type of child offender who makes a distinction regarding

Box 9.1 *July 2001*

In Salem, Massachusetts, a former church youth leader and a swim coach pled guilty to multiple counts of molesting children. In court, Christopher Reardon, age 29, admitted to molesting 29 children and pled guilty to 75 charges. A former religion teacher at the St. Agnes Catholic School, he is only one of several child abusers who have become known to the criminal justice system in widespread publicity cases. For example, in Dallas, Texas, the Catholic Church agreed to spend $30 million to 11 former altar boys of a former priest who was then sentenced to life in prison. In nearby Boston, the Church allegedly paid millions to nearly two dozen molestation cases by a former priest.

Reardon admitted that he wanted to plead guilty to the charges so the children would not have to undergo embarrassing testimony in court. He was sentenced to life in prison for eight charges of raping a child, each of which carried a life sentence.

SOURCE: APB News.com, 7/11/01

victimization solely on age (American Psychiatric Association, 2000). An illustration of this is seen in Box 9.1. This may seem to be a minor point, but when one is involved in the investigation of a case, the small, minor parts often become the pivotal detail for a successful resolution.

An added dimension, and one often confusing to law enforcement, is the sex of the offender and the sex of the child-victim as it concerns the issue of homosexuality and heterosexuality. Consider the following scenario. The police go to a home to arrest a man suspected of molesting several young boys. The police are convinced the offender is a homosexual because of the sex of his victims. They arrive at the door and discover he is married and has several children. He has a self-definition of being heterosexual; he would never consider himself to be homosexual and would view having sex with an adult male as repugnant. The other suspected possibility is that he is gay or bisexual and is in his heterosexual marriage because of special circumstances. The point here is that we should not automatically believe we are looking for a gay male if only young males are victimized. Consider the case of John Wayne Gacy, the executed killer of 33 young males in Chicago. John did not consider himself to be gay and he was rankled when this was suggested (authors' files). He may have been more accepting of the term *bisexual*. If the focus of the Gacy investigation had been centered solely on the gay community, the resolution would have been impeded.

There is yet another consideration here before we look at other elements to be appraised. Women can be child molesters and pedophiles. They receive meager attention in the media and the courts and also tend to attract less rage from parents of the victimized children, especially when an adolescent male is the victim. Some may even condone this behavior as a young boy's "rite of passage."

Regardless of the manner in which most Americans view children, the majority of citizens are opposed to those who regard children in a sexual manner and who wish to victimize children in a sexual way. Vast resources have been expended in the investigation of individuals as well as organizations intent on the sexual victimization of children. But it is also a truism that those who molest children are different. Just as it is impossible to compare exhibitionists with lust killers, it is also impossible to believe that all pedophiles molest in the same fashion and that they have the same social core variables background.

TYPES OF PEDOPHILES

As noted above, it would be a drastic mistake to assume that all pedophiles are the same. Just as all members of a given group are somehow and in some fashion different, pedophiles are different in their behavioral patterns, selection of victims, usage of lures, and propensity toward violence, even fatal violence.

Burgess, Groth, and Holmstrom (1978) report a topology of child molesters. The initial distinction is made between "situational" and "preferential" child abusers. This topology includes "subtypes" with distinguishing traits.

The Situational Child Molester

The first broad category is the "situational" type. The situational pedophile typically has fewer victims than the preferential type. This child molester does not have a "true sexual interest" in children but will experiment with children when stress is introduced into his life. Also, this type of sexual molester will not only molest children but will also abuse the elderly, the impaired, or the sick. Within the situational type are several subtypes.

The Regressed Child Molester

The first is the regressed type. This pedophile has a situational occurrence that impels him to turn to children as a temporary, not permanent, object for sexual gratification. If one examines the word *regressed*, then it is easily understood that this molester turns to children as substitute sexual partners. Something has occurred in the molester's life that challenges his or her self-image and results in poor self-esteem. This type of molester may collect child pornography, but is not as likely as the fixated pedophile to do so. The regressed pedophile has been traditionally involved with adults in normal relationships. Certainly, some interpersonal problems are extant, but from an outward perspective, no great problems exist in relating with adults in personal as well as sexual relationships. Psychologically, this type of child offender experiences the child as a pseudoadult because of some type of situational stress (e.g., breakup in a marriage, a negative employment occurrence, etc.) (Burgess, Groth, & Holmstrom, 1978). Often this type of child molester is married and lives with his family but something happens in his life that propels him into a circumstance in which he feels more comfortable in the presence of children, which in turn results in the sexual victimization of children. Witness the following case.

> I had never thought of molesting children. I was a deacon in my church, a Cub Scout leader, and a youth minister. I had been around children all my life with no intent to harm them. One day, I came home from work and my wife said that there was something she wanted to talk to me about. She said, "Tony, you physically disgust me and I never want you to touch me again!" This really affected me as you can imagine. In the next two weeks, I was coming up for a big promotion and I knew that if I did not get it I would never be promoted before I retired. I'm 60 years old and this would have been my last shot. It came down to me and a young fellow at work who was only 30 years old. He got the job.

I was crushed. That weekend, I and the Cub Scout troop went on a camping trip. As usual, there were two people to a pup tent, and there was a young nine-year-old sharing a tent with me. It started raining and thundering and the boy got scared. He asked if he could come over to my side of the tent and climb into my sleeping bag. Well, one thing led to another and before long, I was fondling him. This led to other young boys, which went on for over a year. (Authors' files)

This abuser was discovered when one child related the experiences to other children and finally to the minister of the church. He was arrested and sent to prison. Holmes and Holmes (2001) report that this molester, the regressed type, is more apt to sexually abuse children he does not know, and the children are typically victims of opportunity (Holmes & Holmes, 2001). Also, this adult is more apt to sexually abuse females, although the above abuser molested young boys simply because they were available. Other traits are prevalent in this type of offender. He is generally geographically stable, employed, married, may have some problems with alcohol abuse, and may have low self-esteem.

The Morally Indiscriminate Child Molester

The morally indiscriminate molester is an abuser of all available persons. Children are just another category of victim; it is not likely that children are preferred as sexual partners with this type of molester. The morally indiscriminate offender has a basic motivation toward sexual experimentation. He is a "try-sexual," that is, willing to try anything. He may be involved in a wide variety of sexual practices including tyndarianism (mate-swapping), bondage and discipline, triolism, and other forms of unusual sexual practices. He may involve his biological children, or children by marriage, in these sexual practices. As one can see, this molester does not have a sexual preference for children; they are simply "there."

The Naive or Inadequate Child Molester

There is another type of situational offender, the naive or inadequate child molester. The molester includes those persons who are suffering from some form of mental disorder that renders them unable to make the distinction between right and wrong in most areas, including sexual practices with children (e.g., retardation, senility, etc.). The people in the neighborhood will know this molester, and he will have a reputation in the community for being "strange" or "bizarre." They are loners, usually not by choice but

TABLE 9.1 Situational Child Molesters

Element	Regressed	Morally Indiscriminate	Sexually Indiscriminate	Inadequate
Basic traits	Poor coping skills	User of people	Sexual experimentation	Social misfit
Motivation	Substitution	Why not?	Boredom	Insecurity and curiosity
Victim criteria	Availability	Vulnerability, opportunity	New and different	Nonthreatening
Method of operation	Coercion	Lure, force, or manipulation	Involve in existing activity	Exploitation of size advantage
Porn collection	Possible	S&M, detective magazines	Highly likely	Likely

SOURCE: Adapted from *Child Molesters:: A Behavioral Analysis* (p. 8), by the National Center for Missing and Exploited Children, 1985, Washington, DC: Author. Reprinted with permission.

because they are not capable of establishing personal relationships with others. This type of sexual predator usually does not physically harm a child and he is more likely to experiment with children with sexual practices that include holding, fondling, kissing, licking, and so on, but not sexual intercourse, oral, or anal sex (Haas & Haas, 1990).

Children are nonthreatening to the molester and he or she feels more in control of this form of relationship as opposed to relationships that involve adults. If he has a collection of pornography, it is typically not of the child porn genre.

As shown in Table 9.1, with each type of child molester certain traits or characteristics are unique to that particular molester. The basic trait of victim criteria, for example, will vary from one molester to the other. With the regressed, for example, simple availability will be the paramount characteristic in the consideration of who will be molested. With the naive or inadequate molester, on the other hand, the selection of the victim will depend on the threat potential to the molester himself.

The Preferential Child Molester

Many cases of severe sexual abuse occur within the situational child molester type, typically the morally indiscriminate and the inadequate. However, there is another large number of child molesters or pedophiles that look at children much differently and perhaps more intensively as providers of pleasure. This group of abusers "prefers" children as the providers of personal and sexual gratification.

The Mysoped Child Molester and Killer

As within the broad category of situational molesters, the preferential type contains several different types of molesters. One type has made the vital connection between sexual gratification and personal violence. This is the sadistic pedophile, the mysoped (Holmes & Holmes, 2001).

Some pedophiles are intent on molesting children with the express desire to harm their victims physically. This type of pedophile, who is usually male, has made a vital connection between sexual arousal and fatal violence. Typically, the child is a stranger to this aggressive and sadistic child offender. It appears also that this offender may stalk the child rather than use any form of seduction (the method typical of many pedophiles).

The mysoped will often abduct a child from places where children gather: playgrounds, schools, shopping centers, and other such places. He will usually not attempt to seduce or otherwise induce the child to go with him; he simply takes the child by force. A scenario that includes pain inflicted on the child, followed by the child's death, comes after the abduction.

This type of pedophile has no "love" of children in the traditional sense. He is interested only in causing harm and death to a vulnerable victim to whom he feels greatly superior. The mysoped inflicts fatal physical harm on the victim and often mutilates the victim's body. If the victim is a young boy, the child's penis may be cut off and inserted into the child's mouth. Small girls are also brutally assaulted and the physical violence is often directed toward the child's genitals. This sexual sadist often terrorizes the child with some type of weapon and the crime is premeditated and ritualized.

An obvious example of the mysoped was Westley Dodd, an executed child killer, considered to have been an aggressive and sadistic child offender. Dodd was regarded as a loner in high school although a member of the high school band and seen as honest and dependable by many of his teachers. The band teacher, for example, remarked that Dodd was quiet, always did what he was told, and was not a behavioral problem. Dr. Al Carlisle, a psychologist from Utah, had interviewed Dodd. Dodd stated that he considered himself a humanitarian sociopath. He said that if a child fell off his bicycle, he would be the first one to reach the child and tender aid. But how, he asked Carlisle, could he intend to do so much pain and suffering to children whom he also loved in the way that he did?

Dodd killed three young boys, two brothers and one five-year-old child. The last victim, Lee Isely, was abducted from a public park while his slightly older brother played with some friends. He took the boy home with him and over a period of several hours sexually abused the boy, which resulted in the child's murder. He placed the body in the closet and, after he came home from work later that afternoon, he retrieved the corpse and committed anal sex and other forms of sexual abuse before he disposed of the body. The police apprehended Dodd as he attempted to abduct a fourth young boy at a neighborhood theater. He was later executed by hanging (his choice) in Washington state.

The sadistic child offender is not rare. Albert Fish, known as the "moon maniac" in the early part of the 20th century, is yet another example. Fish, an elderly grandfatherly type, was finally arrested after years of careful investigation in New York. When arrested, police found body parts that apparently came from various children. Fish took his final victim, Grace Budd, from the Budd home under the pretense of attending a birthday party on Long Island. Taking her to an abandoned area, he killed her and then cooked portions of her body for his own consumption. More than a pedophile and a cannibal, Fish was also involved in infibulation, self-torture of one's own sexual body parts. When he was executed in the electric chair at Sing Sing, the autopsy discovered twenty-nine sewing needles implanted in his penis and scrotum (Schechter, 1990).

There are two other types of preferential molesters: the seduction and the introverted molester. The seduction molester entices the child by courting them with attention, affection, and gifts. This molester is involved in courting the children over an extended period and may be involved with several children at the same time. This type of molester is similar to the fixated molester or pedophile, desiring "a cynical need for affection" (Johnston, French, Schouweiler, & Johnston, 1992, p. 6).

This type of child offender is not really developed past the point where he, as a child, found children attractive and desirable. In other words, he has become "fixed" at an early stage of psychosexual development (Burgess, Groth, & Holmstrom, 1978). The fixated type of child molester's pedophiliac interest started in adolescence; unlike the case of regressed child offenders, there is no precipitating cause in his child abuse. His interest in children is persistent and compulsive. Male victims are the preferred targets of abuse.

The Fixated Child Molester

The fixated child offender has little or no activity with people his own age, usually is single, and is considered to be immature and uncomfortable around other adults. This offender is often childlike in his lifestyle and behaviors. Burg (1983) found that many pedophiles select children as sexual objects because youths are less demanding, more easily dominated, and less critical of their partners' performance than are adults.

The fixated child offender is not interested in physically harming the child. He loves children and does not desire to do anything that might harm them. He courts a child, buys the child gifts as a seduction ploy, and slowly becomes intimate with the child. Oral-genital sex is the norm and actual intercourse develops only after a generous period of time has passed (Holmes & Holmes, 2001).

TABLE 9.2   Typology of Child Molesters

Element	Immature Offender	Regressed Offender	Sadistic Offender	Fixated Offender
Harmful to the child	No	No	Yes	No
Aggressive personality	No	No	Yes	No
Antisocial personality	No	No	Yes	No
Child sexual preference	No	Yes	Yes	Yes
Knows the child	Yes	Yes	No	Yes
Intercourse occurs	No	Yes	Yes	No

PROFILING CHILD MOLESTER TYPES

When examining the various types of child molesters, it is important to remember that each molester is different, particularly in the following three areas: victimization ritual, method of selection, and the abduction process (Knight, Carter, & Prentky, 1989; Okami & Goldberg, 1992). To aid in some understanding of the various types of child molesters, we have decided to examine only a few kinds of child molesters and ones who may be more likely to abuse children and also come into contact with the criminal justice system. We have chosen the following examples of abusers: the immature offender, the regressed offender, the sadistic offender, and the fixated offender.

Table 9.2 contains selected elements or traits that are important in the profiling process. These traits are considered to be important when in the process of investigating crimes against children, and the alert investigator must consider some of these items when examining a case such as a child abduction, a molestation of a child, or even the murder of a child.

From the information contained in the Table 9.2, differences are readily apparent in the various traits attributed to certain types of child molesters and pedophiles. Consider the first listed trait: Harmful to the Child. Is the child abuser physically harmful to the child? We are not certain of the mental and psychological damage that is done to a child by an adult who uses a child for gratuitous pleasure. Children victimized by adults often will repeat this abuse on children when they reach their adult years (Holmes, 1983). This is a dismal conclusion, if true, but must be considered important in the investigatory process. Only the sadistic offender purposely intends to inflict physical harm to the child. This harm eventually results in the death of the child. Again, witness the case of Westley Dodd; he was intent on performing exploratory surgery after he killed his abducted, helpless victim.

The Sadistic Offender

The sadistic offender has an aggressive and antisocial personality and is best considered to be a sociopath. Because of the sociopathy and aggressive personality, he may also possess a criminal record. His personality and temperament may necessitate his involvement with the criminal justice system because of crimes such as rape, assault, and various other violent acts.

For some child molesters, the sex of the child normally does not matter (Harris, 1994; see descriptions of the other types of offenders below). The sadistic offender will have a sex preference: He will choose young boys. The molester and fatal abuser often will mutilate the young victim even to the extent of decapitation and cutting off the penis that is then inserted either into the victim's mouth or anus. This is not to say this offender will not victimize young girls, which is sometimes the case. The sadistic offender is the only offender who attacks a child.

The sadistic offender is more likely to be geographically transient. He is more likely to hold sporadic employment positions, less likely to form long-lasting personal relationships, and is more likely to move on very quickly after a fatal victimization.

The Fixated Offender

The fixated offender has young boys as his preferred sexual target. It may be that the fixated pedophile selects children as sexual objects because youths are less demanding, more easily dominated, and less critical of their partners' performances than are adults (Burg, 1983). As we have already seen, fixated pedophiles may account for a great number of pedophiles and may have a tremendous effect on the number of homosexuals who are pedophiles versus heterosexuals who also may be termed as pedophiles. Freund and Watson (1992) report that the ratio of heterosexual pedophiles to homosexual pedophiles is 11:1. This certainly needs further empirical research.

The Immature and Regressed Child Offenders

Immature and regressed offenders are more apt to be geographically stable. There are reasons for this, which are readily apparent. On the other hand, the fixated offender may move from one area of the country to another in his search for victims, taking some time in the area to cultivate and find the children to victimize. This molester is more apt to move into an area, victimize children, and then move on to another area. He may leave on his own accord; the community may give hime a choice to stay and face prosecution or move on to another area. In one community, for example, a molester of more than 100 young boys was arrested. The judge offered the defendant a choice: return to England or stay in the community and face prosecution. The offender, of course, chose the former. In effect, it became another community's problem. The immature or naive offender does not have a sexual preference for the child-victim. The regressed offender, however, does have a sexual preference. In most cases, the sexual preference is female. The case of Tony was an exception, but it must also be remembered that there was a "pool" of vulnerable victims, the young boys in his Cub Scout pack. Consider, in the case of the regressed offender, that most of the time he has been married and then there occurs a situational stress that results in his movement away from adults to a position in which he can exert power and control over other human beings, this time children. However, if the offender uses sex for control and the victim is a male, then many would believe that the offender is a homosexual including, perhaps, the offender himself.

As the age of technology advances even into the world of child sexual victimization, two types of child abusers will use the computer in their search for child victims: the sadistic and the fixated. Computer bulletin boards advertise sexual proposals, which may also include veiled ads for children. For example, Detective Walt Parsons of the Arvada (Colorado) Police Department has been most successful in using the bulletin boards in his investigation of child abuse cases.

The possession of child pornography may be more a domain of the preferential child molester. For example, the fixated and the sadistic pedophiles are far more likely to possess child pornography than are the situational types. The victimization of children, even to the extreme of homicide, is more a "style of life" to the preferential molester. Because this appears to be the case, it would be far more likely that child porn plays a more integral part in the fantasy life of the molester. The character of the pornography is more likely to consist of violent sex acts. One pedophile interviewed stated that the pornography he desired most came from detective story magazines that spoke of violence directed toward children (authors' files). Knowing this, the alert investigator could include this in the search warrant.

The number of children abused by a molester will vary. True, there may be a few child molesters in prison who have abused only one child, but it is also certain that this is the exception rather than the rule. Some believe that many pedophiles abuse hundreds of children (Briere & Runtz, 1989; Holmes & Holmes, 2001). In addition to this dismal statistic, even more disturbing news concerns the rehabilitation possibilities of the child molester (Conners, 1992, p. 401; Freeman-Longo & Wall, 1986, p. 58; Proulx, Cote, & Achille, 1993, pp. 140–147).

CONCLUSION

The sexual abuse of children in American society cannot be tolerated. One major task in the criminal justice enterprise is to detect and apprehend those who exert violence against our most treasured, yet vulnerable, citizens. The profiling process needs to be placed in a position so that it will aid in the investigation and, later, the apprehension of those who victimize our children. There should be a concentrated effort to identify those social and demographic parameters that, coupled with behavioral and criminal activities, will assist in the arrest of such offenders (Abel, Lawry, Karstrom, Osborn, & Gillespie, 1994). This includes the very violent or those who have no intent of physically harming the children but do immeasurable psychological and permanent damage nonetheless.

AUTOEROTICISM

Perhaps no other sex behavior is more baffling than autoeroticism. Typically we find cases of this kind of eroticism (that which restricts breathing) only when some type of failure results in some harm and often death. What is known is that those who practice this form of sex play put themselves in imminent danger of death. What we know about autoeroticism, other than masturbation of course, is what we have learned from the fatal victims of autoerotica. And how many deaths arise from this type of sex play? There is no reliable number to cite here because many are ruled suicides or accidental deaths instead of a death associated with autoeroticism. In some cases, cardiac arrest is a consequence of this form of activity. It is not the purpose of this chapter to relate the medical and physiological conditions surrounding the individual involved in autoeroticism; rather, it is intended more for the criminal justice practitioner investigating a suspected case of autoeroticism. Consider the following case.

As the husband caught his ride to work at 8:00 a.m. with three friends, the wife, Barbara W., waved good-bye from their front door. The wife of less than one year told the husband that she was not going to work that day and was going "to hang out with my girl-friends." The husband told the police later that he tried to call her a couple times during the day with no success.

The same three friends drove home with him and he encouraged them to come in the apartment and have a beer. The four entered the apartment and the husband called the wife's name, but there was no response. He told the men to help themselves to a beer and he went down the hallway to their bedroom. The wife was not there. On the way back to the kitchen, the husband looked into the bathroom. He saw his wife on her knees, leaning over into the bathtub filled with six inches of water. She was dead.

The police investigated the case and thought it to be a homicide. The victim's ankles were bound by a telephone cord tied with a knot. Her wrists were also bound with another telephone cord wrapped 21 times but not knotted. She was wearing her nightgown and a brown, terry cloth robe, the same robe that she was last seen wearing by the husband and his friends who picked him up for work that same morning. She also had one of her husband's brown knit ties around her neck. Her face was in the water and the medical examiner later ruled the cause of death was drowning.

Because of an officer's suspicion, this case was submitted for a psychological profile. The profile indicated that this may have been a case of aqua autoeroticism. The profile indicated that further investigation should be made into the apartment itself. What was troubling was that the victim drowned in only six inches of water, the necktie around her neck, and the manner in which the telephone cord was wrapped and not tied around her wrists.

The profile suggested that this was a case of autoeroticism and, therefore, recommended that the investigators return to the apartment and examine the doors, the doorknobs, and the bedroom for any collateral evidence of this type of sexual paraphilia. The police did find rope burns on the top of the door in the bedroom. Rope fibers were also found on the door knobs on the inside of the closet door. The victim had practiced autoerotic asphyxiation before, on many occasions, and had placed a rope around her neck (the husband's heavy necktie around her neck was used to prevent ligature marks), then the rope was placed over the door and tied to the knob on the closet side of the door.

The husband, who was not considered a suspect in the case because he had a perfect alibi, finally admitted that his wife had shared with him her practice of this form of autoerotic asphyxiation. He added that he had never personally witnessed this. He also stated that he was not aware of any interest in aquaeroticism. It was assumed that this was the first time and she failed in her attempt at sexual gratification using water. He suspected that she had tried to expand her sexual repertoire but was hesitant to say anything to the police because her parents were fundamentalist Christians. He believed that the parents would be better suited to handle a suspicion that their daughter had been murdered rather than killed through an autoerotic sexual act that many consider sinful.

WHAT IS AUTOEROTIC SEX BEHAVIOR?

The strict definition of autoerotic sexual behavior would include sex behaviors done by oneself. Masturbation as a form of autoeroticism is not included in this section.

We have found at least four forms of autoeroticism excluding simple masturbation. One is autoerotic hanging, another is aquaeroticism, and a third is chemical eroticism. A fourth type of autoeroticism is self-suffocation. A common theme connects all these sexual practices. When someone practices autoerotic asphyxiation, a deficiency of oxygen occurs in the brain, inducing cerebral anoxia. This lessening of oxygen to the brain is done by self-applied suffocation methods usually in conjunction with some form of genital self-manipulation. The restriction of blood supply to the brain with some can intensify sensations because the lack of oxygen may produce lightheadedness, giddiness, or a sense of euphoria. There may also be a sense of excitation with the realization of the potential danger and the very real possibility of death.

We know little about the various practices of autoerotic behavior, regardless of the format it takes. This sexual behavior is done in private and only becomes public when the person commits an error and then accidentally dies.

Forms of Autoerotica

Autoerotic Asphyxiation

Although several types of autoeroticism were mentioned in the previous section, we will now strictly consider autoerotic asphyxiation as sexual hanging. In this form, different types of bindings are used around the neck. What is important is that the material used—rope, ties, and the like—exert equal pressure on either side of the neck on the carotid arteries to induce cerebral anoxia.

One can practice this form of autoeroticism in various ways. One method is to place a part of the rope over a pipe, a beam in a ceiling, over a door, or some similar support. In one case, a woman placed a rope around her neck with the other end around a doorknob. She knelt with her back to the door, and then she simply leaned forward until she passed out. Her body was found by her parents when they came home from work. In another case, a young man was found dead in the attic of his parents' home. He had tied a rope around his neck then over a beam in the ceiling of the attic and then around his ankles. He pulled on the rope with his feet but the beam broke. He fell through the drywall and was left hanging only a few feet from the dining room floor. His back had broken.

Aquaeroticism

The second type of autoeroticism is aquaeroticism. We have already mentioned the case of the young woman who was found by her husband in the bathtub. With this form of paraphilia, the practitioner will deliberately place himself or herself in water. The intent is to place oneself in a position to drown but raising one's head out of the water before the loss of consciousness.

Recently, a man placed himself in a sleeping bag alongside the bank of a river. Inside the sleeping bag he had tied his feet and wrapped his hands in duct tape. He had in one hand a pair of scissors. One end of a rope was placed around a small tree on the bank and the other end was placed around his neck. He was able to crawl and move into the river and soon the sleeping bag was under water. The plan was apparently to cut the tape around his wrists before he drowned. Unfortunately the rope broke from the tree on the bank, the man was pushed into the middle of the river, he was run over by a speedboat, and he died. This was a case of someone involved in aquaeroticism that was verified by collateral evidence found in his home—pornography, stories, pictures, and videos.

Chemical Eroticism

Some cases involve a person practicing autoeroticism using some form of chemical to induce a sense of lightheadedness, a giddy feeling, and other sensory apparitions—much the same feelings that result from erotic asphyxiation. Freon is one such chemical.

An air conditioning appliance repairman made a house call to a couple's home where the air conditioning unit was not working properly. The lady of the house left for a few minutes to go to the grocery store. When she got back, she found the repairman dead. He had placed a plastic tube in his mouth from a tankard of freon. He had lowered his pants and underwear and turned on a grinder that vibrated against his penis and scrotum. Apparently the freon was swallowed too quickly which then resulted in his death.

In another case of chemical eroticism, a man was dressed in panties and bra with a plastic tube running under a plastic baggie over his head. Divorced but having custody of a 16-year-old daughter, the daughter came home from school to find her father dead on the kitchen floor.

Suffocation

In some cases of autoeroticism, the person will deliberately attempt to suffocate to the point of almost losing consciousness. Unlike autoerotic asphyxiation, this form of solitary sex may be the safest manner of manual strangulation. In some cases, a partner is chosen with a key word agreed on ahead of time to stop the suffocation. This is, nonetheless, a risky situation.

Take, for example, the following case. In a southern town, a woman was found dead in her bed. She had a towel around her neck and her right hand was on her stomach. Her left hand was under her back and she was on the bed, face up. The police were investigating this case as a homicide. After further inspection, the police decided to seek a psychological profile. In their investigation, they found some information about sadism and masochism. There was also a swinger's magazine with circles around some names. The profile suggested that this may have been a murder but the appearance of the towel around the neck and the position of her left hand may have been indicative of some form of autoeroticism. Because of these findings, the direction of the inquiry changed from a murder investigation to one of accidental death. It was discovered that the victim had found a date with a man. When he was interrogated, he said that she had suggested that he slap her, which he did several times at her insistence. She then told him a fantasy she had about being strangled. He related that he agreed to do that and they had arranged a release word. He started to strangle her but never heard the release word and she died. The man was charged with a lesser charge of manslaughter and was granted probation.

TRAITS AND CHARACTERISTICS OF AUTOEROTIC PRACTITIONERS

In viewing this form of sexual behavior, certain traits and characteristics have become evident. How representative these attributes are of the total universe of those involved in erotic asphyxiation is unknown. This data is obtained because these individuals—who usually suffer an accidental death as a result of participation in such activities—then come to the attention of the criminal justice system. Nonetheless, it is a starting point and until further information can be garnered by more objective and scientific studies, these remain as the only facts we have.

In the course of researching this topic, we have gained some information from the Eulenspiegel Society. This organization is located in New

York and was founded in 1971. One of its main goals is to support sexual liberation in all formats between and among consenting adults. They sponsor classes for autoerotics as well as classes that deal with S&M, B&D, group sex, and other topics.

Gender

Generally when one speaks of autoerotica, males are the overwhelming practitioners, although the exact ratio is unknown. Females sometimes practice this form of paraphilia, but the setting and circumstances are different.

Age

From the information available, it appears that autoeroticism is predominantly a young person's practice. We must be very careful in this assumption because other than scarce stories of self-reports, the cases seen are those in which injury or death occur. Thus, what may be happening is that as one ages and becomes more experienced in this sexual paraphilia, the chances of error diminish. The attention to details and what accounts for safety as well as sexual gratification becomes more of a ritualized event and ensures that the practitioner will be safe from a fatal mishap. Thus, early in a person's career in autoerotica, mistakes are likely to be made that result in tragic consequences.

Race

In the overwhelming number of cases involving autoeroticism, we have found the practitioners to be Caucasian. This not to say that other races do not practice autoeroticism, but in the cases resulting in death because of something gone wrong, the victims are almost exclusively white. Why this seems to be the case is unknown at this time. Statistics, however, are missing in this analysis.

Socially Isolated

When interviewing family and friends of some fatal victims of autoerotica, the reports suggest these individuals were shy, introverted, often having few friends and personal associates, and few interests and hobbies.

If particularly young and in high school, teachers and counselors reported they were loners despite efforts to get them involved in school activities like clubs and athletics. The person may also have been shy and timid around people of the opposite sex because they lacked the social skills to interact adequately.

Overachiever

Some involved in this form of sexual paraphilia are described as overachievers. This would be evident in the school situation or, for an older practitioner, the workplace setting. This person will devote attention to detail to almost everything in his or her life, which partly accounts for success in school or the workplace. This extends into the person's health and appearance. Many of these individuals whom we have examined were in good physical condition, neat and clean in personal appearance, with well-kept homes.

Upwardly Mobile

Many of the practitioners found as a result of a sex act that resulted in a death often were from middle-class backgrounds. This suggests that perhaps the background of the parents often have an impact on the personality of the practitioner. The parents often are professionals in the community and if the practitioner is a student, he or she is often involved in academic programs or, if already in the workplace, has a professional occupation.

This person may also appear to be an intellectual, conversant in many topics, regardless of age. The list of topics, however, seldom includes the sexual practices of autoerotica. This is a personal topic, not to be discussed in public or even with most close personal friends.

Often Religious

Ironically, someone who is involved in some type of sexual aberration such as autoeroticism is often a churchgoer and is therefore judged to be a devout person by those who attend the same religious services.

Another side of the religious appearance accounts for some dissonance in the religious life of the person. On the one hand, although the picture presents an image of social and religious conformity, the private life of aberrant sex practices is diametrically opposed to acceptable sexual practices. Whereas sex is viewed as a pleasurable and procreational act, autoeroticism has one purpose—solitary sexual hedonism.

Suicidal Tendencies

In many cases, the person has suicidal tendencies. Police will often find comments about the feelings of guilt, shame, and remorse about the acts involving autoeroticism in notes left by those committing suicide. We are not certain of the number of people who commit suicide and do not leave this form of note, but the notes that are found contain statements such as "I'm sorry I am this way," or "Please don't tell my parents. Let them think I was just tired of living." (authors' files).

AUTOEROTIC SCENE INDICATORS

Gender

Gender differences require consideration when examining scenes in which an autoerotic fatality has occurred. Let us first deal with women who are involved in this form of sexual behavior. Women are much different than men in their habits of autoeroticism. First, women will often practice the acts in their bedrooms or bathrooms. Seldom will women become involved in autoeroticism outside or in open areas. They will not typically move furniture or use sexual paraphernalia as do many male practitioners.

Crossdressing

Crossdressing is very prevalent with males involved in autoerotica. This simply mirrors transvestism in American society. Women do not generally crossdress for the same reason as men. For women, when they crossdress, it is most often a matter of fashion or comfort. However, when men crossdress, it is a sexual matter, at least initially (Holmes & Holmes, 2001). The men who crossdress will either be in "high drag" (dressed completely in women's clothing) or "low drag" (dressed in a few articles of clothing such as panties and a bra).

Mirrors

In many cases involving erotic hanging, the investigator will find a mirror somewhere within the visual field of the deceased. This may be a full-length mirror, a mirror on the wall, or even a small, hand-held mirror. The investigator should assume the position of the deceased. What might be seen is a reflection of the individual from the neck down. This is especially true when the deceased is involved in crossdressing. Why? As one looks at the mirror and views this scene, the person can imagine himself or herself to be anyone he or she wishes to be. This feeds into the fantasy system of the individual.

Pornography

Pornography is present in many cases of autoerotica. The character of the pornography will reflect the fantasy of the individual. With this said, few cases develop in which pornography is present and women are the practitioners. The pornography will be within the vision of the person and may be on the floor, a table top, or some other resting place.

Pornography may be of a commercial variety (that which can be purchased) or a relationship variety (the kind of pornography one can make on one's own). It may be an advertisement of underwear for women or even children, something that feeds into the fantasy of the practitioner. In one case of erotic asphyxiation, a man had placed in front of himself an advertisement from the newspaper for women's nightgowns and leisure wear. For him, these ads provided a form of erotic arousal, allowing him to move into sexual excitation.

Genital Binding

The investigator viewing a scene that has resulted in a death may sometimes see bindings around the genitals of a male practitioner. This binding may come in many different formats. Some asphyxiates may use rope, some may prefer nylon cord, and others use clothing in strips as forms of binding.

Body Marks and Bruising

A close examination of the body of the person involved in this form of sexual practice will oftentimes show two forms of marks on the body. The first mark could be around the neck. The practioner sometimes conceals the "burn" marks by high collars, scarves, or other items of clothing that are placed around the neck. This is true for both males and females and some styles of clothing are certainly better suited for this concealment.

The other marks that may become evident are around the wrists. The locations of the bruises become extremely important. For example, in erotic practitioners who have some preference for being tied around the wrists, the bruising is more apt to occur on the wrists below the thumbs. If a person was tied by the wrists against that person's will, the bruising is more likely to occur on the outer wrists below the dorsima; this indicates that the person has struggled, trying to separate the wrists from each other and thus bruising the wrists below the back of the hand. Bruises of this sort may indicate that death was not the result of autoerotic asphyxiation.

In addition to marks around the wrists and neck, other bruising may have appeared, especially around the ankles.

Bondage

Bondage is a common practice, especially with males. As anticipated, arms and legs typically are used for bondage but may occur in other places as well. For example, in a northern city, a 16 year-old-male was found in the attic of his home. His parents called him for dinner and then went to look for him. He was dead in the attic with a rope around his neck, over a rafter in the ceiling, and the other end of the rope wrapped around his ankles; additional binding, fashioned from the vacuum cleaner tubing and duct tape, was found around his waist.

Diaries and Writings

As a form of collateral evidence, diaries and writings are often found in the possession of the practitioner. These writings will contain descriptions of the fantasies and practices of the person involved in this form of paraphilia. Some contain dates of practice as well as the various methods used during instances of autoeroticism. One person found dead by his 16-year-old daughter kept a diary of the various manners in which he practiced his sexual preference for sexual asphyxia. He also mentioned the times of his sex acts as well as various new things he tried such as crossdressing, trying freon, and aquaeroticism.

EVIDENCE OF PAST AUTOEROTIC BEHAVIORS

Rope Burns in the Residence

Sex is very ritualistic. What works well and provides sexual gratification and satisfaction will likely be repeated, if possible. A case in the midwest, for example, involved a young husband, age 21, who accidentally killed himself by hanging from a pole mounted across a doorway from the apartment's kitchen to the living room. The wife and young child had left only an hour earlier to do some grocery shopping. The wife found him dead when they returned and called the police. The police found fibers on the bar from previous actions as well as burns on the bar itself. In another case, a 50-year-old man was found in his kitchen by his married daughter who had not heard from him in a week. She opened the door and found him lying on the kitchen floor with a nylon rope around his neck, tied over the door and then to a mounted lock on the other side of the door. Fibers, rope burns, and other signs of former practice were discovered.

Videos and Pictures of Self-Practice

Similar to the custom of keeping diaries and writings, some practitioners will video themselves in their sex play. For example, in Florida a man was discovered by his wife and father-in-law as they opened the garage door. The man had set up a video camera on a tripod and took a video of himself hanging. It shows him placing the noose around his neck, stepping off a step of a stool, and hanging. As he tries to step back on the stool, the stool is accidentally kicked aside and he is unable to stop his death. The police found several other videos of his sex acts in the crawl space of his home.

In another case, a man was found dead in his apartment. The police found three photo albums with more than 500 pictures of him in various scenarios of autoerotica, many in drag. The purpose? To relive the experiences of his sexual paraphilia.

Position of the Knot in Erotic Hanging

In the practice of erotic hanging, the investigator should look at the position of the knot. In a true case of erotic hanging, the knot usually will be in the back of the neck. This ensures that equal pressure will be placed on either side of the neck for sexual pleasure and gratification. This is one of the first items at the scene the investigator should inspect.

If the knot is on the side of the neck, it should be determined if the deceased is right-handed or left-handed. If the person was right-handed and the knot is on the right side of the neck, the death may be the result of a suicide. If the knot is on the left side, this may be an indication of foul play of some type. Of course, if the person is left-handed, the process would be reversed.

A deliberate placement of the knot on one side of the neck, below the ear and arranged so the running end goes behind the neck and then around the front of the neck could be found. With the rope tied this way, some blood flows through the carotid artery so the person can, with some effort, open an air path that can lead to a much longer experience. This, however, comes with some practice and experimentation. If an individual is found like this, the investigator will have to rely on other scene evidence in order to rule a suicide or accidental death. Because of the rapid loss of consciousness, brain damage can occur within four minutes, and death within 10 to 15 minutes. But the heart may stop before this.

Facial Coverings

In many cases of autoeroticism, the face is covered in a variety of fashions. In a previously cited case—the young man who died while his wife and child went to the grocery store—the wife's panty hose was placed over his face. In the case where freon was ingested, the man had placed a plastic baggie over the face as did the man who was found in the river in the sleeping bag. The purpose of the placement of something over the face is to complement the experience of losing consciousness and for some becomes a part of the ritual of the autoerotic experience.

Anal Insertion

Objects inserted into the anal opening of the practitioner are common among males. A variety of objects are used, from dildos that are purchased at adult stores to other objects. One man was freebasing cocaine and placed himself into a closet with his head and shoulders in the closet but his buttocks and feet outside. He had placed a condom on the handle of a vacuum machine, turned the vacuum on, and inserted the handle into his anus. The drug exploded in his face and he died. When found by a relative, the handle was still inserted. Most objects are not as ingenious as this last example. Most are commonplace, such as bottles, tools, and other similar items.

Decorative Symmetry

Perhaps one of the most interesting aspects of physical evidence is decorative symmetry. That is, when a person involved in autoerotica and body decoration is a part of the fantasy and ritual, the decorations tend to appear on both sides of the body. For example, if duct tape is wrapped about the right calf, the left calf is also decorated. If a belt is placed around the upper right thigh, the upper left leg will also be decorated in the same manner. Why this is done in this manner is unknown, but this appears time and again in the investigation of autoeroticism cases.

CONCLUSION

Perhaps no other sexual behavior is more complex, considered more bizarre, and yet less known than cases of autoerotica. The very manner in which an individual learns about this paraphilia and develops a need for this activity are also unknown. Certainly few of the person's friends and acquaintances practice it. Even adult bookstores carry little information. What we have found, however, is on the Internet: Web sites give instructions as well as precautions for those wishing to become involved in this potentially dangerous sex behavior. The Eulenspiegel Society offers classes on a variety of different sex practices including autoeroticism. The classes are offered at the headquarters in New York City, but the society does offer information over the Internet concerning breathing exercises, "buddy sex," and other items of sexual interests for those who may visit the Web site.

Keep in mind that the information in this chapter was gathered from those who have in some way "failed" in their sexual practice. They have died by accident and we have gathered data from their deaths. Common sense tells us that there are other, perhaps more experienced, autoerotics who have been practicing autoeroticism for years with no complications. What are their traits and characteristics? We may never know because this is a solitary sexual act and the practice of it is seldom shared with others. Nonetheless, it is important for the investigator to know the scene indicators to properly evaluate the scene itself. With this information an investigator can determine if it is the scene of an autoerotic, a suicide, or even a homicide.

PROFILING SATANIC AND CULT-RELATED MURDERS

When the popularity of *Rosemary's Baby* and *The Exorcist* reached pandemic proportions more than three decades ago, consciousness about the occult was stimulated to a height probably unknown since the time of the Salem witch hunts. These two movies made a case for Satanism existing among a group of followers not too different from us. One consultant and actor in *Rosemary's Baby,* Anton LaVey, a former rock musician, later became better known as the founder of the Church of Satan.

What accounted for this sudden rise in popularity in the occult? More than the 1960s as an era—with its emphasis on sex, drugs, and rock-and-roll—something about the time stimulated us, as a society, to look around for stability and a complete distinction between right and wrong, good and evil. As crime may be a social event that helps us identify instantly those who are good and those who are not (and even perhaps to be feared), it may be that the occult is a social invention that arises periodically to provide for some a sense of stability and individuality. For youth, the involvement may be a cry for attention whereas for adults it may be an attention to the myths of yesteryear, the time of werewolves, vampires, and the devil.

Regardless of the reason some become involved in Satanism, Satanic crimes and activities once again appear to be on the increase. With interest at a peak, a moral panic has redeveloped in the last few years and what we are seeing is a resurgence in the existence, interest, and practice of Satanism (DeYoung, 1998). Regardless, law enforcement at the initial phase must investigate alleged crimes of occult groups and determine if youth or adults are involved (the importance of this lies in the manner in which the crimes are committed, the spatial mobility of the people involved, etc.; see Bernet & Chang, 1997; Crews, 1996). Despite reports by police and other authors, Satanists apparently are not as involved in serious crimes as once suspected. Of course, some murders are committed by dabblers but these are relatively few. Most satanic crimes committed deal with cemetery desecrations, vandalism, writing of graffiti on public and private property, and other such minor crimes. Nonetheless, we still need to be concerned with their activities even if their crimes are not as serious as once supposed.

ROOTS OF SATANISM

This interest in Satan as an alternative to popular religion did not gain popularity overnight. Roots of Satanism date back to the Old Testament. In addition, the practice and belief in magic, spells, and curses, as well as divination of the future, were found among all primitive people. Demon worship was widely practiced in ancient Egypt and Mesopotamia. Originally not considered evil, demons were simply attendant spirits, only later developing a harmful character.

The Jewish rabbis of the Old Testament era condemned the belief in Satan because the devil was part of a non-Jewish religion. Second, rabbis saw demonology as an attempt to influence the destiny of man rather than accepting man accepting the will of God. As the Jewish faith moved closer to the time of Christ, Satan was used to protect the ideal of a perfect God. After all, how could a good God create evil? The credible answer was that he did not; Satan would be the responsible culprit.

Early Christian theologians believed that Satan, now a "reality," had no control over the followers of Christ, only pagans and apostates. The Gnostics saw the world as being evil and life on earth as a "prison sentence" imposed on them by the Yahweh of the Old Testament. Because the world was evil, the one who created it must also be evil. Ergo, Yahweh was evil. The good God must live far away in some distant heaven and they were in bondage to the evil god, now called the devil, Satan, Lucifer, Papablas, or any other of the multitude of demonic names.

SATANISM IN THE UNITED STATES

The greatest influence on those who find Satanism so attractive undoubtedly is Aleister Crowley. Raised in a traditional Christian family, Crowley became attracted to the occult while still quite young. Crucifying a dead toad, Crowley offended many of his own followers, who made mud casts of his form and killed him in effigy. Despite his unpopular status among

TABLE 11.1   LaVey's Nine Statements of the Devil

1. Satan represents indulgence, instead of abstinence!
2. Satan represents vital existence, instead of spiritual pipe dreams!
3. Satan represents undefiled wisdom instead of hypocritical self-deceit!
4. Satan represents kindness to those who deserve it, *instead of* love wasted on Ingrates!
5. Satan represents vengeance, instead of turning the other cheek!
6. Satan represents responsibility, instead of concern for the psychic vampires!
7. Satan represents man as just another animal, sometimes better, more often worse, than those who walk on all fours, who because of his divine and intellectual development has become the most vicious of all!
8. Satan represents all of the so-called sins, as they lead to physical, mental or emotional gratification!
9. Satan has been the best friend the church has ever had, as he has kept it in business all these years.

SOURCE: From *The Satanic Bible* (p. 25), by A. LaVey, 1969, New York: Avon. Reprinted with permission.

many of his disciples, the social conditions of the time combined with his charismatic authority helped maintain the influence of Satanism.

In 1966, Anton LaVey founded the Church of Satan on the Satanic feast day of Walpurgisnacht, April 30. Gaining great popularity from LaVey's performing marriages and burial rites, the Church of Satan has grown to a membership that some estimate at 20,000 people.

As a youthful runaway, LaVey worked in a circus as a carney barker, a cage boy for Clyde Beatty (a hypnotist), and a bump-and-grind organ player for a stripper named Marilyn Monroe. He finally moved to San Francisco where he was photographer for the San Francisco Police Department. Tiring of the alleged inconsistencies of traditional Christianity, LaVey founded a new religion predicated partly on the premise that "the strong shall inherit the earth."

THE SATANIC BIBLE

The writings of LaVey provide the faithful with a written dogma and liturgy of the Church of Satan. *The Satanic Bible*, available in paperback, has sold thousands of copies. It illustrates rituals, rites, holy days, and lists the nine "statements" of the devil (see Table 11.1). The basic teachings of LaVey concern a worship of the trinity of the devil: Lucifer, Satan, and the devil. The Church of Satan is actually a human potential movement. Each member is encouraged to actualize his or her own potential, which can be reached through magic, spells, rituals, and incantations to the demonic trinity.

The Satanic Bible includes an invocation employed toward the conjuration of lust, invocation employed toward the conjuration of destruction, invocation employed toward the conjuration of compassion, a list of holy days, chapters on the Black Mass and rituals, as well as a chapter titled "On the Choice of a Human Sacrifice."

LaVey passed away recently. He is succeeded in power and office by his daughter.

Definitions in Satanism

To understand Satanic worship and rituals, it is necessary to understand the terms used. Table 11.2 reviews some fairly commonly used terms in Satanic worship and rituals.

TYPES OF PERSONAL INVOLVEMENT IN SATANISM

As in any religious movement, some members are more involved and indoctrinated into the liturgy and rituals than others. In personal *interviews* with two high priests and several coven members of Satanic cults, they report three types of personal affiliation. Table 11.3 graphically delineates these types in terms of involvement and participation.

Type

The first type resembles religious affiliation as with any church. Members are similar to other, more traditional church members, with an affinity for worship, familiarity with church ritual and liturgy, and recognition of church hierarchy and bureaucratic lines of authority. Regular attendance of church-related functions, observance of feast days, and organizational maintenance through contributions by members are all characteristics of this type of membership, be it of a traditional, recognized religious organization (Catholic, Baptist, Jewish, etc.) or a member of one of the Satanic churches: LaVey's Church of Satan, Dr. Michael

(Text continues on page 190)

TABLE 11.2 Words, Rituals, and Rites of Satanists

Terms

Antichrist	Enemy of Christ
Archfiend	A chief or foremost fiend (Satan)
Black Magic	Basically the same as sorcery
Black Mass	A ritual of the Church of Satan which is a mockery of the Roman Catholic Mass
Circle	A declaration of sacred ground
Coven	An assembly of 13 witches
Equinox	First day of autumn or spring
ESBAT	Coven meeting
Fire	Symbolizes Satan
Goat	Satan appears in the form of a goat
Hectate	Goddess of the Lower Region and patron of witchcraft
Hexagram	Evil sign in the occult world; six pointed star in a circle
Incubus	A male demon that copulates with human females
Lilith	Adam's first wife and later the wife of Lucifer
Lucifer	The archangel cast from heaven for leading a revolt of angels. He is the "father" of the trinity of the devil
Mass	A ceremony
Necromancy	The art of controlling the spirits of the dead
Pentagram	A five-pointed star that is used as a barrier against evil. The pentagram with one point upwards repels evil, but a reversed pentagram, with two points upward, Is a symbol of the devil and attracts sinister forces. In this case, the two points represent the horns of the goat, which is the symbol of the devil
Sabbath	Holy days and celebrations, of which there are eight in a year; assemblies of witches in honor of the Archfiend
Satan	A member, the "son," of the trinity of the devil
Solstice	First day of summer or winter
Sorcerer	Male practitioner
Sorcery	The use of supernatural power over others through the assistance of evil spirits

(Continued)

TABLE 11.2   (Continued)

Succubus	A female demon that copulates with human males
Talisman	An object believed to hold magical powers
Voodoo	A form of primitive sorcery that was organized in Africa and is generally associated with fetishes (dolls, etc.)
Walpurgisnacht	The eve of May Day believed in medieval Europe to be the occasion of a witch's sabbath
Witch	Female practitioner
Witchcraft	The process of using the forces of the unseen world through potions, incantations, or ceremonies for the purpose of controlling or changing conditions or situations

Important Dates

September 22	Autumn Equinox
June 21	Summer Solstice
March 20	Spring Equinox
December 21	Winter Solstice
February 2	Candlemas
April 30	Walpurgisnacht
October 31	Halloween
November 1	Festival of Hecate

Numbers of significance

One	Equates with primal chaos
Three	Triple repetitions, effective in incantations
Five	Symbolizes justice
Seven	Possesses mystic implications
Thirteen	Number of members in a coven
Four x Four	The devil's own number
7 + 9	Multiples of these possess thaumaturgical potency
666	Mark of the Beast, the devil's calling card. Pentacle: Five-pointed star

Aquino's Temple of Set (also headquartered in San Francisco), or Robert and Mary Anne DeGrimston's Church of the Final Judgment. Many instances occur in which children are born into this religious affiliation. There may be movement of membership from one Satanic "denomination" to another. Unlike the more traditional religions, there is no evidence of a "baptism," although in *The Satanic Bible*, it does state that for a person to be baptized, the liquid used is salt water. But in reality, it appears

---

TABLE 11.3   Organizational Elements and Types of Personal
Involvement with Satanic and Devil Worship

Type I

Large membership	Fiscal organization maintenance
Stable membership	Long-term membership
Formalized rituals	Lateral sect transfer
Ecclesiastical hierarchy	Human and animal sacrifice
Recognized authority	Converted and familial membership
Official holy days	

Type II

Limited membership	Transient membership
Informal rituals and liturgy	No ecclesiastical hierarchy
Personal authority	No holy days
Total fiscal commitment	Moderate-term membership
No lateral religious transfer	Human and animal sacrifice
Converted membership	

Type III

Individual and solitary membership	No rituals
No ecclesiastical authority	No external authority
No holy days	No fiscal maintenance
No lateral religious transfer	Human and animal sacrifice
Self-styled membership	

---

that if one wishes to become a member in the Church of Satan, for example, one needs only to complete an application (see Figure 11.1) and mail in the required fee.

We must stress that no firm evidence exists that organized churches are responsible for crimes such as homicide, forced suicides, child abuse, or other serious offenses. They may be responsible for some animal sacrifices but when examining *The Satanic Bible*, sections demand the true believer not break the law in certain areas including the sacrifice of adults and children. However, there may be small, splinter groups led by someone who demands obedience to a set of rules that may be contrary to the Church of Satan or the Temple of Set or other churches of this ilk.

Type II

The second type of personal affiliation is membership in a cult, although not all cults are Satanic. A cult is comprised of people bound together by

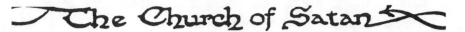

The Church of Satan

Post Office Box 210082   San Francisco, CA 94121

Regarding request for information on affiliation with
The Church of Satan

As an elitist organization, The Church of Satan grants Active Membership to only those individuals who meet its requirements. If you are sincerely interested in affiliating with us, or simply credit the Church of Satan with establishing the world's most formidable threat to hypocrisy, the first step is simple.

We make no false claims of altruism; we realize what we have, what we are, and what we shall become. Knowing relatively little of you, we accept your professed interest or dedication at face value. We have every desire to incorporate valid members into our plan for the future, so we suggest that you join us as a Contributing Member.

For $50.00 you will receive an identification card, an amulet bearing the symbol of the Church of Satan, your first year's subscription to our publication; The Cloven Hoof, information on how to progress more deeply into Satanism—its philosophy, rituals, locations and means of meeting other Satanists, and sources of supply for working materials unique to basic magic. You will also receive a questionnaire, should you wish to apply for Active membership status.

Our scope is unlimited, and the extent and degree of your involvement is based upon your own potential. All names and addresses are held confidential and you are under no other obligation as a Contributing Member, unless you desire otherwise.

Please use the form below for registration.

URCH OF SATAN
st Office Box 210082
n Francisco, CA 94121; U.S.A.

ase enroll me as a Contributing Member of the Church of Satan.   Enclosed is $50.00.
                                                                  (Couples: $75.00)

me (Mr./Mrs./Miss/Ms)

eet

y   / State   / Zip (or other) Code   / Country

FIGURE 11.1 Application for the Church of Satan

the acceptance of a leader, a less sophisticated system of beliefs, and less formal ritual. The charismatic quality of the leader is essential because this person will obviously lend direction to the cult's activities. The membership in the cult is modally short term and will depend largely on the persona of the leader.

Some excellent examples of cults have existed in America during the last few decades. The Charles Manson Family is probably the most infamous instance of a cult based in no small part on the charismatic authority of Manson himself. One theory contends that David Berkowitz (also known as the Son of Sam) was involved in the same Satanic cult as Manson, even though they belonged to that cult at different times (Terry, 1999); however, no firm evidence supports this claim by Terry. A serial killer in a prison in California who knows Manson said the cult leader denied any involvement with the Process Church in New York at the time of the Son of Sam killings or any other time.

Another cult that recently came to the attention of the American public was the Heaven's Gate cult headed by Do. He convinced his small group of followers that they were living in a foreign body, a pod, that was awaiting space transportation to another planet, their home. Each member of the cult committed suicide becaue they believed Do. This was not a criminal cult, a cult such as Manson's family.

David Koresch lead another cult, many of whose members were killed in a fatal confrontation with U.S. law enforcement agents in Texas. Apparently a strong personality, Koresch convinced many people to leave their homes, families, jobs, and other social and personal ties to follow him. Ultimately, Koresch's charismatic persona convinced his members to fight the police.

In a southwest state, police are finding bodies wrapped in aluminum foil in the desert. The intelligence gathered suggests that all the people are members of a cult that share beliefs similar to the Heaven's Gate group. They do differ, however, in at least one respect. These people believe that after they die of natural causes and their bodies are placed in a pod of foil, the corpse eventually is destroyed by the sun and the weather, and then the essence is taken by space beings and transported back to their home planet. From all indications, these groups are not criminal or Satanic in inclination. Other cults, on the other hand, may be.

Henry Lucas admitted to membership in a devil cult, along with Ottis Toole, his alleged accomplice to multiple murders in various states. Both convicted serial killers, Lucas said he was also involved in the kidnapping of small children and paid several thousands of dollars to deliver the children for human sacrifice or prostitution; others were reportedly sold to wealthy Mexicans (authors' files). This story was never verified. Lucas died in prison without admitting further details. Lucas at one time admitted to more than 300 murders across the United States. He went with police officers and told them stories that were sufficient for them to close scores of unsolved murders. Lucas may have suffered from some kind of mental or emotional disorder, causing him to confess to crimes he did not commit so that he would have some time in the social spotlight.

Type III

The third tier of participation manifests itself in a personal, self-styled form. It may take the format of Satanism, a Gothic lifestyle, or other type of cult membership. This involvement may either be on an individual dimension or in a small group. Ritualism is quite limited, if it exists at all.

The younger person is more inclined to participate in this measure of Satanism. This type of member has little knowledge of the liturgy of Satanism and may be quite heavily involved in animal sacrifice, especially small dogs and cats.

Few members exist in any one particular self-styled aggregate. With no liturgy or religious hierarchy, the participant is set up as the authority and proceeds to "worship the devil" as deemed appropriate. There is no need for fiscal organizational maintenance; there are no tithing or collections. There are no buildings, schools, churches, or a religious bureaucracy to financially subsidize. This "Satanist" is a loner with little knowledge of the Satanic oath, Satanic prayers, hierarchy of hell, or the personalities of the trinity of the devil.

Richard Ramirez, the Night Stalker, is a self-styled Satanist. On his left palm he displayed a tattoo of a pentagram and, as he walked out of the court at his arraignment, he shouted, "Hail Satan." One Satanist related during an interview that he was personally offended that people would put Ramirez into the same category as a Church of Satan member (authors' files).

As with any religion, not all people who practice Satanism truly believe the same nor practice the same liturgy. It is also true that some believers are more immersed in Satanism than others without an awareness of the nuances of membership and doctrine. These occult members, sometimes referred to as "dabblers," create their own form of the occult. They may set up a small and simple set of dogma, ceremonies, and rituals. They may also sacrifice small animals like as dogs and cats.

Ricky Kasso was a high school student who declared to anyone who would listen that he was a self-styled Satanist. He practiced the drinking of blood and other types of rituals and ceremonies of a Satanic dogma. He stabbed one student to death and afterward, on several occasions, he brought other high school students to the site where he dumped the young boy's body. Finally, one student informed on him and Kasso was arrested. The night he was arrested and placed in jail he hanged himself with his t-shirt. He committed the ultimate sacrifice for his Satanic belief. Thankfully, there are few like this young person.

GENERAL BELIEFS IN SATANISM

Within Satanism, many belief elements are prevalent. First, most Satanists acknowledge the existence of God. After all, they profess, there could be no Satan without God. Just as every person has a good side and a bad side, there are interesting parallels when one examines the belief system of the Satanic church.

Trinity of Satanism

Consider, initially, the trinity of Satan. As Christians firmly believe in God the Father, God the Son, and God the Holy Spirit, the Satanists believe in Lucifer, Satan, and the devil. They are three different parts of one being (Authors' file).

Lucifer

Lucifer holds the position of the primary godhead and the ruler of hell. He is the god of power and can give power to his followers or take the power from them. Lucifer has more power than Satan, who has more power than the devil. Lucifer, functioning in the same role as God the Father, has never been personally seen. He can, it is believed, take any form, animal or human. He is the Leader of Hell, the Worker of Evil, and the Ruler of Evil. Lucifer, once the shining angel of God, was cast out of heaven with his wife, Lilith. They later had one son, Mendes. Lucifer demands human and animal sacrifices.

Satan

The second personality of the trinity of the devil belongs to Satan. His parallel in the Christian Trinity is God the Son. Satan is the son of Lucifer, not a son in the same sense as Mendes but in the same sense as Jesus is the Son of God the Father. Satan is the leader of the "wasteland," the spiritual realm that surrounds the earth. He is called on by devoted Satanists for special favors.

The Devil

The main purpose for the devil is to serve as a liaison between the people and Satan. As is characteristic of any bureaucracy, certain lines of communication must be followed; this is evidently true also in the god-head of the devil. Satan communicates with Lucifer and the devil communicates with Satan. The particular role of the devil is to tempt people to do the work of Lucifer and Satan. He wants to pull people into hell.

Human Sacrifice

Human sacrifice takes two forms: blood or burning. According to some Satanists (personal interview with a priest of the Church of Satan, May 11, 1990, Utah State Prison), a blood sacrifice is usually reserved for those whose souls will be relinquished to Lucifer. This soul, which has been "martyred," will someday be reincarnated into the "wasteland" that is Earth and later occupy a revered place in hell. A blood sacrifice occurs in several of the ceremonies of Satanism. The sacrificial victim is usually cut from the upper part of the chest to above the pubic bone. The heart is often removed and mixed with blood, urine, and feces to become an anthropophagous mixture. This victims' soul will go directly to Lucifer, who will make a determination when it will be reunited with its body in a next life.

A burning sacrifice is considered a killing of vengeance or destruction. This type of human execution is reserved for those who have done something against the coven or church and as such, they deserve to be killed. People who are not Satanists may also be killed. With Type I members, however, these non-Satanist human sacrifices have seen some secret ritual or ceremony.

A victim burned to death can never be reincarnated, a vital concern to the Satanist. Moreover, the soul from the sacrificed goes directly to Lucifer, making him stronger with each burned victim and each blood victim.

How often are there sacrifices? Fortunately, the answer is very few. If one does occur, it is important to know about the doctrine and dogma if one is to understand the full picture of the crime. For example, in Michigan, a young female, age 16, was killed allegedly by two young men, one a juvenile. Her face was skinned, a finger was cut off of her left hand, and there were several tattoos on her body, including the 666 symbol. An alert investigator knowing the contents of *The Satanic*

Bible would immediately know the significance of the crime scene elements.

Hierarchy of Hell

Some Satanists believe that the earth on which we all live is surrounded by a spiritual "wasteland." Satan commands the wasteland, and the devil serves as a liaison between hell, earth, and the wasteland. Earth is hell. People can choose right or wrong; a "free agency" permits one to choose between right and wrong. A person could live life and be good and plentiful, survive this life, and after death, go to heaven. If one does not live life according to certain orthodox principles, that person would go to hell.

Many Satanists believe in reincarnation. If the member does what Lucifer, Satan, and the devil command, when physically dead, the member will be reincarnated. One will never move downward in class in the next life. A high priest, for example, would not come back in the next life as simply a coven member. He would come back as at least a high priest. But the members of the Church of Satan believe there is only one "high priest" and that person is the high priest of the Church of Satan.

Hell is like the heaven Christians envision. In other words, hell is where good Satanists will receive all of their wishes. Lusts will be satisfied and in hell they will reside with Lucifer, Satan, the devil, demons (Satanists' answer to Christianity's angels), and humans. Interestingly enough, two classes of humans are in hell: faithful Satanists form one class and fallen Satanists and sinful Christians the other. The faithful Satanists will receive all of their demands and their servants will be the sinful Christians and fallen Satanists.

The Demons

The demons are at the service of the devil. The demons, then, are lower in the hierarchy in hell than the trinity of the devil but they are higher than the humans in hell. Sometimes the demons will appear in spiritual form and carry spells of good (white) magic or bad (black) magic to the people on Earth.

Devices Used in Satanic Rituals

Any form of religion, whether it is Christianity, Judaism, or Satanism, relies on rituals and ceremonies; this is true even for the self-styled

TABLE 11.4	Religious Elements in Satanic and Devil Worship Rituals and Ceremonies	
Vestments		Altar
Phallus		Candles
Bell		Chalice
Elixir		Sword
Symbol of Baphomet		Gong

Satanist. A ceremony typically recognizes a unique happening, marking an important event. A ritual is more. It is repetitive, traditional, and has a certain prescribed set of behaviors that is intended to symbolize and reinforce a system of beliefs. Satanic rituals certainly fit into this operational definition. Table 11.4 lists the devices necessary for Satanic rituals (LaVey, 1969, pp. 134–139).

Vestments. Cowled or hooded black robes are worn by male participants. Females are to wear sexually appealing apparel for the purpose of arousing and intensifying the adrenal or bioelectrical energy of the males.

Altar. The purpose of the altar is to serve as a focal point. A nude woman is used on the altar because the female is the natural passive receptor and represents the earth mother. The altar is to be three to four feet high and five and one-half to six feet long. The front of the altar will face west and the feet of the altar will face south.

Symbol of Baphomet. In Satanism, the pentagram is inverted to perfectly accommodate the head of the goat, its head representing duality and the other three points inverted to symbolize the Trinity denied. This Symbol of Baphomet is placed on the wall above the altar.

Candles. The candles represent the light of Lucifer. Only black and white candles are used and never more than one white candle can be used. As many black candles as needed can be used to illuminate the ritual chamber. One black candle is placed to the left of the altar and the white candle is placed to the right of the altar.

Bell. The bell is used to mark both the beginning and the end of the ritual. The high priest rings the bell nine times while turning counterclockwise.

This is done at the beginning of the ritual to clear and purify the air and at the end to intensify the workings and indicate finality.

Chalice.   The chalice should be made of silver, glass, or crockery but not of gold. Gold is traditionally identified with Christianity. Therefore, anything that is identified with Christianity is to be avoided. The contents of the chalice are to be drunk first by the priest.

Elixir.   A stimulating fluid is used but wine is not necessary. The elixir is to be ingested immediately following the Invocation to Satan.

Sword.   The sword is the symbol of force and is held pointing toward the Symbol of Baphomet by the priest. If a sword is not available, a long knife, cane, or something similar can be used.

Phallus.   The phallus is held in both hands and shaken twice toward each cardinal point of the compass. The phallus may be made of wood, clay, or plaster.

Gong.   The gong is used to call on the forces of darkness.

SATANIC MASSES

Satanic masses are offered several times during the course of the year and several days of the week are appropriate for a particular service: Thursdays, Fridays, and Saturdays. Thursdays are especially appropriate for witches. With each mass, there is an accompanying ritual. Colors, prayers, chants, words, meditation, and drugs may accompany each type of mass.

Initiation Mass.   This mass is offered when new members are accepted into the Satanic group, either Type I or Type II. The new member will participate in the Mass as an acolyte and once the new member has passed through the rite of initiation, he or she is sworn to secrecy.

Gnostic Mass.   This type of Satanic mass is frequently open to Satanic members who have shown an interest in joining the Satanic group. Demons are called on to intercede and convince interested nonmembers to join.

Mass of Angels.   The manifest purpose of this mass is to seek power from Lucifer to protect the high priest from demonic powers. Because demons can do what they wish, they are not restricted by Lucifer-Satan-devil. On the eve of this mass, a black cock is killed and the heart, eyes, and tongue are cut out and become a potion for the participants to share.

Mass for the Dead.   The purpose of this mass is to petition Lucifer to free the celebrant from the fear of hell and to make the demons obey. A lamb will be sacrificed, its throat cut, and the heart, eyes, and tongue removed and ground into powder and then buried with the lamb.

The Black Mass.   This is probably the most bizarre and famous of all Satanic masses. A parody and a mockery of the Roman Catholic mass, this ritual is done for evil purposes only.

During the Black Mass, men wear black robes and women wear black sexually erotic dress. The Black Mass is presided over by a priest who celebrates this mass to recall a spirit, to gain power, or to ask for insight into the future. A nude female lies on an altar with her head facing south and her feet facing north. All the males in the grotto have sexual intercourse with the woman and each member, male or female, then inserts a bread wafer into her vagina, which is then ingested.

In *The Satanic Bible*, LaVey (1969) denies the practice of a Black Mass. But the members of Type I who were interviewed admitted the existence of such a ceremony. In addition, they said that there were no sacrifices of any type; it was mainly a sexual ceremony.

SATANIC CEREMONIES

Night of the Beast

Unlike the Black Mass, which lasts one night, the Night of the Beast is a three-week ceremony. The ceremony commences at the third full moon of the year with the purpose of replenishing power and gaining new power to foresee the future. It is a great time of happiness and, strangely enough, emotionally similar to the Christians' Christmas. At this time, the newly indoctrinated Satanists are invited to participate in the oath to Satan, with the new member making a pact with Satan to give his or her soul to Lucifer. Second, the inductee will learn the principles of black magic. Third, the initiate will learn the vocabulary of Satan; and last, he or she will participate in simulated human sacrifice.

The celebration of the Night of the Beast is the opportunity for a high priest to suffer symbolic martyrdom, his soul dispatched to Lucifer for his uses, and reincarnated at some future time. It is also an opportunity for parish members to assume the position of priest because someone will be needed to fill the now-vacant position.

The ceremony begins with the slaughter of a goat. A cloven-hoofed animal is necessary for this ceremony because it symbolizes Satan. The goat will be slaughtered and hung on an inverted cross, which has been suspended over the altar. Thirteen priests will march *counterclockwise* around an inverted pentagram, which has been drawn near the altar. As the priests walk slowly in procession, the hope of each is that a drop of blood from the goat will fall on him. This is taken as a sign that Lucifer has selected this minister as his chosen one; he is to be symbolically martyred.

Once this drop of blood from the goat has fallen on a high priest, he will be "martyred" midway through the Night of the Beast ceremony. His wife, if he is married and she is a believer, will be "killed" as well. If he is single, or if his wife is not a member of the church, a woman must be chosen from the grotto. Grotto women have been specially trained and educated, much like nuns. One will be chosen by the priests to join the "sacrificed" male victim.

The male is always sacrificed first. His abdomen is "opened" from below the throat to the pubic bone. His heart is cut out because this is the life source. The eyes are also removed because the eyes are to see the future. The blood is drained and the blood, heart, eyes, and urine are all mixed with wine into a potion, which the members of the church will drink. The removal of the body parts is all done symbolically; the "murders" are simulated. The procedure is repeated for the chosen woman, and again for the closing night's ceremony.

The Night of the Beast is presided over by an "Overlord." This person was once a priest, but because of his "martyrdom" in a past life, has been elevated to the present status of Overlord or "bishop." As with many other satanic rituals and ceremonies, including the Black Mass, no evidence indicates that this ceremony occurs with any great frequency. The ceremonies described by the two men in prison in Utah were independent of each other.

The Passover

Every six months, in February and August, the Passover Rite is celebrated. The purpose of this ceremony is to reaffirm the Satanists' belief in the dead and hell. This rite lasts only one night, and there will be two "human sacrifices": a high priest and his wife (also known as the "Bride of Lucifer").

The May Day Rite

This occurs on May 1. The general purpose of this ceremony is to celebrate the beginning of the new year and also to celebrate the new life of Satanism. We believe symbolic animal and human sacrifice transpires (like in the other rituals, the humans "sacrificed" are a high priest and a woman). As with the Passover, the rite is presided over by 13 priests and the participants are the Overlord, the coven members, and, according to belief, demons.

CRIME SCENE ELEMENTS

In Satanic killings, from any of the three dimensions of personal involvement, certain elements may be present. The extent of the evidence will vary according to the type of personal involvement in Satanic ritualism and personal affinity. Less evidence is *left* at the scene of a Satanic killing than there is in a devil worship murder perpetrated by a self-styled Satanist, primarily because the latter is less careful of the crime and the crime scene. Conversely, the coven of an organized Satanic cult will be very careful in the covering up of the scene itself.

Circle of Salt

In a Type I affiliation, and in fewer scenes of Type II and Type III, two circles of salt may surround the ritual scene. The investigator should be aware that the circles of salt, or any amount of salt found at a suspected ritualistic crime scene, would be a sign that a Satanic sect or a devil worship cult had been involved. Bowls of salt of different colors may also be found around the altar. The colors of salt, as well as banners and other symbols, all have expressive meanings. Table 11.5 lists the meanings of the various colors.

Candles

Candles comprise an important role in the Satanic ritual. As stated earlier, black and white candles are used by Satanic sect members. Never more than *one white* candle is used. Therefore, wax drippings found at the

TABLE 11.5	Significant Colors in Satanic and Devil Worship Rituals and Ceremonies
Black	Darkness, evil, devil, night, Satanism, occult
Blue	Tears, water, sadness, pornography
Green	Vegetation, restful, nature, soothing
Orange	Personal aura
Purple	Summons spirits, summons spirits of destruction
Red	Blood, life, energy
White	Cleanliness, purity, innocence
Yellow	Perfection, wealth, glory, power

ritualistic crime scene may serve as an index of Satanic involvement. If candle wax is found in colors other than black or white, then it can be assumed that the participants are Type II or Type III worshipers.

Mockery of Christian Symbols

The inverted cross is a sign of Satanic or devil worship rituals. Often the inverted cross is made of stone and hung above the altar. An animal may be sacrificed above the altar, and blood may be found on the ground below the cross and altar. Christian symbols may be desecrated. Statues, crosses, crucifixes, chalices, and other symbols associated with Christianity may all be broken and in pieces.

Satanic Symbols

Drawings of a hexagram or the inverted pentagram may be present. The pentagram or hexagram is always enclosed by a circle, which serves as a protective device from harm and danger from the demons. In addition, other Satanic symbols used are presented in Figure 11.2.

The Satanic alphabet may also be present, with the letters drawn on the ground to spell a prayer, statement, or warning. The Satanic number of the beast, 666, may be present, but this is so well known that accepting this as an unimpeachable indication of direct Satanic involvement may be in error. Also, the swastika, older than the Nazi Party itself, is primarily a symbol of Satanic worship. If the swastika is present alone without any other visible Satanic symbols, the inference of Satanic involvement should be diminished.

AC/DC	Anti-Christ, Devil Child
S	Satan-Stoner
MARKOS	Abracadabra
FFF	Anti-Christ
666	Anti-Christ
NATAS	Satan Reversed
6,9,13, XIII	Occult Numbers

卐   Swastika

Pentagram, White Magic

Pentagram, Sign of Occult

Lucifer, Morning Star

Ank

FIGURE 11.2 Symbols of Satan

Blood

Because of the emphasis by Type I participants on blood sacrifice, both human and animal blood may be present at the ritual scene. If, however, everything occurs as ritualistically planned, little blood will be found of either humans or animals. The blood is drained from the victim and mixed with certain body parts, urine, and feces, and made into a potion thought to have magical powers for Satanic purposes. Of course, when burning is the method of execution used, blood most likely will be missing.

The reason for burning, however, must be kept in mind for the various types of Satanic involvement.

Bodies

If a group does practice human sacrifice, and we encourage the reader to remember this seldom happens, bodies will usually not be found at the ritual scene. This is especially true if evidence at the crime scene reflects Type I participation. If the method of murder involves bloodletting, the body is going to be moved and hidden so that at some future time the soul will be reunited with the body at Lucifer's command. The burned body, however, will often be left at the scene after the artifacts of the ritual have been carefully removed.

A body found at a crime scene in which death has been caused by evisceration and cutting is not the result of a Satanic sect; rather, it is a cult or self-styled killing. Positioning of the body, foreign objects inserted into body orifices, or bodies found where parts of the body have been removed will all reflect Type II or Type III involvement.

With a bloodletting sacrifice, the body typically will be cut from the pubic area to the upper chest. The heart, parts of the intestines, and other parts of the body (such as fingers and ears) will be removed, as well as the eyes. The body will be mutilated as a result of this action. There may be fecal matter smeared over the body and the body may also be anointed with oils and incense.

With a Satanic sect, however, it is unlikely that the body will be found at the kill site. If discovered, its recovery will probably be more by accident than through investigation.

Animals

Small animals, such as dogs, cats, frogs, rabbits, and so on, are all favorite targets of sacrifice for Type III Satanic cults or devil worship. Perhaps one reason for this choice of animal is the lack of sophistication or knowledge of the dogmatically correct animals of sacrifice.

Sect members will make every effort to secure the "proper" animal to offer Lucifer, who demands blood. Usually, the goat is the desired animal of sacrifice. If this animal is not available, another cloven-hoofed animal can be substituted. If, however, the animal is a dog, cat, or other "inappropriate" sacrifice, this might indicate a younger

TABLE 11.6   Elements in Satanic and Devil Worship Ritualistic Killings

Ritual Elements	Satanic Sects	Devil Worship Cults	Self-Styled Devil Worship
Animal sacrifice	yes	yes	yes
Human sacrifice	yes	yes	yes
Victims	members	strangers	strangers
Blood sacrifice	yes	yes	yes
Burn sacrifice	yes	no	no
Executioner	priest	leader	self stylist

perpetrator or one who has been involved in the group a relatively short period of time.

CONCLUSION

As in any crime scene, there is a mixture of profiling elements. It would be safe to assume, however, that the preponderance of Satanic elements indicates a type of participation in Satanism. This participatory involvement, which entails to some degree a belief system and knowledge component, will reflect not only the amount of worship liturgy but also the method and selection of the total Satanic ritual.

Table 11.6 describes the elements in sacrificial rituals and personal involvement, whether it is through sects, cults, or self-styled devil worship. There are fundamental differences between goals, motives, rationalizations, methods, and drives, according to the type of ritualistic offender. If a body is found at a crime scene with fecal matter spread on the corpse, and if Satanic pentagrams and numbers are present, one would suspect a devil worship killing. If this proves to be the case, a young offender with a limited amount of active involvement in an official Satanic church could be suspected. After all, a bloodletting victim is a martyred "saint" for the church and his or her body would be cared for in the appropriate, revered fashion. In other words, it would not simply be left at the scene. If this were done, then Lucifer would not reunite the soul with the body at a future time.

A burned body would be deliberately placed at a site that would accelerate its discovery. A victim burned by a sect sends a message to other sect members that this member has violated the confidentiality of the sect. The sect will not tolerate a member's disobedience and the burning execution not only conveys this message but will also negate any potential for reincarnation.

A careful examination of the crime scene will yield some information regarding the type of participation. Conceivably, a sect-related crime will be committed by a person who has been in the Satanic community for some time and is intelligent. On the other hand, a ritualistic crime perpetrated by a self-styled devil worshiper will offer a profile of a younger perpetrator, maybe a transient, and probably less educated and lower in the socioeconomic scale. Also, self-styled and cult offenders are more of a danger to society because their victims are almost entirely strangers. They will kill not for worship purposes but because of their quest for power.

The elimination of a person's life can never be taken lightly. An investigation must take into account all parameters. Because there has been mutilation, anthropophagy, or any other bizarre act that would, on the surface, indicate a sex crime, further investigation may indeed yield a different result.

Chapter 12

GEOGRAPHY, PROFILING, AND PREDATORY CRIMINALS

Psychological profiling has been used as an investigative tool for a relatively short time. It would be untrue to say that profiling has been universally accepted by the law enforcement community, but the procedure is becoming increasingly endorsed by police officers. It is still vital to practice the time-proven methods of successful investigation: careful preservation of the crime scene, meticulous collection of physical evidence, thorough interviewing of all witnesses, and so on. However, the investigator must also be aware of the latest scientific techniques, such as DNA fingerprinting and linguistic profiling, in order to maximize the chances of successful case resolution. One such novel investigative approach within the profiling field is the analysis of geographic patterns in an effort to determine the location of the offender's residence.

THE ROLE OF GEOGRAPHY

What sort of role does geography play in the criminal profiling process? This is still unclear and the question deserves a great deal of research and study. Up to now the importance of geography has not been stressed, but many indications suggest that the analysis of criminal mobility and an understanding of the geographical characteristics of crime scenes hold significant promise for the advancement of investigative profiling.

Author's Note: This chapter was cowritten with Kim Rossmo.

TABLE 12.1   Elements in the Perception Of Distance

Method of transportation
Attractiveness of origins, destinations, and travel ways
Familiarity of roads and highways
Number and types of barriers
Alternative routes
Actual distance

SOURCE: From "The Measurement of Mental Rape: An Experimental Model for Studying Conceptual Spaces," by D. Stea 1969, in K. Cox & R. Golledge (Eds.), *Behavioral Problems in Geography*. Evanston, IL: Northwestern University Press. Reprinted with permission.

Distance

Distance means different things to different people and we are sometimes surprised at the sundry attitudes displayed by people living in various parts of the country. A colleague from Utah, Dr. Al Carlisle, thinks little of driving several hundred miles, interviewing someone, and then driving home the same day. In another part of the country, a distance of 100 miles might necessitate an overnight stay at a local hotel before the return trip the next day. So distance is a relative concept and its perception depends on a variety of elements (Douglas, Burgess, Burgess, & Ressler, 1992). Table 12.1 lists some of these influences.

Method of Transportation

One's perception of distance will be influenced by mode of transportation. For example, if a killer has to walk or depend on public transportation, his range of activities will be more constricted than if he has a vehicle. One murderer, whose case we profiled, traveled by city bus because he had neither a driver's license nor an automobile. He killed and assaulted within the immediate area of his home because his range of travel was restricted to within his own neighborhood. The hunting area was immediate to his personal activities and was determined not only by his daily actions but also by his personality. He was a "disorganized" personality who saw visions and heard voices. His restricted comfort zone was defined by his daily activities, limited by the range and mode of his travels, and by his own personal inadequacies.

Attractiveness of Origins, Destinations, and Travel Ways

As we all know, we prefer to travel certain roads and highways for reasons that vary from person to person. It may be that there are fewer regulated stops along one route than along another. It may be that a road is particularly scenic. There is an expressway in Kentucky, for example, that wanders through the thoroughbred horse farms. Another highway cuts through a strip mining area, characterized by huge, gaping holes in the earth. Which of these is preferable, based only on the criteria of visual attractiveness?

Of course, other factors will enter into the decision of which route to choose. The origin and the destination must also be considered. These exert, respectively, "push" and "pull" factors on the individual. What is the exact nature and character of such forces in a given case? Only the individual offender knows this answer—but the alert investigator must be able to get into the mind of the criminal, just as Will Graham did in *The Red Dragon.*

Familiarity of Roads and Highways

We are all, to one degree or another, creatures of habit. We will repeat those things that are familiar and comfortable to us. Some families take their vacations in the same places year after year. Reasons for this are obvious. Familiarity brings comfort. The routes of travel become memorized and road maps are no longer needed. Landmarks are easily recognized and anticipated as a means of validating the route traveled.

As one gets to know the roads and highways along with topological elements and landmarks, familiarity leads to comfort and reassurance. This affects the subjective perception of distance and can affect where an offender cruises for victims or searches for places to dispose bodies. The more familiar the offender is with a highway or road, the more locations he will be aware of that will serve his criminal purposes.

Number and Types of Barriers

Geographical barriers and boundaries affect our chosen methods of travel. These include such things as rivers, freeways, railroad tracks, jurisdictional and state lines, national borders, and so on. An offender facing such a decision—whether or not to cross a river in the hunt for victims, for example—must weigh certain factors. How much of a barrier is the river? What is the distance to the nearest bridge? Is he comfortable enough, psychologically, to operate on the other side of the river? Is there a county or state line involved, and, if so, what are the advantages and disadvantages and the various legal issues involved? The investigator must take into account these types of considerations that the offender makes when examining the geographical landscape surrounding the crime areas.

Alternative Routes

If only a few major roads exist in a community, an offender will quickly become aware of not only the avenues of travel but also of the possibilities for criminal behavior held by each. When several arterial routes are found in a community, however, additional elements need to be considered. Which road is the most direct one? Which is the most pleasant to travel? Which has the lowest risk of detection? These are all important considerations. The existence of multiple routes of travel will enhance the capability of the offender to find, and flee, desirable locations.

Actual Distance

Not surprisingly, the actual distance between two points, as measured objectively, also has an influence on the perception of distance. For some offenders, further distances are an advantage, whereas for others, like the disorganized asocial type, straying too far from their home bases is not feasible. Jeffrey Dahmer, for example, stayed within the confines of his Milwaukee neighborhood. On the other hand, Ted Bundy traveled considerable distances in search of his victims.

Mental Maps

Everyone possesses a "mental map." This is a cognitive image of our spatial surroundings that has been built up over time by our daily activities and experiences. Most of these activities occur in the areas around our homes, workplaces, recreation sites, shopping districts, and the like, causing these neighborhoods to become known and familiar. Connecting our centers of activity are various routes such as paths, streets, bridges, and highways; separating them are various physical and psychological barriers, such as buildings, rivers, ravines, brush, and lakes.

TABLE 12.2 Elements of a Spatial Mental Image

Paths—routes of travel (e.g., streets, railroad tracks, paths)
Edges—border or lines (e.g., river edge, lakeshore, city limits)
Districts—distinct and identifiable areas (e.g., financial district,
  Chinatown, Skid Row)
Nodes—focused centers of activity (e.g., intersections, subway stations,
  plazas)
Landmarks—geographic reference points (e.g. mountains, towers,
  billboards)

SOURCE: From *The Image of the City*, by K. Lynch, 1960, Cambridge: MIT Press. Reprinted with permission.

Based on this spatial information, we choose paths that we use during our daily routine travels. Our activity sites, familiar areas, travel routes, and barriers all influence the development of our mental maps. Table 12.2 lists some of the elements comprising a spatial image (Holmes & Holmes, 1998).

Because mental maps are affected by activity sites, we should remember that for the experienced criminal, such locations could include court houses, prisons and jails, criminal justice agencies, areas of prostitution, previous crime sites, and the like. It may be that we should return to an examination of the "concentric zone theory" of years past to develop some theory of the relationship between criminal profiling and geography; but perhaps it is just as effective to consider our thoughts regarding our own mental maps and spatial behavior.

Criminals and Mobility

One of the main items of interest to us in the examination of the Ted Bundy case, in addition to the number of victims that he admitted to having killed during a 17-year successful murder career, was the manner in which he drove the highways of our nation. In *Serial Murder* (Holmes & Deburger, 1985b), the authors termed Bundy a *geographical-transient* serial murderer. This means that he killed first in one area and then moved to another area and killed again. In an interview (R. Holmes' files), Bundy stated that "this person we are talking about [himself]" may have killed in as many as nine states. Only the night before his death did he admit to a tenth state, Idaho!

The highway system makes it possible for a predator to travel long distances, not only in the search for potential victims, but also in an effort to confuse law enforcement. In addition, expanded road networks have opened up opportunities for the disposal of bodies. In the case of the Hillside Stranglers in California (O'Brien, 1985), most of the victims' bodies were dumped close to the freeway, allowing the killers to be back on the road within seconds.

Questions considering why the killer decided to search that particular neighborhood for a victim, choose that particular area to dump the body, and pick that particular route to travel are important to ask. What were the geographical characteristics that made those victim selection areas, body disposal locations, and routes of travel so attractive? We should not consider these choices to be the mere result of accident.

Consider the following case of a serial rapist who admitted, after his arrest, to more than 30 rapes. The attacks commenced when his wife refused to engage in sexual relations because she was fearful of pregnancy. Her refusal, he later admitted, launched him into a mental state in which he both feared and hated women. To ventilate his hatred and to help control his fear, he repeatedly raped but with little additional overt violence. From the model of personal violence discussed earlier in this book, we can see that he progressed from the distorted thinking stage to the fall.

The serial rapes of this offender took on an interesting geographical pattern. The first rape occurred on the direct route from his home to work. It was less than one block from his commuting path to the apartment of the victim. He admitted to police that he often left home early to search for suitable victims along the route he traveled to work. The next few victims were attacked further away. After moving to a new address, he began to explore other directions but again, never traveled more than a block from the main thoroughfare. This rapist is best categorized as a power reassurance rapist with many personal traits of the disorganized asocial personality type (Knight & Prentky, 1987). He felt most comfortable and personally secure traveling along familiar routes.

We have evaluated more than 800 murder cases and have found some interesting results regarding journeys taken and distances traveled. When cases of serial offenders, rapists, murderers, and child abusers are plotted, we have noted that offender mobility and crime site geography are not only important but are also predictable.

As the neophyte criminal progresses in the "industry of offending," he gains experience that leads to increases in both comfort and confidence levels. With this increasing sense of comfort and confidence comes an expansion in predatory spatial activity, increasing travel distance, and enlarging the victim search area. When an offender starts to hunt, the first few acts are usually situated relatively close to the locations of either his home or work. As initial successes lead to increased confidence, the offender becomes more willing to prey further and further from home.

If the investigator is convinced that the crimes have been committed by a serial offender, special consideration should be given to those locations connected to the first few crimes. If it appears that the crimes are the responsibility of a single person and if the site pattern is spreading, then it may be that the locations of the earliest crimes are close to the home or workplace of the offender. The focus of the investigation should then be concentrated in the area of the original crime sites as it is likely that this contains the offender's "comfort zone." Obviously, this has important implications for the successful investigative resolution of a crime series.

Geography and Victim Selection

Crimes suitable for geographic analysis are those in which the offender exercises some spatial decision-making process. The most obvious of these involve crimes of a predatory nature in which the criminal hunts for his victims, choosing the neighborhoods in which he plans to seek out suitable targets. Not only must the perpetrator pick the areas in which he will look for his victims, but he must also determine where he will dump or bury the body, what routes he will travel, and the mode of transportation that he will use. The degree of offender movement or travel varies depending on the type and characteristics of the perpetrator (Hickey, 1991). Serial crimes are the easiest to geographically profile because each different crime site contains new spatial information, providing the profiler with multiple sources of data. Serial murder, serial rape, and serial arson are the most common offenses profiled in this manner, but the principles can be applied to a variety of other crimes.

Rossmo (1995) speaks of a series of geographic zones, derived from the Brantingham and Brantingham model of target selection, within which an offender is most likely to commit his or her crimes (Brantingham & Brantingham, 1981). The areas of "home," "work," and "shopping and entertainment" comprise comfort zones that allow predatory offenders to cruise and commit their crimes under a psychological blanket of protection. Bundy created cemeteries in places such as Taylor Mountain and

Home   Work

Shopping and Entertainment

FIGURE 12.1   Offender Activity Space

Lake Sammanish State Park. The dumpsites were close to the Washington state highway system, situated in areas that he was familiar with and that conveyed a sense of psychological comfort.

The predator has a zone of behavioral activity, an activity space that contains both activity sites and the connecting paths between them. The rapist earlier discussed had activity sites situated within his home and work neighborhoods and shopping and entertainment areas. His connecting routes were the main streets that ran from one activity site to another (see Figure 12.1.).

Rossmo (1995) notes that geography plays an important role in the offender's selection of "suitable victims." What defines a suitable victim? Why is it that some predators will let one potential victim pass and wait for another? It has to be more than the physical characteristics of the victim; there has to be a "click" within the mind of the predator which alerts him to a sense of "rightness" for attack.

When a criminal selects a target, there must be a suitability for victimization that may have something to do with "the rightness of the place." Is the area appropriate for predation? Does it contain sufficient and suitable victims? Is it familiar? Does it possess a feeling of comfort? Is the risk of apprehension low? Are there escape routes? As the offender considers these factors, so must the profiler.

THE NATURE OF GEOGRAPHIC PROFILING

A geographical analysis is only one potential source for information and strategies in the successful investigation of a crime series. There are many

---

TABLE 12.2   Elements to Consider in Geographic Profiling

Crime location type
Arterial roads and highways
Physical and psychological boundaries
Land use
Neighborhood demographics
Routine activities of victims
Displacement

SOURCE: From "Place, Space, And Police Investigations: Hunting Violent Serial Killers," by D. Rossmo, 1994, in J. Eck & D. Wesiburd (Eds.), *Crime Prevention Studies* (Vol. 4). Monsey, NY: Criminal Justice Press. Reprinted with permission.

---

others. Table 12.2 lists several steps in an investigative process involving the use of profiling tactics (Rossmo, 1994). Certain of the above-mentioned elements are well known to police and citizens alike. We are all alerted to the possibilities of similar crimes being committed by the identification of modus operandi or signatures. As discussed earlier, the method of operation may change but the signature will remain the same (Rossmo, 1994).

When a series of crimes show similarities that suggest that they were committed by the same offender, police agencies now have a variety of investigative options at their disposal. Traditional investigative techniques will always be the mainstay of all detective work. In addition, linkage analysis can identify connections between similar crimes committed in different jurisdictions. Such analyses are usually performed at the state or national level through the use of computerized systems such as the Federal Bureau of Investigation Violent Criminal Apprehension Program (VICAP), the Royal Canadian Mounted Police Violent Crime Linkage Analysis System (VICLAS), the New York State Police Homicide Assessment and Lead Tracking Project (HALT), or the Washington State Attorney General's Office Homicide Investigation Tracking System (HITS).

Not only can linkage analysis systems locate possible suspects from records of similar past offenses, but they also provide, through the identification of similar crimes, maximum information for psychological and geographic profiling efforts. The development of both psychological and geographical profiles, used in a complementary fashion, will hopefully lead to new investigative strategies that can be employed to help solve the crime series.

TABLE 12.3 Types of Crime Locations
Encounter site
Attack site
Crime site
Victim disposal site
Vehicle dump site

Geographic Profiling: Nature and Considerations

No one method will identify an unknown offender; therefore, it is beneficial to consider the various elements as complementary to each other. This is especially true when one considers the impact of geography on criminal profiling. What are some of the factors that are important in such an analysis? Table 12.2 lists several important elements that need to be considered in the construction of a geographic profile and will be discussed in more detail in the following sections.

Crime Location Type

What constitutes a crime site location? This depends on the particular offense and the perpetrator's modus operandi. Many violent crimes involve different locations. Table 12.3 lists the various types of crime sites which might be connected to an offense of murder or rape (Rossmo, 1995). The geographic pattern of these crime sites will be influenced by the mode of travel available to the criminal. An offender who walks, for example, will have a more constricted hunting area than if he had access to a vehicle.

The location where the offender first contacts the victim is termed the encounter site. This may be in a bar, a street or park, a red light district, or any other location where the victim and the offender share physical and psychological space. The attack site is the location where the offender first attacks the victim. It is often the same as the encounter location. In such cases, it may be that the offender lives relatively close to this position. Two different locations suggest that the personality of the offender may be more developed, indicating a capability for growth in the range of travel in the search for victims. In other words, this type of offender is more likely to be the "organized personality."

The crime site is the location of the actual crime—the murder or rape scene in this case. The victim disposal site is the location where the offender dumps or releases the victim. If the victim disposal location is different from the encounter, attack, or crime locations, then we would suspect that the offender has a more organized personality; not only would he be capable of elaborate planning, but he would also be willing to travel further distances. If all the crime locations are the same, then we have reason to believe that the offender is more disorganized. This type of personality is most comfortable in familiar (i.e., nearer) neighborhoods. Because the more organized offender usually travels longer distances to stalk, attack, or dispose of his victims, it is more likely that this type of offender lives further from the initial contact site (Barrett, personal communication, February 19,1990). The same argument can be applied to the other types of crime locations. It should be stressed that often these different crime sites are in the same location. Every case has to be viewed separately because each crime is unique, even if the offender and his signature are the same.

Arterial Roads and Highways

In any area, people have preferences for the roads that they travel. These preferred routes depend on a variety of things. There may be, for example, one road more pleasant to the view than another. Some people travel by car or public transportation, others by bicycle or on foot. Choice of street may depend on the number of stop signs or stop lights that one might encounter along the way, or by the directness of the route traveled. It is safe to say that no one road, despite how planners have laid out the thoroughfare, will be the favorite way to travel.

Camelback Road is one of the main routes between Phoenix and Scottsdale, Arizona. Along this street are numerous businesses, new and used car dealers, restaurants, and stop lights. Asking for directions while there on a speaking engagement, we were told that the best way to get "there" from "here" was another road, less traveled, less direct, but with little to detract the view of the driver and passenger, and with not as pleasant a topology. Which is the better way? It depends. What does one desire? The quickest way? The most visually appealing? The answer will depend not only on the person but on the circumstances and the purpose of the trip. Would a person travel one road to work and a different one to commit a crime? The answer may depend on the personality, circumstances, or personal organization, of the offender.

Physical and Psychological Boundaries

Physical and psychological barriers and boundaries also exist in our travels. Rivers and railroad tracks act as physical barriers to travel. In some cases, the barriers cannot be physically crossed, whereas in others it depends more on the choice of the traveler. Such choices may not be initially comprehensible to us, from our perspective as investigators, but it makes sense from the criminal's standpoint. People often feel uncomfortable in unfamiliar areas, such as neighborhoods of different socioeconomic or racial composition. The hunting patterns of offenders may therefore be distorted by such influences.

Land Use

The dominant land use in those areas surrounding, and between, the crime sites is important in a geographical analysis. What is the zoning in those areas—residential, commercial, industrial, or parkland? Are there major close-by attractions such as shopping centers, bars, entertainment sites, parks, office towers, factories, or the like? Are there important transportation sites within those areas, such as train stations, bus routes, freeways, jogging paths, or subway stops? The way that the surrounding areas are used can provide vital information—in effect, geographic clues—that may significantly assist in the crime series investigation.

Neighborhood Demographics

Related to land use information is demographic and census data. What are the characteristics of those populations that reside in the neighborhoods of the crime sites? Information on sex ratios, racial composition, age breakdowns, occupational groups, socioeconomic status, crime rates, and other demographic variables is important in any profiling process.

Routine Activities of Victims

The behavior, travels, and habits of the victims are critical elements in the profiling process, especially in any geographical analysis. Certain inferences can be drawn if the body dump site in a murder case is found in a location that would not be expected considering the victim's normal range of behaviors and interests. It may be assumed, in such a case, that the location of the dump site has more significance to the offender than to the victim. It is important to consider the manner in which the body was dumped or displayed as that information may give us some indication of the characteristics of the offender.

Displacement

Spatial patterning may change as the offender progresses through his crime series, maturing and gaining confidence, and learning how to expand his hunting areas. But there is also an additional factor that can affect the location of crime sites. Geographic displacement occurs when the offender moves the locations of his criminal activities (e.g., victim hunting areas, body dump sites, etc.) in response to some action taken on the part of the criminal justice system. Patrol saturation efforts by the police in targeted neighborhoods is the most common cause of displacement. Inappropriate media disclosures have also led to changes in modus operandi and geography by the organized offender. Profilers must be aware of, and take into the consideration, the possible influences of these types of factors.

Investigators may ask, "Now what?" We would suggest that profilers should be aware of the geography of relevant areas. Plot the crime locations on a map. Look for patterns. Are there industries, residential areas, or shopping and entertainment centers along the routes between the crime sites? This may seem to be an old-fashioned approach, but what is new is the manner in which the areas of activity and their relationships are considered.

COMPUTERIZED GEOGRAPHICAL ANALYSES

At a national criminal justice conference, speakers discussed psychological profiling, geographic profiling, and other new scientific advances. Rossmo noted that there now exists a computerized program called CGT (Criminal Geographic Targeting) that assesses spatial characteristics of crimes. He described the computerized analysis as a strategy for information management in cases of serial major crimes. The underlying mathematical process involves the scanning of every point in the offender's hunting area and then the assigning of probabilities based on the distances from the point to each of the crime sites (Rossmo, 1995). The result is presented in a manner similar to a topographic map of a mountain range, with the high points representing the most likely areas for the location of the offender's residence.

Most major crime cases that are serial in nature suffer from the problem of information overload. Often thousands of tips will be received and hundreds of suspects developed, placing tremendous demands on limited police resources. One of the major values of profiling is that it can provide a means for prioritizing leads and suspects. Because many of our sources of information are address-based, geographic profiling is particularly useful for strategic information management.

Because the CGT process produces a map that shows probability of offender residence by area, it can be employed as the basis for a variety of investigative strategies, the use of which depends on the specific details of the case. Some of these strategies include the following:

- patrol saturation and static stakeouts
- door-to-door canvassing, grid, and area searches
- suspect prioritization
- computerized searches of police information and record systems
- searches of outside agency databases
- task force tip prioritization
- zip/postal code prioritization

In one series case, a child was abducted from near her home, murdered, and her body dumped in the outskirts of the city. Investigators had only a brief description of the suspect vehicle from a young playmate of the victim. A geographic profile was constructed using the CGT program and the prioritized zip/postal codes were used, in conjunction with the vehicle description, in an off-line data base search of Department of Motor Vehicles owner registration records. The end result was that thousands of potential suspect vehicles were narrowed down to only a few dozen, greatly facilitating the investigative process.

Rossmo states that the typical construction of a geographic profile involves the following process:

1. a thorough perusal of the case file including investigation reports, witness statements, autopsy reports, and psychological profile (if available);

2. detailed examination of crime scene and area photographs;

3. interviews with lead investigators and crime analysts;

4. visits, when possible, to each of the crime sites;

5. analysis of demographic data and neighborhood crime statistics;

6. study of street, land use, and transit maps;

7. computerized analysis (if appropriate); and

8. interim and final report writing.

In this whole process, which takes on average about two weeks to complete, the computerized analysis involves less than 5% of the total time and its use requires judicious decision making on the part of the profiler. So although computers play an important role, their function should be placed in the proper perspective. We must always remember that profiling is still more of an art than a science. It is only viable when the human element comes into play. This provides profiles with their richness. A computer system, regardless of its sophistication, cannot include all the multitude of details involved in a given case or comprehend the complete range of potential human behavior. Although the development of computerized profiling programs involving expert systems has been discussed, their widespread availability is some years away. For now, we still need humans who are schooled in the disciplines of criminology, sociology, psychology, geography, and psychiatry. And a little luck.

CONCLUSION

The role of geography has been ignored too often in the profiling process. This chapter has examined some of the general principles of geographic profiling and crime scene assessment. Much of the material has been gleaned from the research and experiences of Rossmo and others who have worked in this area. Some of the insights have been gained by the authors through the process of profiling cases for police departments across the nation. By blending all this information, a plan has been presented that allows for a consideration of the role of geography and topology in the profiling process. It is critical, however, to retain the human factor in our understanding of the influence of geography. Then, and only then, can we be successful.

Chapter 13

JACK THE RIPPER

A Case for Psychological Profiling

From August through November, 1888, the east end of London, especially the Whitechapel section, was swathed in a state of dread and foreboding. The residents feared an unknown killer who called himself "Jack the Ripper." First called "Leather Apron" by the police and the press, a letter sent to media alerted them of his existence and he signed the letter "Jack the Ripper." This name of the unidentified murderer has become famous, or infamous, in the annals of serial crime and serial murder.

This was a time when interest in crime was at all-time high. Only a year had passed since the first novel by Sir Arthur Conan Doyle depicting the crime resolution efforts of Sherlock Holmes was published. And although Mr. Holmes and his companion, Dr. Watson, were able to resolve the most bizarre crimes within the confines of the pages of the book, the murders by Jack the Ripper remain unsolved even into the 21st century.

After the murder of the first victim, Polly Nichols, the subsequent killings became more famous, especially when the name of Jack the Ripper became known. Then, even the west enders of London became a part of the frightened populace. This was unusual because London was a divided city. The west end was a society of the wealthy men and women of this town that dated to even before the Middle Ages. The west enders were people of wealth, taste, and power. Their children were taken care of by nannies. They attended plays, operas, and partook of all the good things offered in the capital city of England. Their queen, Victoria, ruled for their benefits and they benefitted greatly in comparison to those who merely existed in the east end of London.

With a population of 900,000 in the east end of London, many were homeless. Here was an area called Whitechapel. It was an island within a ghetto largely ignored by business leaders and the power brokers of government. Overcrowding, unemployment, disease, and other social maladies affected thousands of people, particularly women. Many had to turn to prostitution for food and shelter for themselves and their often fatherless children. A man could purchase the services of a woman for the price of a loaf of bread. Because conditions were so bad, no one thought ill of the women who had to resort to the streets for subsistence.

Such deplorable conditions, combined with one man terrorizing the streets of Whitechapel, caused ever-increasing alarm to the citizens of London. The women of the west end wrote a letter to the queen asking for protection from Jack the Ripper lest the killer come into their own section and start killing the affluent women of London.

In general, this sense of pandemic fear enveloped London. Five women, and perhaps at least three more, had been murdered, and, although there were viable suspects, no arrests were forthcoming.

In this chapter we will examine the case of Jack the Ripper. We will introduce the five victims with as much information as is available about their backgrounds, habits, behaviors, and so on to provide a victimology report. We will also offer forensic information about the murders including geoforensic information, and finally certain information concerning viable suspects in the Jack the Ripper case. The last section of this chapter deals with the development of your own profile for the identity of Jack the Ripper. This allows you to enhance your profiling skills because of the emerging knowledge of the profiling process gleaned up to this point.

VICTIM: MARY ANN "POLLY" NICHOLS

Personal History

Some disagreement surrounds the actual number of victims killed by Jack the Ripper. We have decided to deal with the five women considered mostly likely Jack's victims (see Table 13.1 for a list of his known victims). The first is Polly Nichols.

Polly Nichols was born Mary Ann Walker on August 26, 1845, in Shoe Lane in London. Polly's father, Edward Walker, was a blacksmith; her mother's name was Caroline. She was christened in 1851 and at the time of her death she was 43.

TABLE 13.1 Known Victims of Jack the Ripper

Victim's name	Age	Date Killed	Comments
Mary Ann Nichols, aka "Polly"	43	August 31, 1888	First of the five victims. Her throat was slashed, she was stabbed in the stomach, and her vertebrae were exposed
Annie Chapman, aka "Dark Annie"	47	September 8, 1888	Organs removed from the body
Elizabeth Stride	45	September 30, 1888	As Jack was killing her, he was interrupted; tried to take her ear with him
Catharine Eddowes	46	September 30, 1888	Same day as Stride killing, only a few minutes later; victim suffered savage mutilation, removal of her kidney
Mary Jane Kelly	25	November 9, 1888	Killed in her apartment, intestines removed, heart taken, skin and body parts placed on a table next to her bed

Nichols was 5'2" tall with brown eyes, dark complexion, and brown hair slightly turning gray. She had five front teeth missing at the time of her death. Her teeth were also slightly discolored, which was common among the poor. She also had a small scar on her forehead, perhaps the result of an accident as a child. People described her as small and clean. She was also an alcoholic.

Nichols married William Nichols in 1864; she was 18. Together they had five children: Edward, Percy, Alice, Eliza, and Henry. The couple did not have a happy union and separated perhaps as many as six

TABLE 13.2 Criminal Record of Polly Nichols	
Date	*Location*
04–24–1882 to 01–18–1883	Lamberth Workhouse
01–18–1883 to 01–20–1883	Lamberth Workhouse
01–20–1883 to 03–24–1883	Lamberth Workhouse
10–25–1887	One night at St. Giles Workhouse
10–26–1887 to 12–02–1887	Strand Workhouse
12–02–1887 to 12–19–1887	Lamberth Workhouse
12–19–1887 to 12–29–1887	Lamberth Workhouse
08–01–1888 to 08–02–1888	Grays Inn Workhouse

times during their 24-year marriage. She separated from William for the last time in 1881. When Nichols' husband learned that she was making her living as a prostitute, he stopped paying her child support. Some believe that she was living with other men during the time of her final separation until she was murdered. William was accused by Polly—and at least one of the children—of having an affair that led to their final separation.

Criminal Background

Nichols had a lengthy police record but all were for minor offenses such as drunkenness, disorderly conduct, and prostitution (see Table 13.2).

Residences and Locations

At the time of her death, Nichols lived with four women in a lodging house at 18 Thrawl Street. Thrawl Street was south of and parallel to Flower and Dean Streets in London's east side. One roommate, Emily (or Ellen) Holland, also had a minor record for prostitution. Nichols moved from this public lodging house to another one a quarter mile away. Here, men and women were allowed to share the same rooms and the same beds. In this new house, the rooms were small, dark, and dank. The area was rampant with disease, squalor, crime, and despair. Many roomers paid on a night-to-night basis; they earned enough money during the day to pay their "doss," or nightly fee, for lodging.

TABLE 13.3   Last Known Sightings of Polly Nichols

Time	Comments
11:00 pm	Polly is seen seeking "dates" for prostitution.
1:30 am	She is asked to leave a public lodging house because she had no money for a bed. As she was leaving, she told the manager that she would be back soon so the manager would save the bed for her. The fee that she demanded for an act of prostitution was 2 or 3 pence, the price of a loaf of bread. She also made some remarks about her new black bonnet.
2:30 am	Ms. Holland, who stated to the police that Polly was very drunk and had staggered along the walls of the buildings as she walked down the street, sees her.
3:15 am	The local bobbie was walking his beat on Buck's Row and saw nothing unusual. This same information was reported by another beat officer at about the same time.
3:45 am	Polly Nichols' body was found by a man on his way to work
3:50 am	A local physician arrives at the crime scene and pronounces Polly dead

The Night of the Killing

Various sources provided information concerning the chronology of the night of Polly Nichols' death (Douglas, Burgess, Burgess, & Ressler, 1992; Evans & Skinner, 2000; Harrison, 1993; Paley, 1996; Rumbelow, 1988). Table 13.3 offers a snapshot of Polly Nichol's last night alive.

Buck's Row was a narrow street with few well-kept houses. Most were shabby, dirty, and in need of major repair. On one side of the street were homes and public lodging houses; on the other were businesses and warehouses. The street in this block where Nichol's body would be found was illuminated by one street light.

Nichol's body was found across from a warehouse in a gateway to a stable. The people who lived next door to the stable and across the street reported that they woke up several times during the night but heard nothing. What she was wearing when she was discovered is noted in Table 13.4.

TABLE 13.4   Clothing Worn by Polly Nichols on Night of Her Death
Black straw bonnet
Aulster of reddish brown
Brown Lindsey frock
White flannel chest cloth
Black ribbed wool stockings
Two petticoats
Brown stays
Men's elastic side boats
White handkerchief

Medical Report

The physician reported that Nichols had five teeth missing and a slight tear at her tongue. She was bruised along her cheek. On the left side of her throat was a circular bruise with a similar bruise on the left side of her face. Starting on the left side of the neck was a 4-inch incision as well as a similar incision about one inch below this, which ran for about three inches. This was below the right jaw and severed all the tissues down to the vertebrae. This incision was about 8 inches long. No blood was found on the body. Across the lower part of the abdomen were several incisions. The physician also reported that there were three or four similar cuts running down the abdomen on the right side. The knife was reported to be sharp and all the wounds made by the same knife.

VICTIM: ANNIE CHAPMAN

Personal History

Not much is known of Annie Chapman's early life. However, we know she married but left her husband and two children to become a prostitute and street vendor, selling flowers and her own crochet. She lived in public housing, earning her daily doss from her work and from prostitution. For about four years after she left her husband she received support from him. The husband had custody of their two children, one in school in France and the other in a mental hospital. The support stopped when her husband died in 1886.

People reported that "Dark Annie" was a hostile person who would often get involved in physical altercations with other women. This was especially true when she drank. Oddly, she drank only on Saturdays. The people on Hanbury Street in Whitechapel knew her well. She was described as a stout woman, about 5 feet tall, with light brown wavy hair, blue eyes, dark complexion, and a flat nose. She was not in good health at the time of her murder, suffering from diseases of the lungs and brain that were considered terminal. She could have also had TB and syphilis.

Criminal Background

Little is known of Dark Annie's criminal background. She did not have the extensive, but minor, criminal background of Polly Nichols. Little doubt, however, exists that she did have an arrest record because of her penchant for fighting while drinking and her general intoxication. Records, as far as we can determine, are missing on Annie Chapman's case.

Residences and Locations

Annie Chapman lived for the last six years before her death in Whitechapel. At one time she lived in a rear room adjacent to Mary Kelly, the last known victim of Jack the Ripper. Records do not show many exact addresses, but she resided several times at 35 Dorset Street, 30 Dorset Street, and on Hanbury Street. All her known addresses were public lodgings, including those on Dorset Street and at Crossingham's Lodging House. She lived with several men during this six-year period. And at one time she called herself Annie Sievey or Siffey.

The Night of the Killing

As can best be determined, Annie had been out drinking the night of her death. She had not come back to the lodging house because the manager said she did not have enough money for her doss. As she left, she said, as had Polly Nichols, that she would be back as soon as she made enough money for a room that evening. Table 13.5 lists the last known sightings of Annie Chapman on the night of her death.

John Davis found the body as he left his own apartment in the rear of 29 Hanbury Street and began his walk to work. He discovered the body in the rear yard of the three story lodging house. She was laying on her back

TABLE 13.5	Last Known Sighthings of Annie Chapman
Time	*Comments*
11:30 pm	Left Crossingham's Lodging House to earn money.
5:00 am	Seen at 29 Hanbury Street.
5:30 am	Seen talking with a man at 29 Hanbury Street.
5:45 am	Her body was discovered by John Davis.

with her face turned to the right. Her intestines were over her right shoulder and her stomach was sliced open. Her left arm was resting on her left breast. There were two rings on the ground next to her. Both rings had been torn from her fingers. In addition, coins were placed at the victim's feet. The right hand was by the right side, the legs were drawn up, and knees were turned outward. The feet were pointed toward a wooden shed. The hands were raised with the palms upward. There was no evidence of a struggle, and no clothing was found ripped or torn.

Mr. Davis alerted the law enforcement officials, who responded in less than five minutes. The rear yard was dark and there was no intent on the part of the killer to hide the body.

Medical Report

The medical information received about the examination of Annie Chapman was sparse. The police physician stated that, in essence, Ms. Chapman was disemboweled; her uterus was removed from the scene, as was one kidney. The abdomen was laid open, the intestines were lifted out and placed over her right shoulder; the intestines were severed. Parts of the pelvis, the uterus, and the upper part of the vagina were removed. Also, two thirds of the bladder was removed.

The physician offered that the knife that was used was very sharp and approximately six to eight inches long. Additional medical information was missing. As in the case of many modern serial killers and their investigations, turf issues were prevalent and information was not shared. However, because this was a publicized case, 16 influential local businessmen formed the Whitechapel Vigilance Committee. It was the committee's responsibility to patrol the area at night and immediately report any problems to the local law enforcement officials. Although nothing is written concerning the effectiveness of the committee, the killings continued.

VICTIM: ELIZABETH STRIDE

Personal History

The third victim of Jack the Ripper was Elizabeth Stride, neé Gustafsdotter. Born on November 27, 1843 in Sweden, she was baptized a Roman Catholic when she was less than one month old. Her father was Gustaf Ericsson and her mother was Beatta Carlsdotter. Stride was 45 when she was murdered by Jack the Ripper. She was reported to be 5' 5" tall, with brown hair, light gray eyes, and a pale complexion. She had no teeth in her lower jaw.

The roomers and friends of Stride called her friendly, outgoing, good hearted, and willing to work when she could find a job. She was not well-educated but could read. However, some reported that she was a drunkard and spent some time in various workhouses in London. She was also reported to use foul language when intoxicated.

She was a registered prostitute but also made some money from sewing and housekeeping. She was treated several times for venereal disease in 1865 in Sweden. In 1866 she moved to London as an unmarried woman. Living with several men before her marriage, she later wed John Thomas Stride, a carpenter, in 1868; he died in 1884. Somewhat of a storyteller, Elizabeth Stride reported that her husband and child had been killed in a shipwreck and that she, too, had almost been killed. This turned out not to be true. Interestingly, John Thomas Stride's nephew, Walter Frederich Stride, was a member of the Metropolitan Police Department in London and identified Elizabeth's body.

From 1882 to the time of her death, Elizabeth lived in common lodging houses in the east end of London. She lived with several men, but perhaps spent more time with Michael Kidney than any other man, about 5 months.

The local churches knew Stride because they would often feed her and give her clothing. Kidney reported that when Stride started drinking she would disappear several days or weeks at a time. She would prostitute herself many times an evening to earn money for a night at one of the lodgings.

TABLE 13.6 Criminal Record of Elizabeth Stride	
Date	*Location/Offense*
March 21, 1887	Poplar Workhouse
September 1888	Arrested for disorderly conduct, spent night in jail

NOTE: Additional records shows that Stride was arrested eight times for various charges in 1887 and 1888.

Criminal Background

Elizabeth Stride did not have an extensive criminal record. Her record is partly detailed in Table 13.6.

Residences and Locations

Elizabeth Stride reportedly lived with many different men from the time she arrived in London until the time of her death. Most of her housings were rented by the night; the residents were often prostitutes who were also alcoholics and many were probably mentally ill. From various sources it appeared that she lived close to Ten Bells, a local tavern, and near 32 Flower and Dean, Commercial Street, and Hanbury Street.

The description of the area was not unlike Polly Nichols's residences: shabby and dirty, public lodgings, businesses, and warehouses on one block followed by a combination of similar buildings in the next block.

Things were better when Elizabeth and John married. They moved into their own residence in another part of London and lived above their own business, a coffee shop. This arrangement lasted until 1882 when she left her husband and started to live in public lodgings and turned to prostitution for her own survival. After her husband's death, she moved in with Michael Kidney, but that arrangement was stressful and she would stay with him only for short periods of time for a total of about five months.

The Night of the Killing

September 30, 1888, would be the last day in the life of Elizabeth Stride. Various people would admit seeing Stride several times during the evening. She was last seen after midnight in the company of a man

> **TABLE 13.7**   Clothing Worn by Elizabeth Stride on Night of Her Death
>
> Long black coat jacket, fur trimmed around the bottom
> Black skirt
> Dark brown velveteen bodice
> Black crepe bonnet
> Checked neck scarf knotted on the left side
> Two light serge petticoats
> One white chemise
> White stockings
> Spring-sided boots

described by two different witnesses as being about 5' 7" tall, with dark hair and a small mustache. He was wearing a long black coat that reached to his heels. Stride had already made sufficient money to buy her a night's lodging in a public house, and one witness stated that he thought he overheard her tell the man that she was not interested in having another sexual date.

At 1:00 a.m., Louis Diemschultz was driving his horse and cart into Dutfield's Yard. The horse refused to enter the premises and the man sensed that there was something wrong but could see nothing because, with no lights, the area was very dark. As he probed the area, his whip came into contact with a body. He thought that the person was drunk and passed out. He went into the neighborhood club and sought help. Two men came to aid him. The three found Stride's body, her throat cut. There were no other mutilations found at that time.

Some thought that Diemschultz frightened Jack off by his sudden arrival at the crime scene. The salesman thought perhaps the killer was still at the scene when he left for help. The reason for this? He said the horse was still acting oddly and the body was very warm as he touched her. The clothing that Elizabeth was wearing at the time of her death is listed in Table 13.7.

Medical Report

The report received by the police physician stated that the body was found lying with the face looking toward the wall and the feet toward the street. The left arm was extended. The right arm was over the abdomen and the back of the hand, as well as her wrists, had blood on them. The body and face were warm when first examined but the hand was cold. The throat had been cut parallel to the left jaw, leaving a deep gash. There was mud on the left side of the face and mud matted in her hair. The cut in the neck was six inches in length and started two and half inches below the jaw. The cut was very clean and the physician thought that the person who had done the incision showed great strength. There was a superficial cut on her right side.

The police offered an opinion apart from the medical report. Some physical evidence indicated that the killer had tried to cut off her head but was unable to do so because of being interrupted.

Other than injuries suffered at the hands of Jack the Ripper, there were no other significant health concerns.

VICTIM: CATHARINE EDDOWES

Personal History

Catharine Eddowes was also known as Kate Kelly. Born in 1842, she was 46 when she was killed. She was 5' tall, with hazel eyes and dark auburn hair. She had a tattoo, "TC," on her left arm. Her father, George, was a tin plate worker and her mother was a homemaker. Catharine had two sisters, Elizabeth and Eliza. After the father went on strike, the family walked to London in 1848. Catharine would be dead 40 years later, murdered at the hands of Jack the Ripper.

At the age of 21, Eddowes lived with an older man, causing some turmoil within the family. She gave birth to a child and decided to come back but her family rejected her. She returned to her former common-law husband. They had two more children. She left him again. She then married another man and this union produced one child. She lived with this husband for only a short time, a time marked with periods of separation. Returning to London after working in the fields of England on temporary agricultural work, she started living in several public lodgings. She mentioned to one manager of a housing unit that she was hoping that she could get some of the reward for catching Jack the Ripper.

Criminal Background

Eddowes was arrested one time for drunk and disorderly conduct. This was on September 29, 1888, the day before her death. She was released from jail at 1:00 a.m. People who knew her said that she was a sober person, easy to get along with but could get angry easily, especially if she had something to drink.

Residences and Locations

Eddowes lived in several public lodgings in Whitechapel. One was Cooney's Lodging House. As with the other victims of Jack the Ripper, Eddowes would stay at various rooming houses but seemed to be more geographically mobile than the other women. She had left her family several years earlier and traveled mostly with other female friends to the countryside—especially during the harvest time and planting months—to earn money for her sustenance and residences. She moved from one area to another around London, including Kent and Maidstone.

The Night of the Killing

The night and early morning hours of September 29 and 30, 1888, found Eddowes seen by several acquaintances as well as neighbors; these are detailed in Table 13.8.

The body was found in a square in front of three empty cottages. The entrance to Mitre Square is a broad entrance. When the police responded to the call, they found Catharine Eddowes' body on its back, the head turned to the left. The arms were by the side of the body. The palms were up and the fingers slightly bent. The abdomen was exposed and the left leg was extended in a straight line. The throat was cut. The intestines were placed over her right shoulder. The right ear was also cut. The police report continued with the mention that the body was still warm. No blood was found on the abdomen, no small feat we would suspect. No blood was found below the middle of the body. As clothing was removed from the body after it arrived for a physical examination, an ear fell from the garments; Jack had cut it off. In addition, he had severed the intestines. The colon was separated and placed in a pile by her side.

Medical Report

The police surgeon examined the body in the late afternoon. The report stated that the body was still not quite cold. A bruise was found on the back of her left hand. No bruises were found on the scalp, the back of

TABLE 13.8   Last Known Sightings of Catherine Eddowes

Time	Comments
8:00 am	Returns to Cooney's Lodging House; sees Mary Kelly.
9:00 am	Pawns a pair of shoes.
10:00 am	Seen eating breakfast with Mary Kelly.
2:00 pm	Leaves Mary Kelly to make some money for lodging.
8:00 pm	Seen drunk and doing imitations of a fire engine.
8:50 pm	Arrested for drunk and disorderly conduct.
1:00 am	Released from jail.
1:35 am	Seen by two men in the company of another man.
1:45 am	Eddowes' body was found in Mitre Square.

the body, or the elbows. The face showed considerable mutilation. A cut through the lower left eyelid, on the right eyelid, and a deep gash in the nasal bone were found. The tip of the nose was cut off. Another cut was found at a right angle on the mouth. On each side of the cheek was a triangular cut about an inch and a half long.

The throat was cut with a slash of about seven inches. Also, another cut was found by her left ear. The larynx was severed to the bone. Jack took the kidney and uterus from the crime scene. The liver was also cut. The womb was sliced horizontally and parts taken. It was the opinion of the police surgeon that the throat was slashed followed by the other attacks. Amazingly, the surgeon stated that he did not think the wounds were self-inflicted!

At the time of her death, the victim was wearing the articles contained in Table 13.9.

VICTIM: MARY KELLY

Personal History

Mary Jane Kelly was 25 years old at the time of her death. She was 5' 7" tall, with blond hair and blue eyes. The reports stated she was pretty but stout. She was called attractive, neat, and clean, and always wore a clean white apron. She was also judged to be a quiet, polite, and industrious person except when she drank. She then became loud and, in some cases, belligerent.

TABLE 13.9 Clothing Worn by and Items Found on Catherine Eddowes on Night of Her Death

Black straw bonnet trimmed in green and black velvet
Black cloth jacket
Large metal buttons
Dark green skirt
Man's white vest
Brown bodice
Gray stuffed petticoat
A very old green alpaca (worn as an undergarment)
A white calico chemise
A pair of men's lace up boots
Gauze used as a neckerchief
1 white handkerchief
1 blue stripe bed ticking pocket
2 short black clay pipes
1 tin box containing tea
1 tin box containing sugar
1 tin matchbox, empty
12 pieces of white rags
1 piece of coarse linen, white in color
1 piece of blue and white shorting, 3 cornered
1 piece of red flannel with pins and needles
6 pieces of soap
1 small tooth comb
1 white handle table knife
1 metal spoon
1 red leather cigarette case
1 ball of hemp
Several buttons and a thimble
A printed handbill
1 red mitten

Kelly was born in Limerick, Ireland, one of several children from the middle-class family of John and Catherine Kelly. Educated for her day, Mary was also judged to be intelligent; she possessed good reading skills and was an artist with some promise.

At 16, she married for the first time and was thought to have one child from this marriage. Her husband was killed in an explosion at

TABLE 13.10 Previous Addresses of Mary Kelly
Providence Row Convent, Crisp Street
Public lodging house on George Street
Public lodging on Paternoster Street
Public lodging on Thrawl Street
26 Dorset Street
13 Miller's Court

work. After spending some time with relatives in various parts of Wales and England, Kelly came to London in 1884. She was thought to have lived in a convent with Catholic nuns when she first arrived. She secured other employment as a maid and housekeeper, and she had been a nursemaid for an illegitimate child of the Duke of Lawrence, a suspect in the Jack the Ripper case. Later she became a prostitute in a high-class brothel in London.

Kelly lived with several men after she arrived in London. The last man was Joseph Barnett. He stated she lived with other men before she moved in with him. They apparently had a good relationship except when they were drinking. Both would become loud and disturbing to others.

Criminal Background

Mary Jane Kelly had no extensive criminal background. She had perhaps one arrest for being drunk and disorderly in a public place. She received a fine from the Thames Magistrate Court on September 19, 1888.

Residences and Locations

When Mary Kelly came to London, she first lived at the Providence Row Convent on Crisp Street in London. She stayed there only a short period. She then became a prostitute and her addresses changed with some rapidity as illustrated in Table 13.10.

The room on Miller's Court was small, approximately 12 feet by 12 feet. Inside the room were two small tables, a small bed, a pail, and a washstand. The windows that faced the outside had two broken panes stuffed with clothing.

TABLE 13.11	Last Known Sightings of Mary Kelly
Time	*Comments*
8:00 pm	Joseph Barnett leaves the room to go to his own abode.
11:00 pm	Seen at the Britannica Bar drinking with another woman.
11:45 pm	Mary Ann Cox sees Kelly talking with a man.
12:30 am	A neighbor is disturbed by Kelly's singing.
1:00 am	A neighbor sees the lights on in Kelly's room.
2:00 am	A neighbor meets Kelly on the street; she seeks money.
3:00 am	Same neighbor sees her in the company of a man.
4:00 am	A roomer hears a cry from Kelly's room.
5:45 am	Someone reported that a man left Kelly's room.
10:45 am	Kelly's body is discovered by the lodging's manager.

The Night of the Killing

Mary Kelly was three months pregnant at the time of her death on November 9, 1888. Several citizens of Whitechapel saw her on the night of her killing and in the early morning hours. These sightings are summarized in Table 13.11.

When the police arrived, Mary Kelly's body was found in her bed. The body was nude and the head was turned to the left. The right arm was slightly moved from the side of the body, elbow bent. The left arm was crossed over the abdomen. Her clothing was found neatly folded on a chair and her boots were in front of the small fireplace. Her legs were spread apart, the left thigh at right angles to her body and the right one askew. The surface of the abdomen and thighs were removed. The breasts were cut off, the arms mutilated, and the face also mutilated beyond recognition. The nose, cheeks, eyebrows, and ears were partially removed. The lips were cut several times. The neck was cut down to the vertebrae. The heart was removed and was not found at the crime scene. In addition, some of her skin was placed on a table next to the bed.

Neighbors reported that when she was seen earlier that night, she was in the company of a man who wore a long dark coat, dark felt hat, dark jacket and trousers, boots, linen short collar, and gloves, and that he had a mustache. He was estimated to be about 35 years of age and about 5' 7" tall.

Medical Report

Medical reports stated that Kelly's face was covered with a sheet at the time of the killing. One breast was found by her right foot and Jack placed a kidney under her head and face. The liver was situated between her feet. The arms and hands displayed defensive wounds, and abrasions were found on the back of the hands. The thorax was opened; the lower part of one lung was ripped and torn off. The cause of death was the cutting of the carotid artery.

WHO WAS JACK THE RIPPER?

Who was Jack the Ripper? This question has, at least at this time, no definitive answer. Competent minds for the last century have pondered this question, and still the case has not been resolved. Table 13.12 contains names of some suspects considered at the time as well as those later regarded as suspects.

Various profiles have been presented. One profile, for example, suggests that:

> Jack the Ripper was a white male, 28–36 years of age, who lived or worked in the Whitechapel area, and probably worked at a sort of job in which he could vicariously experience his destructive fantasies, such as a butcher. He would have come from a family with a weak, passive, or absent father, and would have probably suffered from some sort of physical disability, such as a speech impediment. He would have displayed a strong dislike to prostitutes, and during the course of the investigation, he would have been interviewed by the authorities, and consequently overlooked or eliminated as a suspect. His ordinary, neat, and orderly appearance would not have fitted the prevailing impression of the Ripper as an odd or somehow ghoulish-looking man. (Paley, 1996, pp. 3–4)

John Douglas, a former agent with the FBI, offers his profile of Jack the Ripper in his book, *The Cases That Haunt Us* (with Olshaker, 2000). Similar to the profile cited above, Douglas says that Jack the Ripper was a white male, 28 to 36 years of age who lived or worked in or near the Whitechapel area. His parents were dysfunctional; the mother was domineering, sexually promiscuous, and possibly an alcoholic. The father was passive or absent. As a child, Jack was a loner and also a firesetter as well as being cruel to animals. As he grows into adulthood, he craves power

TABLE 13.12   Selected Suspects in the Jack the Ripper Killings

Dr. Thomas Cream	Cream was at one time considered a viable suspect as Jack the Ripper. Later information revealed that he was hanged in 1892 but was in prison in the United States at the time of the killings.
Jill the Ripper	Sir Arthur Conan Doyle, creator of Sherlock Holmes, believed that Jack the Ripper was a woman. He thought she was a nurse and had medical knowledge to remove the body parts taken by the killer.
George Chapman	He was hanged in 1903 for the murders of his wives by poison. No evidence ties him to the murders of Jack the Ripper. But just as he was about to swing from the gallows, he shouted, "I am Jack ..."
Dr. Roslyn Donston	A surgeon in a hospital two blocks from the murder scene of Polly Nichols. He was also known to associate with prostitutes and one news clipping identified him as Jack the Ripper. No evidence supported this accusation.
Prince Edward Albert	The Duke of Clarence and the grandson of Queen Victoria. A theory proposed that the royal household was covering up the Prince's involvement in the murders. He died in 1892 of natural causes.
Montague Druitt	School teacher, barrister, drug user, Druitt was strongly considered to be Jack the Ripper. He allegedly committed suicide by jumping into the Thames River, from which his body was later recovered.
James Maybrick	Maybrick is a new suspect because of the alleged "Jack the Ripper Diary." He was a cotton broker, moving about England from Liverpool to London and doing business in the Whitechapel area. He appears to be a main suspect in many people's minds.
Dr. Francis Tumblety	An Irish American outlaw, he was in London at the time of the murders. After being arrested in 1888, he escaped custody and left London. Many people believe he is Jack the Ripper.
Aaron Kosminski	A Polish Jew and a resident of Whitechapel, he was considered insane and held great hatred for women. He spent his final years in an insane asylum where he died. Many people believe him to be Jack the Ripper.

and domination over others. He works as a butcher, mortician's helper, a hospital worker, or a morgue attendant. An asocial personality, he dresses well to show his wealth and social status. He carries a weapon because he is paranoid. He has been married in the past and infected with a sexually transmitted disease. Outwardly he appears to be quiet, shy, obedient, and neat in appearance. He also frequents the local pubs in Whitechapel.

But what do you think? We have provided you with information not only here but also in the previous chapters to help you examine this case and develop your own personal profile of this famous unresolved murder case.

CONCLUSION

The case of Jack the Ripper has fascinated criminologists and other interested persons throughout the world for the last century. Despite being closed by the local police, Web sites, books, articles, conferences, and seminars about the case have been offered for public consumption, all attempting to disclose the identity of Jack. None has been successful. One of the latest endeavors has been the publication of the diary of Jack the Ripper in the book, *The Diary of Jack the Ripper: The Discovery, the Investigation, the Debate* (Harrison, 1993). In this book, an alleged diary of James Maybrick—a cotton dealer who had ties to London, Liverpool, and the United States—is suggested as Jack. Serious debate is now dedicated to the authenticity of this diary. If the diary is legitimate, the case of Jack the Ripper may soon be closed.

JONBENET RAMSEY

The Murder of a Beauty Queen

T he people of United States were shocked when they learned that 6-year-old JonBenet Ramsey was killed in her home in Boulder, Colorado. The young beauty queen had been savagely murdered and her body was found in her parents' home. Immediately, suspicions arose that the parents were somehow involved; other theories considered that a neighbor or someone else broke into the home and murdered JonBenet.

Perhaps because of the beauty of this young girl or the wealth of the parents or even the location of the murder itself, the case galvanized the attention of all those who are interested in murder or mystery. This case had both. JonBenet's mother, Patsy, was a former Miss West Virginia; her father was a wealthy businessman. Three siblings, two brothers and a sister, survived JonBenet. Another sister had tragically been killed in an automobile accident only a few years before. Patsy had been diagnosed with cancer but with treatment and her will she seemed to have defeated the disease. So, despite their wealth and power, this family had been touched with tragedy. Their misfortunes were topped by the death of JonBenet.

THE PRINCIPAL PLAYERS IN THE RAMSEY MURDER CASE

The Family

JonBenet Ramsey. The victim. JonBenet was a 6-year-old beauty queen, the former Little Ms. Colorado and National Tiny Miss Beauty. She was killed either on December 25 or 26, 1996. Her body was found in the basement of her parents' home.

Patricia Ramsey.   The mother of the victim. She won the title of Miss West Virginia in 1977. Perhaps because of her own experiences in beauty pageants, Mrs. Ramsey involved JonBenet in a variety of different beauty pageants in several states. In addition, she funded some of the contests in which JonBenet was involved. Patsy also was on several local community boards and was a volunteer at the local elementary school.

John Ramsey.   The father of JonBenet. Ramsey is a wealthy business-man, president, and chief executive officer of Access Graphics, a com-puter services company and a subsidiary of Lockheed Martin. Mr. Ramsey stated that he found JonBenet's body in the basement of their 15-room home in Boulder.

Burke Ramsey.   The 10-year-old brother of JonBenet. He was home at the time of the killing. He is the first child of John and Patsy Ramsey.

Melinda Ramsey.   John Ramsey's daughter by his first marriage. The police verified that she was out of town at the time of the murder of JonBenet.

Elizabeth Ramsey.   John Ramsey's daughter from a previous marriage. She was killed in an automobile accident in 1992.

John Andrew Ramsey.   John Ramsey's son from a previous marriage. He was found to be in Georgia at the time of the murder of JonBenet.

Donald and Nedra Paugh.   Patsy Ramsey's father and mother. At the time of the murder, they lived in Georgia.

Lucinda Ramsey Johnson.   John Ramsey's first wife. At the time of the murder, she lived in Georgia.

Linda Hoffman-Pugh.   The Ramsey's housekeeper.

Rev. Rol Haverstock.   The minister of the church the Ramsey's attended.

Dr. Francesco Beuf.   JonBenet's Boulder pediatrician for the last three years of her life. He has said he saw no evidence of abuse of JonBenet before the murder.

Fleet White Jr. and Priscilla White. Ramsey family friends who were with John Ramsey when he found his daughter's body. Police have said that the Whites are not suspects.

John and Barbara Fernie. Friends of the Ramsey's. They were called to the Ramsey home in the early morning hours of December 26.

Law Enforcement Officials

Linda Arndt. Police officer with the Boulder Police Department. She resigned from the police department on March 19, 1999.

Patrick Burke. Boulder attorney who was hired to represent Patsy Ramsey.

John Douglas. Former FBI agent hired by the Ramsey's to develop a profile for the Ramsey family. He stated that the Ramsey's were not involved in the murder and suspected that the killer was a former disgruntled employee of John Ramsey.

Leslie Durgin. The mayor of Boulder, Colorado.

John Eller. Former lead detective on the case who was replaced by Mark Beckner in October 1997. He later announced his resignation from the Boulder police force.

George Epp. The Boulder County sheriff who handled the investigation into the release of crime scene photos to a tabloid newspaper. His investigation resulted in arrest of a former sheriff's deputy and a photo lab employee. Epp is not directly involved in the Ramsey investigation.

Donald Foste. Literature professor at Vassar who analyzed the alleged ransom note. He determined that Patsy Ramsey had written the note (Douglas & Olshaker, 2000, p. 325).

Officer Rick French. First responding Boulder police officer.

Patrick Furman. A University of Colorado criminal law professor reportedly hired to represent Patsy Ramsey.

Detective Ron Gosage.   Detective with the Boulder Police Department.

Hal Haddon.   Leader of John Ramsey's legal team.

Alex Hunter.   Boulder County district attorney.

Thomas Koby.   At the time of the murder, he was the chief of police.

Henry Lee.   Forensic expert brought into the JonBenet case. He had also worked on the O.J. Simpson case as well as several other high profile cases.

Sergeant Larry Mason.   Detective of the Boulder Police Department. Commander Eller removed him from the case for allegedly leaking information to the news media (Douglas & Olshaker, 2000, p. 308).

John Meyer.   The coroner of Boulder County.

Bryan Morgan.   John Ramsey's attorney. A well-known Denver criminal defense attorney.

Sergeant Paul Reichenbach.   Patrol supervisor of the Boulder Police Department. He was the second officer on the scene at the Ramsey house.

Barry Scheck.   A New York lawyer who specializes in the use of DNA in legal proceedings. He was also on the defense team in the O.J. Simpson case.

Lou Smit and Steve Ainsworth.   Two investigators for the Boulder District Attorney's Office. Smith resigned on September 20, 1998.

Steve Thomas.   A lead detective for the Boulder Police Department in the murder case. Thomas (along with coauthor Don Davis, 1999) wrote a book about the case, *JonBenet: Inside the Ramsey Murder Investigation.* He resigned from the police department on August 6, 1998.

Figure 14.1 and Table 14.1 show the ransom note and time line for the crime. (See Figure 1.1 in Chapter 1 for a reproduction of the actual ransom note.)

Because the ransom note was thought to be of paramount importance, the police department decided to seek professional help in interpreting the contents of the note itself. The company selected provided the profile that became a part of the investigative file (see Figure 14.2).

TABLE 14.1   Time Line of the Crime

1996	
December 25	JonBenet is last seen at 10:30 pm when parents put her to bed.
December 26	Patsy Ramsey calls 911, reports that her daughter has been kidnapped. She tells the dispatcher that she has found a kidnap note on the stairs.
	The police arrive at 5:52 am. JonBenet's body is found at 1:00 pm.
December 27	Autopsy was conducted.
December 31	JonBenet is buried in Marietta, Georgia.
1997	
January 4	Police found a notepad similar to the tablet used for the ransom note.
March 6	The adult children of John Ramsey are removed as suspects.
March 14	Police determine that John Ramsey did not write the ransom note; they determine a female wrote it.
September 29	Police execute search warrants on the Ramsey home and find duct tape, rope, and fibers that match those found on the body of JonBenet.
1999	
October 13	The grand jury announced that it has found insufficient proof to indict anyone in the death of JonBenet Ramsey.

THE MORNING OF THE MURDER, DECEMBER 26, 1996

Early Monday morning of the murder, Patsy Ramsey made a call to 911 at 5:52 a.m. She reported that her daughter was missing from the house and that she found a note indicating that JonBenet had been kidnapped. She stated that the note was found on the stairs after she had left JonBenet's bedroom after finding her missing from her bed. She will later change this story. Illustrated in Figure 14.3 is the transcript of the call to 911 on that morning.

Mr. Ramsey,

Listen carefully! We are a group of individuals that represent a small foreign faction. We do respect your business (sic) but not the country that it serves. At this time we have your daughter in our possession (sic). She is safe and unharmed and if you want her to see 1997, you must follow our instructions to the letter.

You will withdraw $118,000.00 from your account. $100,000 will be in $100 bills and the remaining $18,000 in $20 bills. Make sure that you bring an adequate size attache to the bank. When you get home you will put the money in a brown paper bag. I will call you between 8 and 10 am tomorrow to instruct you on delivery. The delivery will be exhausting so I advise you to be rested. If we monitor you getting the money early, we might call you early to arrange an earlier delivery of the money and hence a (sic) earlier delivery pickup of your daughter.

Any deviation of my instructions will result in the immediate execution of your daughter. You will also be denied her remains for proper burial. The two gentlemen watching over your daughter do not particularly like you so I advise you not to provoke them. Speaking to anyone about your situation, such as Police, F.B.I., etc., will result in your daughter being beheaded. If we catch you talking to a stray dog, she dies. If you alert bank authorities, she dies. If the money is in any way marked or tampered with, she dies. You will be scanned for electronic devices and if any are found, she dies. You can try to deceive us but be warned that we are familiar with law enforcement countermeasures and tactics. You stand a 99% chance of killing your daughter if you try to outsmart us. Follow our instructions and you stand a 100% chance of getting her back. You and your family are under constant scrutiny as well as the authorities. Don't try to grow a brain John. You are not the only fat cat around so don't think that killing will be difficult. Don't underestimate us John. Use that good southern common sense of yours. It is up to you now John!

Victory!

S.B.T.C.

FIGURE 14.1 The Alleged Ransom Note

SOURCE: Thomas, S., & Davis, D. (1999). *JonBenet: Inside the Ramsey Murder Investigation* (p. 17). New York: St. Martin's Press. Reprinted with permission.

Officer Rick French was the first responding officer; he found the parents and several friends at the house. It took less than ten minutes for the police to arrive. When police arrived, they found Patsy Ramsey wearing the same clothing that she wore to a Christmas Eve dinner at the White's home. She answered the door in response to the police completely

(Text continues on page 252)

In 1997 our company was contacted by the Boulder Police Department to assist them in the investigation of the murder of JonBenet Ramsey. We were asked to submit an analysis of the ransom note and in 1998 we were asked to write a psychological profile on Patsy Ramsey. Here are those reports.

PROFILE REPORT
Analysis of $118,000 ransom demand in Ramsey case

To: <u>Det. Ron Gosage</u>
Reference: <u>Psalm 118:27b, Biblical reference Old Testament</u>

"The Lord is our God, Who has shown and given us light. Decorate the festival with leafy boughs and bind the sacrifices to be offered with thick cords to the horns of the altar."

Based on my experience, this second section of verse 27 has been used by several white supremacy groups such as the Christian Identity movement and the Aryan Nation to justify their killing of blacks, Jews, and other minorities. In **their** non-orthodox view, the verse is speaking of offering a person as a sacrifice to God and God is accepting their sacrifice on his altar as atonement. No conservative or liberal Christian theologians interpret the verse in this way.

We have consulted with several theologians about the verse and all have agreed that the verse is a metaphor concerning praise and redemption.

As a historical note, the Hebrews were required to offer a blood sacrifice to God to atone for their sins as a nation. A lamb or sheep would be placed on the altar and tied to the four extended horns of the altar with thick cords. The animal was then cut and bled until it was dead. The blood was then used in ceremony for the "washing away by the blood, the sins of the people."

White supremacists use the redemption and sacrifice ideas to form a justification for killing "animals" [minorities] and offering them to God.

In 1987, I met a FBI agent who told me about a case in the late 1970s that involved this verse of scripture. The case involved a woman with a very conservative Christian background, who strangled her daughter and used this verse as a justification for the killing. Her belief was that the child would be better off in "heaven with God" and that the daughter would be a redemptive sacrifice to God for her [the mother's] sins. We have tried to find information about this case but have been unsuccessful. I would suggest a call to the Psychological Crimes Unit of the FBI in Quantico, VA.

My assessment of this verse and it's possible relevance to this case is as follows: The person using this verse would be from a conservative Christian

(Continues)

FIGURE 14.2 THE PROFILE ANALYSIS OF THE RANSOM NOTE

SOURCE: http://www.seraph.net/jonbenet.html (retrieved August 10, 2001)

FIGURE 14.2 (Continued)

background, i.e. Southern Baptist, Presbyterian, etc. They would see themselves as having committed a grievous sin that requires more than a prayer of forgiveness. Their disgust for their sin would lead to anger towards themselves and towards the person that they felt they had wronged—in this case, the girl.

By killing the child they believed that they were taking the child from a dark world or a dark existence and sending the child to a better place. This blood sacrifice would in their mind bring them redemption for their sin and rid them of their guilt as it related to the child.

I have spent over twenty years studying extreme conservative Christian ideology. Based on my experience and research, this belief in para-redemptive acts manifests itself in many ways, some extreme and some more philosophical.

From my limited knowledge of the killing [news reports of forensic findings], I believe that the individual who committed this act had no previous experience with the killing of a human being.

If the information is correct, the strangulation and blunt trauma to the skull meant that the offender tried one method of killing the girl and then changed to a different method out of frustration. One of these methods failed and the person resorted to a second method to kill the victim. The contusions and other secondary injuries may have been attempts to control the victim during a struggle or strikes of frustration when the child did not die on the first attempt.

Based on my experience, this crime was done by an intimate, a person who knew the victim and had an emotional attachment to the victim. If the forensic information that I have is correct, the offender attempted strangulation first. The offender was in my opinion connected to the victim in an emotional way.

I hope that this information assists you in your investigation. If you need additional information, please feel free to contact me.

Submitted: 29 July 1997
Dale Yeager

Part II

Psalm 118:18 - 27
1/1a As we stated in our first report, we believe that Patsy Ramsey's mindset before and after the murder of JonBenet was heavily influenced by the charismatic theological subculture that she had embraced during her bout with cancer.

Psalm 118 is a biblical chapter that is used quite often in the Charismatic/ Pentecostal movement. This subculture of the Christian Religion has many unwritten fundamentals that they adhere to. One area in which they divert from main stream Christian theology is in the area of biblical interpretation. Because of their extreme emphasis on spiritual gifts, they tend to have a more flexible view of interpretation compared to the more scholarly approach taken by their fellow Christians in main stream denominations.

Rather than believing the scriptures to be the general will of God being presented to all believers, they take a more mystical approach by viewing the scriptures as a prophetic tool used by God to speak to individual believers. This flexible attitude leads to extraordinarily diverse views theologically. We believe that Patsy Ramsey took this approach from the Osteen, Hickey, and Barnhill books that she was introduced to during her illness.

1/2a　Several words and phrases that appear in the ransom note also appear together and with great frequency in these books and in the Charismatic subculture. The following list explains their importance in this case.

1. CORDS OR BINDINGS - Binding is a significant word used frequently in the Charismatic subculture. It stems from the belief that Satan/Evil does not operate without God's permission. This tenant of Charismatic theology requires that Individual believers verbally "bind" Satan's power over their lives through prayer, verbal affirmations to other believers during worship, and in some cases through the ceremonial tying of physical cords or ropes around themselves or others. It is possible that the tying of JonBenet's body with cords was linked to Patsy's view of JonBenet's death, whether accidental or deliberate, as a para-redemptive sacrifice similar to the request by God to Abraham regarding his son.

2. S.B.T.C. - In the Charismatic subculture, acronyms are quite common and used quite frequently as teaching tools and on banners [in church icons]. S.B.T.C. is a well-used acronym that represents the words Saved By The Cross. In our extensive database of terroristic groups, we find no use of this phrase with White Supremacy or International Organizations. The author of the ransom note uses this acronym along with the word *victory*. The word victory is used in the Charismatic subculture as a verb. It is seen as the result of actions taken by believers to bind and overcome Satan's power primarily in the areas of physical health.

(Continued)

FIGURE 14.2 (Continued)

3. SACRIFICE - The concept of sacrifice is prominent in all Christian theology most clearly in the idea of Jesus being sacrificed on the cross for the remission of the world's sins. In Charismatic theology sacrifice is connected to chastisement. The idea that believers must sacrifice to be truly repentant is emphasized heavily. Charismatic theology holds that true confession involves sacrificial action by the believer. This sacrificial action is usually benign, such as asking forgiveness from a person you have offended.

> We believe that Patsy Ramsey is a delusional sociopath. Based on our experience with religious sociopaths, we believe that she saw JonBenet's death as a sacrifice for sins she had committed. Obviously Psalm 118 does not ask for human sacrifice but in her delusional mindset she interpreted verse 27 as a request by God for a para-redemptive act.

1/3a Our conclusion is that you are investigating a child's murder with ritualistic overtones. Mrs. Ramsey's motives and post-incident actions cannot be understood with rational thought. This crime was committed by a delusional individual who has convinced herself of her own innocence. Sociopaths always view their violent actions as justified. When a divine intervention is added to this justification pathology, you have a highly volatile individual.

We do not believe as has been theorized that this murder was the result of sexual assault. The autopsy report clearly states that the vaginal trauma was superficial and not consistent with known forensic profiles of sexual assault. There is no evidence in pedophile research of strangulation as a means of sexual gratification for a child molester. Strangulation and sexual assault are most commonly seen in sadomasochism between heterosexual and homosexual adults. Or by late adolescent and young adult males during masturbation.

We do not believe that John Ramsey was involved in a sexual relationship with JonBenet. We do believe that he played a role in the cover up that followed the murder.

---

dressed, including face makeup. This appears to indicate that she was fully dressed and made up when she started down the stairs that morning to make coffee and found the alleged ransom note. She stated that John Ramsey was in the shower and she screamed for his assistance. Patsy Ramsey was on the first floor of the house and John Ramsey was reported by Patsy Ramsey to be taking a shower on the third floor of the house and we are led to believe that he heard her scream.

PATSY RAMSEY: (inaudible) police.
BOULDER POLICE DISPATCHER: (inaudible)
PATSY RAMSEY: Seven fifty-five Fifteenth Street
DISPATCHER: What's going on there, Ma'am?
PATSY RAMSEY: We have a kidnapping. . . . Hurry, please.
DISPATCHER: Explain to me what going on, OK?
PATSY RAMSEY: There we have a. . . . There's a note left and our daughter's gone
DISPATCHER: A note was left and your daughter is gone?
PATSY RAMSEY: Yes.
DISPATCHER: How old is your daughter?
PATSY RAMSEY: She's six years old, . . . she's blond, . . . sex years old.
DISPATCHER: How long ago was this?
PATSY RAMSEY: I don't know. I just found the note and my daughter's (inaudible)
DISPATCHER: Does it say who took her?
PATSY RAMSEY: What?
DISPATCHER: Does it say who took her?
PATSY RAMSEY: No . . . I don't know it's there . . . there's a ransom note here.
DISPATCHER: It's a ransom note.
PATSY RAMSEY: It says SBTC Victory. . . . Please.
DISPATCHER: OK, what's your name? Are you . . .
PATSY RAMSEY: Patsy Ramsey. I'm the mother. Oh my God, please . . .
DISPATCHER: I'm . . . OK, I'm sending an officer over, OK?
PATSY RAMSEY: Please.
DISPATCHER: Do you know how long she's been gone?
PATSY RAMSEY: No, I don't. Please, we just got up and she's not here. Oh my God, please.
DISPATCHER: OK.
PATSY RAMSEY: Please send somebody.
DISPATCHER: I am, honey.
PATSY RAMSEY: Please.
DISPATCHER: Take a deep breath (inaudible).
PATSY RAMSEY: Hurry, hurry, hurry, hurry (inaudible).
DISPATCHER: Patsy? Patsy? Patsy? Patsy? Patsy?

FIGURE 14.3 Transcript of Patty Ramsey's 5:52 a.m. Call to 911

SOURCE: Thomas, S., & Davis, D. (1999). *JonBenet: Inside the Ramsey Murder Investigation* (pp. 14–15). New York: St. Martin's Press. Reprinted with permission.

As Officer French talked with Patsy Ramsey, John Ramsey had joined her at the door; they stated that someone had kidnapped their daughter. They added that their 10-year-son, Burke, was asleep upstairs. Officer French followed them into the kitchen where the three-page ransom note was spread on the floor. Sergeant Paul Reichenbach, patrol supervisor, then arrived at the scene. The father told both officers that he had gone into JonBenet's bedroom at 5:45 a.m. to awaken her for their flight to Michigan for a vacation. The officers noted that there was no sign of forced entry and were told that the alarm system had not been set that night. He then went outside and found no footprints in the light snow that had fallen during the evening and early morning hours. He also found no signs of a forced entry on the outside of the house.

The police noted that Patsy Ramsey made two more phone calls— apparently immediately after calling the police—to her close friends, Fleet and Priscilla White and John and Barbara Fernie. It was reported that the Whites and the Fernies had arrived at the house by 6:30 a.m. Mr. White walked through the house and into the basement where he noted a small window was broken. Mr. Ramsey would later say that he had broken the window when he lost his keys and got into the house in this manner. Mr. Ramsey also went to a small white door in the basement, the same one that Officer Reichenbach would also check. He went inside the small room but could not see anything clearly because it was dark. JonBenet was on the floor. Officer Reichenbach checked this door later that morning.

Soon afterward, the minister of the Ramsey's church (St. John's Episcopal Church), Rol Haverstock, had arrived. He, too, was allowed into the house, further contaminating the crime scene. Detectives Fred Patterson and Linda Arndt then arrived. At 8:03 a.m., Sergeant Whitson called John Eller, the detective division commander, to inform him of the case. He was on vacation with his family in Florida. The officers were starting to develop their own ideas about who would have kidnapped JonBenet. One viable, but temporary suspect, would be Linda Hoffman-Pugh, the housekeeper.

The police noted that the time was passed from the announced time of the "kidnapper's" telephone call, between 8 a.m. and 10:00 a.m. Detective Arndt thought it strange that no one, even the parents, seemed to pay attention to that passing. She was left alone with the seven adults in this house and there was no way she could maintain visual control over all of them. At 1:00 p.m., she asked Fleet White to go with John Ramsey to search the house from "top to bottom" (Thomas & Davis, 1999, p. 27). They started in the basement and Ramsey opened the white door and immediately found the body of JonBenet. White ran to him and saw JonBenet. Her arms were straight above the top of her head. A piece of duct tape was on a blanket next to her and a long cord was attached to her right wrist. She had a rope around her neck that was attached to a handle of a paintbrush used as a garrote. Later investigation would show that the handle of the brush was broken off from a paintbrush that was found in the mother's hobby room.

John picked up her body wrapped in a white blanket and carried her upstairs. When Arndt saw Ramsey with JonBenet, she told him to place her down on the floor, near the front door. She then moved the body, after determining JonBenet was dead, and moved it in front of the Christmas tree in the living room.

Arndt placed another call to 911, telling the dispatcher the information. At 1:20 p.m., Officer Barry Weiss entered the home. Sergeant Bob White arrived only a short time later and asked for handwriting samples of the parents; both complied. Sergeant Larry Mason, the acting detective bureau commander, arrived with an FBI agent from Denver. Another officer overheard John Ramsey call to get his private plane ready to fly to Atlanta. Mr. Ramsey later canceled this plan.

By 2:35 p.m., the house was empty except for the corpse of JonBenet.

AFTERMATH OF THE INVESTIGATION

When the first author interviewed Ted Bundy, one of the comments he made was that the police who investigate homicides take the cases too personally. The case will ruin their health, their marriages, and their careers. This was certainly true in the case of JonBenet Ramsey. Table 14.2 lists what happened to many of the leading investigators in this case.

There are other casualties in the JonBenet Ramsey case. Certainly the main casualty is the victim, the young 6-year-old girl. The children of the Ramsey family have also been affected by the homicide and the subsequent investigation. The legitimate media, as well as tabloids, have not treated the parents of JonBenet well. If they are truly without fault, they have been victimized in a brutal fashion.

THE AUTOPSY REPORT

One tool needed to develop a psychological profile is an autopsy report. The following was released in court and to the public concerning the postmortem medical report on the victim. Careful attention should be paid to the injuries done to JonBenet and that which the pathologist believed to be the cause of death. The complete text of the JonBenet Ramsey autopsy report, released by Boulder County Coroner John Meyer, follows.

TABLE 14.2 The Aftermath of the JonBenet Ramsey Case

Detective Steve Thomas resigned from the Boulder Police Department. He was apparently unhappy with the manner in which the case was being handled.
Investigator Lou Smit resigned as a protest against the manner in which the prosecutor's team was handling the case.
Detective Linda Arndt resigned from the Boulder Police Department in reaction to the manner in which the case was being handled by the criminal justice system in Boulder.
John Eller resigned from the Boulder Police Department.

NAME: Ramsey, JonBenet
DOB: 08/06/90
AGE: 6Y
SEX: F
PATH MD: MEYER
TYPE: COR
AUTOPSY NO: 96A-155
DEATH D/T: 12/26/96 @1323
AUTOPSY D/T: 12/27/96 @ 0815
ID NO: 137712
COR/MEDREC# 1714-96-A

FINAL DIAGNOSIS:

   I. Ligature strangulation
  A. Circumferential ligature with associated ligature furrow of neck
  B. Abrasions and petechial hemorrhages, neck
  C. Petechial hemorrhages, conjunctival surfaces of eyes and skin of face

  II. Craniocerebral injuries
  A. Scalp contusion
  B. Linear, comminuted fracture of right side of skull
  C. Linear pattern of contusions of right cerebral hemisphere
  D. Subarachnoid and subdural hemorrhage
  E. Small contusions, tips of temporal lobes

  III. Abrasion of right cheek

IV. Abrasion/contusion, posterior right shoulder

V. Abrasions of left lower back and posterior left lower leg

VI. Abrasion and vascular congestion of vaginal mucosa

VII. Ligature of right wrist

Toxicologic Studies
blood ethanol - none detected
blood drug screen - no drugs detected

CLINICOPATHLOGIC CORRELATION

Cause of death of this six-year-old female is asphyxia by strangulation associated with craniocerebral trauma.

John E. Meyer M.D.
Pathologist
jn/12/27/96

The body of this six year old female was first seen by me after I was called to an address identified as 755 - 15th street in Boulder, Colorado, on 12/26/96. I arrived at the scene approximately 8 PM on 12/26 and entered the house where the decedent's body was located at approximately 8:20PM. I initially viewed the body in the living room of the house. The decedent was laying on her back on the floor, covered by a blanket and a Colorado Avalanche sweatshirt. On removing these two items from the top of the body the decedent was found to be lying on her back with her arms extended up over her head.

The head was turned to the right. A brief examination of the body disclosed a ligature around the neck and a ligature around the right wrist. Also noted was a small area of abrasion or contusion below the right ear on the lateral aspect of the right cheek. A prominent dried abrasion was present on the lower left neck. After examining the body, I left the residence at approximately 8:30PM.

External Exam

The decedent is clothed in a long sleeved white knit collarless shirt, the mid anterior chest area of which contains an embroidered silver star decorated with silver sequins. Tied loosely around the right wrist, overlying the sleeve of the shirt is a white cord. At the knot there is one tail end which measures 5.5 inches in length with a frayed end. The other tail of the knot measures 15.5 inches in length and ends in a double loop knot. This end of the cord is also frayed. There are no defects noted in the shirt but the upper anterior right sleeve contains a dried brown-tan stain measuring 2.5×1.5 inches, consistent with mucous from the nose or mouth. There are long white underwear with an elastic waist band containing a red and blue stripe. The long underwear are urine stained anteriorly over the crotch area and anterior legs. No defects are identified. Beneath the long underwear are white panties with printed rose buds and the words "Wednesday" on the elastic waist band. The underwear is urine stained and in the inner aspect of the crotch are several red areas of staining measuring up to 0.5 inch maximum dimension.

External Evidence of Injury

Located just below the right ear at the right angle of the mandible, 1.5 inches below the right external auditory canal is a $3/8 \times 1/4$ inch area of rust colored abrasion. In the lateral aspect of the left lower eyelid on the inner conjunctival surface is a 1mminmaximum dimension petechial hemorrhage. Very fine, less than 1mm petechial hemorrhages are present on the skin of the upper eyelids bilaterally as well as on the lateral left cheek. On examining the left upper eyelid there are much smaller, less than 1mm petechial hemorrhages located on the conjuctival surface. Possible petechial hemorrhages located on the conjunctival surfaces of the right upper and lower eyelids, but livor mortis on this side of the face makes definite identification difficult.

Wrapped around the neck with a double knot in the midline of the posterior neck is a length of white cord similar to that described as being tied around the right wrist. This ligature cord is cut on the right side of the neck and removed. A single black ink mark is placed on the left side of the cut and a double black ink mark on the right side of the cut. The posterior knot is left intact. Extending from the knot the posterior aspect of the neck are two tails of the knot, one measuring 4 inches in length and having a frayed end, and the other measuring 17 inches in length with the end tied in multiple loops around a length of a round tan-brown wooden stick which measures 4.5 inches in length. This wooden stick is irregularly broken at both ends and there are several colors of paint and apparent glistening varnish on the surface. Printed in gold letters on one end of the wooden stick is the word "Korea." The tail end of another word extends from beneath the loops of the cord tied around the stick and is not able to be interpreted. Blonde hair is entwined in the knot on the posterior aspect of the neck as well as in the cord wrapped around the wooden stick. It appears to be made of a white synthetic material. Also secured around the neck is a gold chain with a single charm in the form of a cross.

A deep ligature furrow encircles the entire neck. The width of the furrow varies from one-eighth of an inch to five/sixteenths of an inch and is horizontal in orientation, with little upward deviation. The skin of the anterior neck above and below the ligature furrow contains areas of petechial hemorrhage and abrasion encompassing an area measuring approximately 3×2 inches. The ligature furrow crosses the anterior midline of the neck just below the laryngeal prominence, approximately at the level of the cricoid cartilage. It is almost completely horizontal with slight upward deviation from the horizontal towards the back of the neck. The midline of the furrow mark on the anterior neck is 8 inches below the top of the head. The midline of the furrow mark on the posterior neck is 6.75 inches below the top of the head.

The area of abrasion and petechial hemorrhage of the skin of the anterior neck includes on the lower left neck, just to the left of the midline, a roughly triangular, parchment-like rust colored abrasion which measures 1.5 inches in length with a maximum width of 0.75 inches. This roughly triangular shaped abrasion is obliquely oriented with the apex superior and lateral. The remainder of the abrasions and petechial hemorrhages of the skin above and below the anterior projection of the ligature furrow are nonpatterned, purple to rust colored, and present in the midline, right, and left areas of the anterior neck. The skin just above the ligature furrow along the right side of the neck contains petechial hemorrhage composed of multiple confluent very small petechial hemorrhages as well as several larger petechial hemorrhages measuring up to one-sixteenth and one-eighth of an inch in maximum dimension. Similar smaller petechial hemorrhages are present on the skin below the ligature furrow on the left lateral aspect of the neck. Located on the right side of the chin is a three-sixteenths by one-eighth of an inch area of superficial abrasion. On the posterior aspect of the right shoulder is a poorly demarcated, very superficial focus of abrasion/contusion which is pale purple in color and measures up to three-quarters by one-half inch in maximum dimension. Several linear aggregates of petechial hemorrhages are present in the anterior left shoulder just above deltopectoral groove. These measure up to one inch in length by one-sixteenth to one-eighth of an inch in width. On the left lateral aspect of the lower back, approximately sixteen and one-quarter inches and seventeen and one-half inches below the level of the top of the head are two dried rust colored to slightly purple abrasions. The more superior of the two measures one-eighth by one-sixteenth of an inch and the more inferior measures three-sixteenths by one-eighth of an inch. There is no surrounding contusion identified. On posterior aspect of the left lower leg, almost in the midline, approximately 4 inches above the level of the heel are two small scratch-like abrasions which are dried and rust colored. They measure one-sixteenth by less than one-sixteenth of an inch and one-eighth by less than one-sixteenth of an inch respectively.

On the anterior aspect of the perineum, along the edges of closure of the labia majora, is a small amount of dried blood. A similar small amount of dried and semifluid blood is present on the skin of the fourchette and in the vestibule. Inside the vestibule of the vagina and along the distal vaginal wall is reddish hyperemia. This hyperemia is circumferential and perhaps more noticeable on the right side and posteriorly. The hyperemia also appears to extend just inside the vaginal orifice. A 1 cm red-purple area of abrasion is located on the right posterolateral area of the 1x1 cm hymenal orifice. The hymen itself is represented by a rim of mucosal tissue extending clockwise between the 2 and 10:00 positions. The area of abrasion is present at approximately the 7:00 position and appears to involve the hymen and distal right lateral vaginal wall and possibly the area anterior to the hymen. On the right labia majora is a very faint area of violet discoloration measuring approximately one inch by three-eighths of an inch. Incision into the underlying subcutaneous tissue discloses no hemorrhage. A minimal amount of semi-liquid thin watery red fluid is present in the vaginal vault. No recent or remote anal or other perineal trauma is identified.

REMAINDER OF EXTERNAL EXAMINATION

The unembalmed, well developed and well nourished caucasian female body measures 47 inches in length and weighs an estimated 45 pounds. The scalp is covered by long blonde hair which is fixed in two ponytails, one on top of the head secured by a cloth hair tie and blue elastic band, and one in the lower back of the head secured by a blue elastic band. No scalp trauma is identified. The external auditory canals are patent and free of blood. The eyes are green and the pupils equally dilated. The sclerae are white. The nostrils are both patent and contain a small amount of tan mucous material. The teeth are native and in good repair. The tongue is smooth, pink-tan and granular. No buccal mucosal trauma is seen. The frenulum is intact. There is slight drying artifact of the tip of the tongue. On the right cheek is a pattern of dried saliva and mucous material which does not appear to be hemorrhaic. The neck contains no palpable adenopathy or masses and the trachea and larynx are midline. The chest is symmetrical. Breasts are prepubescent. The abdomen is flat and contains no scars. No palpable organomegaly or masses are identified. The external genitalia are that of a prepubescent female. No pubic hair is present. The anus is patent. Examination of the right extremities is unremarkable. On the middle finger of the right hand is a yellow metal band. Around the right wrist is a yellow metal identification bracelet with the name "JonBenet" on one side and the date "12/25/96" on the other side. A red ink line drawing in the form of a heart is located on the palm of the left hand. The fingernails of both hands are of sufficient length for clipping. Examination of the back is unremarkable. There is dorsal 3+ to 4+l livor mortis which is nonblanching. Livor mortis is also present of the right side of the face. At the time of the initiation of the autopsy there is mild 1 to 2+ rigor mortis of the elbows and shoulders with more advanced 2 to 3+ rigor mortis of the joints of the lower extremities.

INTERNAL EXAM

The anterior chest musculature is well developed. No sternal or rib fractures are identified.

Mediastinum

The mediastinal contents are normally distributed. The 21 gm thymus gland has a normal external appearance. The cut sections are finely lobular and pink-tan. No petechial hemorrhages are seen. The aorta and remainder of the mediastinal structures are unremarkable.

Body Cavities

The right and left thoracic cavities contain approximately 5 cc of straw colored fluid. The pleural surfaces are smooth and glistening. The pericardial sac contains 3–4 cc of straw colored fluid and the epicardium and pericardium are unremarkable. The abdominal contents are normally distributed and covered by a smooth glistening serosa. No intra-abdominal accumulation of fluid or blood is seen.

Lungs

The 200 gm right lung and 175 gm left lung have a normal lobar configuration. An occassional scattered subpleural petechial hemorrhage is seen on the surface of each lung. The cut sections of the lungs disclose and intact alveolar architecture with a small amount of watery fluid exuding from the cut surfaces with mild pressure. The intrapulmonary bronchi and vasculature are unremarkable No evidence of consolidation is seen.

Heart

The 100 gm heart has a normal external configuration. There are scattered subepicardial petechial hemorrhages over the anterior surface of the heart. The coronary arteries are normal in their distribution and contain no evidence of atherosclerosis.

The tan-pink myocardium is homogeneous and contains no areas of fibrosis or infarction. The endocarium is unremarkable. The valve cusps are thin, delicate and pliable and contain no vegetation or thrombosis. The major vessels enter and leave the heart in the normal fashion. The foramen ovale is closed.

Aorta and Vena Cava

The aorta is patent throughout its course as are its major branches. No atherosclerosis is seen. The vena cava is unremarkable.

Spleen

The 61 gm spleen has a finely wrinkled purple capsule. Cut sections are homogeneous and disclose readily identifiable red and white pulp. No intrinsic abnormalities are identified.

Adrenals

The adrenal glands are of normal size and shape. A golden yellow cortex surmounts a thing brown-tan medullar area. No intrinsic abnormalities are identified.

Kidneys

The 40 gm right kidney and 40 gm left kidney have a normal external appearance. The surfaces are smooth and glistening. Cut sections disclose on contact corticomedullary architecture. The renal papillae are sharply demarcated. The pelvocaliceal system is lined by gray-white mucosa which is unremarkable. Both ureters are patent throughout their course to the bladder.

Liver

The 625 gm liver has a normal external appearance. The capsule is smooth and glistening. Cut sections disclose an intact lobular architecture with no intrinsic abnormalities identified.

Pancreas

The pancreas is of normal size and shape. Cut sections are finely lobular and tan. No intrinsic abnormalities are identified.

Bladder

The bladder is contracted and contains no urine. The bladder mucosa is smooth and tan-gray. No intrinsic abnormalities are seen.

Genitalia

The upper portions of the vaginal vault contain no abnormalities. The prepubescent uterus measures 3 x 1 x 0.8cm and is unremarkable. The cervial contains no abnormalities. Both fallopian tubes and ovaries are prepubescent and unremarkable by gross examination.

Gallbladder

The gallbladder contains 2-3 cc of amber bile. No stones are identified and the mucosa is smooth and velvety. The cystic duct, right and left hepatic duct and common bile duct are patent throughout their course to the duodenum.

G.I. Tract

The esophagus is empty. It is lined by gray-white mucosa. The stomach contains a small amount (8-11cc) of viscous to green to tan colored thick mucous material without particulate matter identified. The gastic mucosa is autolyzed but contains no areas of hemorrhage or ulceration. The yellow to light green-tan apparent vegetable or fruit material which may represent fragments of pineapple. No hemorrhage is identified. The remainder of the small intestine is unremarkable. The large intestine contains soft green fecal material. The appendix is present.

Lymphatic System

Unremarkable.

Musculoskeletal System

Unremarkable.

Skull and Brain

Upon reflection of the scalp there is found to be an extensive area of scalp hemorrhage along the right temporoparietal area extending from the orbital ridge, posteriorly all the way to the occipital area. This encompasses an area measuring approximately 7×4 inches. This grossly appears to be fresh hemorrhage with no evidence of organization. At the superior extension of this area of hemorrhage is a linear to comminuted skull fracture which extends from the right occipital to posteroparietal area forward to the right frontal area across the parietal skull. In the posteroparietal area of this fracture is a roughly rectangular shaped displaced fragment of skull measuring one and three-quarters by one-half inch. The hemorrhage and the fracture extend posteriorly just past the midline of the occipital area of the skull. This fracture measures approximately 8.5 inches in length. On removal of the skull cap there is found to be a thin film of subdural hemorrhage measuring approximately 7–8 cc over the surface of the right cerebral hemisphere and extending to the base of the cerebral hemisphere. The 1450 gm grain has a normal overall architecture. Mild narrowing of the sulci and flattening of the gyri are seen. No inflammation is identified. There is a thin film of subarachnoid hemorrhage overlying the entire right cerebral hemisphere. On the right cerebral hemisphere underlying the previously mentioned linear skull fracture is an extensive linear area of purple contusion extending from the right frontal area, posteriorly along the lateral aspect of the parietal region and into the occipital area. This area of contusion measures 8 inches in length with a width of up to 1.75 inches. At the tip of the right temporal lobe is a one-quarter by one-quarter inch similar appearing purple contusion. Only very minimal contusion is present at the tip of the left temporal lobe. This area of contusion measures only one-half inch in maximum dimension. The cerebral vasculature contains no evidence of atherosclerosis. Multiple coronal sections of the cerebral hemispheres, brain stem and cerebellum disclose no additional abnormalities. The areas of previously described contusion are characterized by purple linear streak-like discolorations of the gray matter perpendicular to the surface of the cerebral cortex. These extend approximately 5mm into the cerebral cortex. Examination of the base of the brain discloses no additional fractures.

Neck

Dissection of the neck is performed after removal of the throacoabdominal organs and the brain. The anterior strap musculature of the neck is serially dissected. Multiple sections of the sternocleidomastoid muscle disclose no hemorrhages. Sections of the remainder of the strap musculature of the neck disclose no evidence of hemorrhage.

Examination of the thyroid cartilage, cricoid cartilage and hyoid bone disclose no evidence of fracture or hemorrhage. Multiple cross sections of the tongue disclose no hemorrhage or traumatic injury. The thyroid gland weighs 2 gm and is normal in appearance. Cut sections are finely lobular and red-tan. The trachea and larynx are lined by smooth pink-tan mucosa without intrinsic abnormalities.

Myocardium

Sections of the ventricular myocardium are composed of interlacing bundles of cardiac muscle fibers. No fibrosis or inflammation are identified.

Lungs

The alveolar architecture of the lungs is well preserved. Pulmonary vascular congestion is identified. No intrinsic abnormalities are seen.

Spleen

There is mild autolysis of the spleen. Both red and white pulp are identifiable.

Thyroid

The thyroid gland is composed of normal-appearing follicles. An occasional isolated area of chronic interstitial infiltrate is seen. There is also a small fragment of parathyroid tissue.

Thymus

The thymus gland retains the usual architecture. The lymphoid material is intact and scattered Hassall's corpuscles are identified. Mild vascular congestion is identified.

Trachea

There is mild chronic inflammation in the submucosa of the trachea.

Liver

The lobular architecture of the liver is well preserved. No inflammation or intrinsic abnormality are identified.

Pancreas

There is autolysis of the pancreas which is otherwise unremarkable.

Kidney

The overall architecture of the kidney is well preserved. There is perhaps mild vascular congestion in the cortex but no inflammation is identified.

Bladder

The transitional epithelium of the bladder is autolyzed. No significant intrinsic abnormalities are seen.

Reproductive Organs

Sections of the uterus are consistent with the prepubescent ages. The ovary is unremarkable.

Adrenal

The architecture of the adrenal is well preserved and no intrinsic abnormalities are seen.

Brain

Sections from the areas of contusion disclose disrupted blood vessels of the cortex with surrounding hemorrhage. There is no evidence of the inflammatory infiltrate or organization of the hemorrhage. Subarachnoid hemorrhage is also identified. Cortical neurons are surrounded by clear halos, as are glial cells.

Vaginal Mucosa

All of the sections contain vascular congestion and focal interstitial chronic inflammation. The smallest piece of tissue, from the 7:00 position of the vaginal wall/hymen, contains epithelial erosion with underlying capillary congestion. A small number of red blood cells is present on the eroded surface, as is birefringent foreign material. Acute inflammatory infiltrate is not seen.

EVIDENCE

Items turned over to the Boulder Police Department as evidence include: Fibers and hair from clothing and body surfaces; ligatures; clothing, vaginal swabs and smears; rectal swabs and smears; oral swabs and smears; paper bags from hands; fingernail clippings; jewelry; paper bags from feet; white body bag; samples of head hair, eyelashes and eyebrows; swabs from right and left thighs and right cheek; red top and purple top tubes of blood.

CONCLUSION

Since the murder of JonBenet Ramsey, the crime investigation has taken many twists and turns. Fortunes have been made by former police officers and federal agents have profited from their involvement in this case. Regardless of the best intentions of those who want to resolve this homicide, the case is apparently no closer now to a resolution since the time of the murder itself. Careers have been altered. Several Boulder police officers have resigned and gone on to other careers. The Ramsey's have been judged in the court of public opinion as having been involved in the murder of their daughter. Others believe in the intruder theory. Some believe that the son, Burke, was the killer even though he was a 10-year-old boy at the time of the murder. John Douglas offers various scenarios including an intruder responsible for the murder of JonBenet (Douglas & Olshaker, 2000). In other words, there are many theories but only one witness to that homicide and JonBenet is not able to tell the world who killed her.

Sites on the World Wide Web provide a variety of information, some verifiable, some not. Persons interested in the case can secure additional information on this case because it captures the attention of many still fascinated by the murder of this young girl. But, unfortunately, we may not be any closer to an arrest than in the early morning hours of December 26, 1996.

What do you think?

Chapter 15

THE VICTIM IN PSYCHOLOGICAL PROFILING

Perhaps no single element in the profiling process has been neglected more than the victim. The Behavioral Science Unit (BSU) of the FBI has been active in securing data regarding the social and behavioral characteristics, as well as the reputations, of victims. These are crucial in the profiling enterprise.

The victim is the last person to witness the crime. If alive, the victim can tell a great deal about the crime. If the victim is deceased, however, the crime scene must tell the story. In either instance, therefore, the profiler should be as interested in the activities of the victim as in any element of the submitted packet of information accompanying the request for a profile. It has been noted that the victim profile and victim activity have been frequently neglected, for whatever reason, as reported elements.

ELEMENTS IN THE VICTIM PROFILING PROCESS

To appraise a crime without some knowledge of the victim is certainly remiss. Unfortunately, however, victim information is frequently lacking in substance. The usual report received from an agency contains varying degrees of information about the type of weapon used, the position of the victim's body, the amount and type of physical evidence, the autopsy, and other important items of the case. It is equally important to include certain cognitive elements concerning the lifestyle, habits, oddities, friends, and so on of the victim. Table 15.1 lists the elements important to victim profiling.

Physical Traits

Perhaps the most obvious element in the profiling process is a physical description of the victim. Much care must be taken in gathering an

TABLE 15.1   Important Elements in Victim Profiling
Physical traits
Marital status
Personal lifestyle
Occupation
Education
Personal demographics
Medical history
Psychosexual history
Criminal justice system history
Last activities

accurate description of the victim's basic physical characteristics. Age, for example, could be a critical victim selection factor. Jerry Brudos, a serial killer and serial rapist from Oregon, selected young women from 19 to 23 years of age.

Sex, male or female, is often the overarching element in the selection process. Because the young and women are typically considered to be more vulnerable, they are recurrently victimized. More than one serial rapist and murderer related a conscious effort to select a victim predicated on perceived vulnerability.

The type of dress may be of some significance for selection. For example, one serial murderer designated his victims because they looked like hookers. None of the four young women he abducted and killed were prostitutes. They were all selected because in his mental reality they appeared to be prostitutes, so they must be prostitutes. Their style of dress signaled their apparent vocation and, in effect, their death.

Hair style and hair color may also be preeminent for the violent personal offender. Recall Ted Bundy's reported fondness for young, college-aged women with long hair parted in the middle. Additionally, most of his victims had dark hair; Laura Aime and Susan Rancourt were exceptions.

Marital Status

As much information as possible should be known about the victim's marital status. Too often, the report will simply state "married." Obviously, this is not adequate. In a recent case, the nude body of a woman was found along a rural road. She had not been raped but was shot five times. Reportedly, she had been happily married for 15 years. There were no children. The police report mentioned the couple had been regarded as pillars of the community and were very community minded. Employed, she was athletic and went to an exercise center two evenings a week. All outward appearances indicated a marriage that was committed and happy.

A statement by the homicide detective said the woman was an introvert and had no close friends and no known enemies. To have an attractive young woman, athletic, a golfer with some promise in her youth but with no known close personal friends seemed unusual. Her sole contact with the other sex was an exercise class at the health center. The detectives discovered several leads predicated on the resolute determination that regardless of how it appeared, all was not well within the marriage. The profiler noted this inconsistency in his report to the police. Closer investigation found a husband with a very jealous disposition and a wife with an outside love interest. One small, seemingly insignificant statement signaled an inconsistency that led to the successful resolution of the case.

Personal Lifestyle

A victim's daily activities could yield vital information concerning the victim's character. These data may also serve as an index of the type of people who not only comprise a circle of friends but also the many others with whom the victim may have come into contact.

Hobbies, sports interests, drug use, frequenting bars, drinking habits, or any recent changes in behavior or personality may also be indicators of consequence. Many victims have significant others who serve as sources of such information. They should be queried regarding any sudden or recent change in the social life or personality of the victim. This information may serve as an index of not only availability but susceptibility.

Occupation

The occupation and employment of a victim expands the network of relationships. The number of people involved in a business relationship with the victim, not only on a professional basis but also on a personal one, can, understandably, be quite large. Nonetheless, a careful examination of the number of persons having frequent contact with the victim may lead not only to a better discernment of the victim's personality but also the victim's personal organizations.

Special training and education may indicate organizations, associations, conferences, or meetings in which the victim may have been active. Groups of people at these occasions share common interests. Special training also indicates an aggregate of people temporarily together for a common purpose.

The investigator should not ignore the past positions and employment of a victim because there, too, has existed a network of friends, enemies, or acquaintances.

A profile was completed recently on a young woman who was repeatedly stabbed in the neck. In the setting where she worked for the past seven years, one fellow worker remarked that there was a male coworker who had tried unsuccessfully to date the victim. Also, the victim had once stated that if anything ever happened to her, "John would probably be the one to kill me." From talking with fellow workers, two viable leads were developed. This is obviously nothing new to experienced homicide investigators. It does help, however, in painting a picture of the victim with an eye toward understanding both the victim's personality and the type of person who would commit such an act.

Education

It is important to realize not only the extent of the victim's education but also the various schools and programs attended. As with occupation, education widens the network of acquaintances. Ted Bundy, for example, was thought to be in the same psychology class as Lynda Ann Healy. Although not verified by school officials at the University of Washington, this connection was reported in several different sources, including in an interview with Ann Rule in 1987. Rule also related that Healy had shopped at the same grocery where Bundy had worked as a stock boy, which was two blocks from where Healy lived and was subsequently murdered. As a law student living on a college campus, Ted Bundy was able to associate with young women who would be vulnerable and easy to kill.

The intelligence of the victim may serve as an indicator of the type of people with whom she or he associated. In other words, very intelligent people often associate with those of like intelligence. This may be especially important when the attack occurs in a process-focused orientation and away from the home. Also remember that many victims are victims of opportunity and therefore little stalking may occur. As more stalking of the victim is evident, certain elements are more viable and helpful than others.

Personal Demographics

The location of the victim's home may play an important role in the manner in which the victim was attacked. It may beundeniably true that many crimes of a violent personal nature occur in a lower-class, high-crime-rate area. If the victim resides in such a neighborhood, then this becomes valuable information.

Past residences are also valid indicators of the victim's housing pattern, selected because of preference or necessity. Useful information may be obtained from a thorough canvassing of the neighborhoods of previous areas of residence. Past neighbors and friends can lend an appraisal of the victim's lifestyle and circle of friends. The same names may appear, connoting a continued relationship.

The investigator must be aware of the neighborhood's complexity. Racial composition is one item that should be carefully taken into account. Although it is true that most rapes and murders occur within the perpetrator's race, if the racial composition of the victim's neighborhood is radically different from the victim's own race, several possibilities may immediately arise that may account for the victim living in a particular area.

Medical History

The obvious benefit from a victim's medical history is that it could yield the presence of communicative illnesses, such as venereal disease. It was stated in one interview that one of Bundy's early victims had gonorrhea; he did not test positive for this social disease. The dental records of a deceased victim could lead to the identification of a corpse, especially if there is an advanced state of decomposition. The dental records proved invaluable in the identification of Susan Rancourt, an alleged Bundy victim, when she was found a year after she was reported missing.

The mental health history of a victim should be carefully investigated. This record could supply valuable information regarding the victim's psychological background as well as other persons with whom the victim could have come into contact. It may also serve as an indicator of the behavior exhibited by the victim consistent with daily life and activities. Some behavior may be commonplace with some people but quite inappropriate with others.

Psychosexual History

All people have some fears. Some people have more than others, but all of us have some irrational fears. Some people may feel quite fearful of high places, elevators, restaurants located on top floors, and so on. A list of such fears gathered from friends, relatives, and acquaintances might supply a personality profile, which will give the profiler and the police investigator a better understanding of the victim's personality.

The victim's sexual history might also provide a clue to the present crime. For example, a young woman dated several men, took showers with them, involved herself in mutual oral sex and masturbation, but would not have coitus with a date because she wanted to save herself for her future husband. The victim was found dead in her bedroom, raped and repeatedly stabbed. The information developed in this case was important because it opened the case for another avenue of analysis. It was determined that the original suspect was not guilty in the commission of this crime; another suspect was developed and the case was resolved.

A firm understanding of the personality assessment of the victim is also significant. The personality, as earlier stated, is the sum total of what the person is. It is not static. The personality of any individual, victim or not, will change over time. The essence of the personality may remain the same but some changes occur over time that will somehow alter the temperament. For this reason, a personality profile should be obtained not only from current sources but also from sources outside the present time frame.

From an examination of the personality of the victim, a picture may be drawn of the type of associates with whom a murdered victim may have been involved or to whom she or he may have been exposed. The importance of a full understanding of the personality cannot be stressed too strongly.

Court History

As vital as it is to understand the type of person the victim was, equally important is to realize the experiences the victim may have had with the criminal justice system. For this reason, the investigator should be aware of any past arrest records, court appearances (as offender, victim, or witness), and any pending cases. In acquiring this information, the profiler will have a more complete portrait of the victim.

Victim's Last Activities

In the development of any psychological profile, special attention should be directed to the victim's activities prior to the crime itself. The routes of travel, social activities, phone calls, meetings made or missed, or anything that appears to be out of the ordinary from the victim's usual pattern of daily living should be noted (Holmes & Deburger, 1988, p. 90). In other words, did the victim do something unique today that alerted someone to the victim's vulnerability and availability?

CONCLUSION

This chapter offers insight into the role of the victim as it relates to the crime itself. It must be borne in mind that regardless of daily activities, lifestyle, interaction with the criminal justice system, or other sociological or psychological reasons that conflict with the lifestyle or personal preferences of the profiler, the victim must be considered an integral component in the profiling process—he or she has an integral part in the crime that has been committed. Just as the crime scene, a disposal site in a murder case, special words stated during the crime, and so on all have import to the profiling process, for a full and complete understanding of the crime, the victim must be added to the picture.

Chapter 16

PROFILING AND THE FUTURE

The future of psychological profiling appears promising. The number of cases profiled over the past decade has risen dramatically, and, once viewed with great suspicion, profiling is now being judged increasingly by police professionals as a useful addition to the tools available in the battle against crime.

Of course, many are still reluctant to accept profiling as a reliable and valuable tool. Godwin (1978), for example, asserts that profiling has served little purpose in solving crimes: "Nine out of ten of the profiles are , . . vapid. They play at blindman's bluff, groping in all directions in the hope of touching a sleeve. , , . They [the police] require hard data: names, faces, fingerprints, locations, times, dates. None of which the psychiatrists [profilers] can offer" (p. 276). He goes on to describe profiles themselves as dull and more than a little tedious, a position shared by Campbell (1976). Levin and Fox (1985) have asserted that psychological profiles are of little use in the identification of murderers: "Unfortunately, this tool, no matter how expertly implemented, is inherently limited in its ability to help solve crimes" (p. 175).

As we have noted, profiling is best considered a starting point for the investigation of particular crimes; we make no claim that it should stand on its own as the sole forensic tool in criminal cases.

ADDITIONAL USES FOR PROFILING

Historically, the preponderance of requests submitted to the FBI's Criminal Personality Profiling Program have sought aid in murder cases (65%) and rape cases (25%) (Howlett, Hanfland, & Ressler, 1986). Other kinds of crimes account for the remaining requests: cases involving child molestation, kidnapping, extortion, obscene telephone calls, suicide, and other criminal activity.

Profiles have been developed for many different kinds of offenders as well as for other categories of actors. Haran and Martin (1984), for example, have developed an interesting profile of armed bank robbers in which they list the following social core variables for these offenders: young (age 26 to 30), white (61%), unemployed (56%), and high school dropouts (49%); only 15% have no criminal record and fewer than one in four acts alone. Rider (1980a, 1980b) has developed a typology of arsonists based on psychological profiling. Casey-Owens (1984) argues that the missives of anonymous letter writers should be examined using a psycholinguistic approach; this researcher distinguishes between the types of letter writers using the following categories: threatening, obscene, racial, extortion, nuisance, stool pigeon, and guilty conscience.

Such novel uses of profiling—apart from the 90% concerned with murder and rape cases, as mentioned above—may indicate that the practice has gained some recognition and appreciation for its usefulness in the resolution of certain crimes and in the investigation of other phenomena. As it gains acceptance, the use of profiling will undoubtedly become more widespread and, in addition to its application to murder and rape cases, it will be used routinely to help investigators deal with such offenders as obscene letter writers and phone callers, arsonists, and even bank robbers.

EDUCATION AND TRAINING FOR PROFILING

There is nothing magical or mysterious about the art of psychological profiling. As academicians, we are always amazed when we hear a student say, "The professor really knows his stuff. He must be really smart—I can't understand what he is saying." On the contrary, we believe that a truly intelligent professor is careful to teach in a comprehensible manner to students. Academicians and other professionals are infamous for creating jargon that protects their knowledge—as well as their status—from close examination. This is true of many fields and disciplines, including medicine, psychiatry, psychology, and law enforcement, and it has recently emerged in profiling. Some would like others to believe that profiling can be done only by a select few who have special and unique education and training somehow gained through osmosis as a result of close association with the "masters."

Our message here is that profiling can be done by many different people. Touted "authorities," many of whom sit behind desks hundreds of miles away from the crime investigations on which they consult, may lend insight into certain crimes, but no preponderance of empirical evidence exists to support the position that police investigators with some knowledge of the social and behavioral sciences cannot just as reliably profile their own cases. Many have done so on a small scale for years. In seminars held across the nation, the first author always stresses that profiling can and should be done by those who are closest to the crimes: the police. Again, we emphasize: There is nothing mysterious about the profiling process.

To develop a profile of the perpetrator of a serious, violent crime, one needs to have knowledge of sociology, psychology, psychiatry, and criminology, and the ability to blend the theories of these disciplines. No one has a monopoly on such knowledge. Common sense combined with sound social and behavioral concepts can yield valuable and reliable results. Unfortunately, sometimes law enforcement turf issues hinder the profiling process and sometimes the successful resolution of a case is impeded by the disease referred to as NIH—"not invented here."

COMPUTERIZED MONITORING

The computer revolution has arrived in law enforcement, as it has in almost every other facet of our lives. The Drug Enforcement Administration (DEA), for example, now uses a computerized tracking system called the Drug Abuse Warning Network (DAWN). This program monitors drug mentions in police records in 26 standard metropolitan statistical areas across the nation. The Automated Reports and Consummated Orders System (ARCOS) yields the data necessary for estimating drug-related law enforcement requirements and alerts investigators to sources of diversion in the illicit drug distribution chain. By combining DAWN and ARCOS, the DEA is able to disseminate information on drug abuse and trafficking trends to law enforcement agencies across the United States.

In New York, the Homicide Assessment and Lead Tracking System (HALT) has been established by the Division of Criminal Justice Services and the Division of State Police. HALT's mission is to collect case data on nondomestic homicides in the state of New York and then disseminate the information within the state. In 1983, Michigan implemented the Homicide Investigative Tracking System (HITS), a statewide computerized system to collect data on homicides that is analogous to the HALT system in New York. When similar crimes are matched up by the system, related police agencies are notified.

The Violent Criminal Apprehension Program (VICAP) of the National Center for the Analysis of Violent Crime has been in operation since the late 1980s. This ambitious program has the goal of collecting nationwide data and analyzing specific violent crimes (Howlett, Hanfland, & Ressler, 1986). As Pierce Brooks (1981), a former homicide detective and currently a consultant to the FBI, has noted

> The lack of a centralized automated computer information center and crime analysis system to collect, collate, analyze and disseminate information from and to all police agencies involved in the investigation of similar pattern multiple murders, regardless of the date and location of occurrence, is the crux of the problem. (p. 201)

VICAP deems appropriate those cases involving (a) solved or unsolved homicides or attempts, especially those that involve an abduction, are apparently random, motiveless, or sexually oriented, or are known or suspected to be part of a series; (b) missing persons, in which the circumstances indicate a strong possibility of foul play and the victim is still missing; and (c) unidentified bodies when the manner of death is known or suspected to be homicide (Howlett, Hanfland, & Ressler, 1986, pp. 15–16).

The officials involved in VICAP are optimistic that the program will be expanded to include rape, child sexual abuse, and arson cases. Part of this hope may lie in the fact that the program has not attracted the volume of cases that the FBI had anticipated (Howlett, Hanfland, & Ressler, 1986, p. 17). To help combat this shortfall, VICAP's administrators shortened and revised the questionnaire that agencies must fill out for cases to be analyzed.

Few empirical data are yet available to support the validity of the results yielded by VICAP; nevertheless, the program could be a valuable starting point for the accumulation of information regarding certain kinds of crime. As noted above, however, turf issues can sometimes interfere with the success of such efforts; these must be resolved before VICAP and other similar programs can be truly successful.

The computer should be viewed as a powerful technological tool that can aid in crime investigation; it is not a substitute for human intelligence or for a solid investigation of crimes by competent law enforcement personnel. What a computer issues after a run of data depends on the design of the program used and the data input; thus, great care should be taken in the handling of data. Further, the key to the efficacy of the computer is the validity of the data input.

COMPUTERIZED PROFILING

Although the profiling process is in part an art that can be practiced only by humans, in the near future a computerized profiling program might help law enforcement personnel to define quickly and efficiently the types of personalities associated with such violent crimes as lust murder, rape, and serial murder. Certainly, the examination of a crime scene requires a human element but computers can be used to analyze the data accumulated by humans and to summarize the analysis in a series of statements that can provide some basic information about an unknown suspect. A profiler makes calculated, educated guesses—these are more than wild guesses but they are guesses nonetheless. A computer program can be used to collate information and even to notify other police agencies participating in similar cases and offer them the same personality profiles.

The design of any computer program developed to create offender profiles must take into account all of the information outlined in this volume—that is, all the same information that is important in "traditional" profiling. The crime scene elements, personality characteristics, deviant behaviors, everyday activities, and other factors associated with violent criminals will be vital components of any such program. The authors of such a program must be aware of and theoretically fluent in the concepts of profiling as well as the disciplines of psychology, sociology, psychiatry, and criminology. Indeed, the authorship of such a program would be best achieved through the joint endeavor of investigators, theoreticians, and computer-literate professionals.

CONCLUSION

The computer revolution is having a dramatic influence on the criminal justice system. Computers have been used for some time now by law enforcement for storage of records, personnel files, and criminal files; for case management; and for management of fiscal matters. Computers are also now being used to track crimes and criminals. Psychological profiling would seem to be the next logical task for the computer. The human art of profiling can benefit from the speed and accuracy of analysis that computer technology represents.

Profiling is finally coming of age in the battle against violent crime. We have stressed in this volume not only the components of profiling but the need for profiling itself. As we noted in Chapter 1, a profile can narrow the range of effort, identify suitable interrogation techniques, and help with the evaluation of the unknown suspect's personal belongings. Profilers should make use of all available, legitimate resources, including sociological, psychiatric, psychological, and criminological theory; the experiences and expertise of law enforcement officials; and computer technology. The computer may be the next major advance in our arsenal of weapons against crime.

REFERENCES

Abel, G., Lawry, S., Karstrom, E., Osborn, C., & Gillespie, C. (1994). Screen tests for pedophilia. *Criminal Justice and Behavior, 21,* 115–131.

Abrahamsen, D. (1944). *Crime and the human mind.* New York: Columbia University Press.

Abrahamsen, D. (1952). *Who are the guilty?* Westport, CT: Greenwood.

Aichorn, A. (1935). *Wayward youth.* New York: Viking Press.

Ainsworth, P. (2001). *Offender profiling and crime analysis.* Portland, OR: Willan Publishing.

American Psychiatric Association. (2000). *Diagnostic and statistical manual of mental disorders.* Washington, DC: Author.

Amir, M. (1971). *Patterns in forcible rape.* Chicago: University of Chicago Press.

Bachman, R. (1998). The factor related to rape reporting behavior and arrest: new evidence from the National Crime Victimization Survey. *Criminal Justice and Behavior, 25*(1), 8–29.

Bartol, C. R., & Bartol, A. M. (1999). *Criminal behavior: A psychosocial approach* (5th ed.). Englewood Cliffs, NJ: Prentice Hall.

Bauman, E. (1991). *Step into my parlor.* New York: Bonus.

Becker, J., & Abel, G. (1978). Men and the victimization of women. In J. Chapman & M. Gates (Eds.), *Victimization of women.* Beverly Hills, CA: Sage.

Bennett, W., & Hess, K. (1994). *Criminal investigation.* Minneapolis, MN: West.

Bergen, R. (1998). Wife rape. *Violence Against Women, 5*(9), 989–1085.

Berkowitz, L. (1962). *Aggression: A social-psychological analysis.* New York: McGraw-Hill.

Berkowitz, L. (1969). The frustration-aggression hypothesis revisited. In L. Berkowitz (Ed.), *Roots of aggression.* New York: Atherton.

Bernet, W., & Chang, D. (1997). The differential diagnosis of ritual abuse allegations. *Journal of Forensic Sciences, 42*(1), 32–38.

Blackburn, D. (1990). *Human harvest: The Sacramento murder story.* New York: Knightbridge.

Blair, D. (1993). The science of serial murder. *American Journal of Criminal Law, 20*(2), 1–12.

Block, J. (1995). On the relation between IQ, impulsivity, and delinquency: Remarks on the Lynam, Moffitt, and Stouthamer-Loeber interpretation. *Journal of Abnormal Psychology, 104*(2), 395–399.

Bradway, W. (1990, September). Stages of sexual assault. *Law and Order,* 119–124.

Brantingham, P., & Brantingham, P. (Eds.). (1981). *Environmental criminology.* Beverly Hills, CA: Sage.

Briere, J., & Runtz, M. (1989). University males' sexual interest in children: Predicting potential indices of "pedophilia" in a non-forensic sample. *Child Abuse & Neglect, 13,* 65–75.

Brooks, P. (1981). *Vi-CAP.* Unpublished manuscript.

Brownmiller, S. (1975). *Against our will: Men, women and rape.* New York: Simon & Schuster.

Brugnatelli, F. (1999, July 4). *Ramsey Case: The ransom note* [On-line]. Available: Retrieved August 22, 2001, from the World Wide Web.

Burg, B. (1983). *Sodomy and the perception of evil.* New York: New York University Press.

Burgess, A., Groth, A., & Holmstrom, L. (1978). *Sexual assault of children and adolescents.* Lexington, MA: Lexington Books.

Cahill, T. (1986). *Buried dreams: Inside the mind of a serial killer.* New York: Bantam.

Campbell, C. (1976). Portrait of a mass killer. *Psychology Today, 9,* 110–119.

Carr, C. (1994). *The alienist.* New York: Random House.

Carr, C. (1997). *The angel of darkness.* New York: Random House.

Casey-Owens, M. (1984). The anonymous letter writer: A profile. *Journal of Forensic Sciences, 29,* 816–819.

Cason, H. (1943). The psychopath and the psychopathetic. *Journal of Criminal Psychopathology, 4,* 522–527.

Child, I. (1950). The relation of somatotype to self ratings on Sheldon's temperamental traits. *Journal of Personality, 18,* 440–453.

Craig, M., & Glueck, S. (1963). Ten years' experience with the Glueck Social Prediction Table. *Crime and Delinquency, 9,* 249-261.

Christiansen, K. (1977). A review of studies of criminality among twins. In S. Mednick & K. Christiansen (Eds.), *Biosocial bases of criminal behavior.* New York: Gardiner.

Classifying Sexual Homicide Crime Scenes. (1985). *FBI Law Enforcement Journal, 54,* 12–17.

Cleckley, H. (1982). *The mask of sanity.* New York: Plume.

Cloward, R. (1959, April). Illegitimate means, anomie, and deviant behavior. *American Sociological Review, 24,* 164–179.

Cochrane, R. (1974). Crime and personality: Theory and evidence. *Bulletin of the British Psychological Society, 27,* 19–22.

Cohen, M., Garofalo, M., Boucher, B., & Seghorn, T. (1971). The psychology of rapists. *Seminars in Psychiatry, 3,* 307–327.

Conners, C. (1992, May 9). Priests and pedophilia: A silence that needs breaking. *America,* 400–401.

Cornwell, P. (1991). *Post-mortem.* New York: Avon.

Cornwell, P. (1996). *From potter's field.* New York: Berkley.

Cornwell, P. (1999). *Black notice.* New York: Putnam.

Cortes, J., & Gatti, F. (1965). Physique and self description of temperment. *Journal of Consulting Psychology, 29,* 432–439.

Cortes, J., & Gatti, F. (1972). *Delinquency and crime: A biopsychosocial approach.* New York: Seminar Press.

Craig, M., & Glueck, S. (1963). Ten years experience with the Glueck Social Prediction Table. *Crime and Delinquency, 9,* 249–261.

Crews, G. (1996). Adolescent satanists: A sensible law enforcement approach. *Journal of Police and Criminal Psychology, 11*(1), 13–18.

Crime Scene and Profile Characteristics of Organized and Disorganized Murders. (1985). *FBI Law Enforcement Bulletin, 54,* 18–25.

Curtis, J. (1953). Gabriel Tarder. In C. Mihanovich (Ed.), *Social theorists* (pp. 142–157). Milwaukee, WI: Bruce.

Craig, D. (1980). *Hip pocket guide to planning and evaluation.* Austin, TX: Learning Concepts.

Dalton, K. (1971). *The premenstrual syndrome.* Springfield, IL: Charles C Thomas.

Dettlinger, C., & Prugh, J. (1984). *The list.* Atlanta, GA: Philmay.

DeYoung, M. (1998). Another look at moral panics: The case of satanic day care centers. *Deviant Behavior, 19*(3), 257–278.

Dollard, J., Doob, L., Miller, N., Mowrer, O., & Sears, R. (1939). *Frustration and aggression.* New Haven, CT: Yale University Press.

Douglas, J., & Burgess, A. (1986). Criminal profiling: A viable investigative tool against violent crime. *FBI Law Enforcement Bulletin, 55,* 9–13.

Douglas, J., Burgess, A. W., Burgess, A. G., & Ressler, R. (1992). *Crime classification manual.* Lexington, MA: Lexington Books.

Douglas, J., & Olshaker, M. (1995). *Mind hunter: Inside the FBI's elite serial crime unit.* New York: Scribner.

Douglas, J., & Olshaker, M. (1999). *The anatomy of motive: The FBI's legendary mindhunter explores the key to understanding and catching violent criminals.* New York: Scribner.

Douglas, J., & Olshaker, M. (2000). *The cases that haunt us: From Jack the Ripper to JonBenet Ramsey, the FBI's legendary mindhunter sheds light on the mysteries that won't go away.* New York: Scribner.

Doyle, A. C. (1891a). The Bascombe Valley Mystery, *The Original Illustrated Sherlock Holmes.* Secaucus, NJ: Castle.

Doyle, A. C. (1891b). A Case of Identity, *The Original Illustrated Sherlock Holmes.* Secaucus, NJ: Castle.

Doyle, A. C. (1891c). The Five Orange Pips, *The Original Illustrated Sherlock Holmes.* Secaucus, NJ: Castle.

Doyle, A. C. (1891d). The Hed Headed League, *The Original Illustrated Sherlock Holmes.* Secaucus, NJ: Castle.

Doyle, A. C. (1891e). The Man With the Twisted Lips, *The Original Illustrated Sherlock Holmes.* Secaucus, NJ: Castle.

Drukteinis, A. (1992). Serial murder: The heart of darkness. *Psychiatric Annals, 22,* 532

Dugdale, R. (1877). *The Jukes: A study in crime, pauperism, disease and heredity.* New York: Putnam.

Dunham, R., & Alpert, G. (1993). *Critical issues in policing.* Prospect Hills, IL: Waveland.

Durkheim, E. (1965). *The division of labor in society* (G. Simpson, Trans.). New York: Free Press.

Edward, K., & MacLeod, M. (1999). The reality and myth of rape: Implications for the criminal justice system. Expert evidence. *International Journal of Behavioral Sciences in Legal Context, 7*(1), 37–38.

Egger, S. (1990). *Serial murder: An elusive phenomenon.* New York: Praeger.

Egger, S. (1998). *The killers among us.* New York: Praeger.

Evans, S., & Skinner, K. (2000). *The ultimate Jack the Ripper companion: An illustrated encyclopedia.* New York: Carroll and Graf.

Ewolt, C., Monson, C., & Kanghinrichsen-Rohling, J. (2001). Attributions about rape in a continuum of dissolving marital relations. *Journal of Interpersonal Violence, 15*(11), 1175–1182.

Eysenck, H. (1977). *Crime and personality* (2nd ed.). London: Routledge & Kegan Paul.

Farrington, D., Biron, L., & LeBlanc, M. (1982). Personality and delinquency in London and Montreal. In J. Gunn & D. Farrington (Eds.), *Abnormal offenders, delinquency, and the criminal justice system.* Chichester, UK: Wiley.

Feldman, M. (1977). *Criminal behavior: A psychological perspective.* London: Wiley.

Fergusson, D., & Horwood, L. (1995). Early disruptive behavior, IQ, and later school achievement and delinquent behavior. *Journal of Abnormal Child Psychology, 23*(2), 183–200.

Ferrero-Lombroso, G. (1911). *Criminal man: According to the classification of Cesare Lombroso.* New York: Putnam.

Fisher, S. (1962). The MMPI: Assessing a famous personality test. *American Behavioral Scientist, 6*, 20–21.

Forehand, R., Wierson, M., Frame, C., Kempton, T., & Aristead, L. (1991). Juvenile firesetting: A unique syndrome of an advanced study of antisocial behavior. *Behavioral Research Therapy, 29*, 125–128.

Fox, J. A., & Levin, J. (2001). *The will to kill : Making sense of senseless murder.* Boston: Allyn & Bacon.

Frank, G. (1966). *The Boston Strangler.* New York: Signet.

Freeman-Longo, R., & Wall, R. (1986, March). Changing a lifetime of sexual crime. *Psychology Today,* 58–64.

Freud, S. (1930). *Three contributions to the theory of sex* (Monograph Series 7). Washington, DC: Nervous and Mental Disease.

Freund, K., & Watson, R. (1992). The proportion of heterosexual and homosexual pedophiles among sex offenses against children. *Journal of Sex and Marital Therapy, 18*, 34–38.

Funtowicz, M., & Widiger, T. (1999). Sex bias in the diagnosis of personality disorders: An evaluation of the DSM-IV criteria. *Journal of Abnormal Psychology, 108*(2), 195–212.

Gammage, J. (1991, September 8). Serial murders are on the rise, say experts. *Philadelphia Inquirer,* p. A1.

Ganey, T. (1989). *St. Joseph's children: A true story of terror and justice.* New York: Lyle Stuart/Carol.

Gerberth, V. (1981). Psychological profiling. *Law and Order, 29*, 46–49.

Gerberth, V. (1983). *Practical homicide investigation*. New York: Elsevier.

Gibbs, N. (1991, June 3). When is it rape? *Time*, 48–54.

Gibney, B. (1990). *The beauty queen killer*. New York: Pinnacle.

Gilbert, J. (1986). A cycle of outrage. Englewood Cliffs, NJ: Prentice Hall.

Glick, L. (1995). *Criminology*. Boston: Allyn & Bacon.

Glueck, S., & Glueck, E. (1950). *Unraveling juvenile delinquency*. Cambridge, MA: Harvard University Press.

Glueck, S., & Glueck, E. (1956). *Physique and delinquency*. New York: Harper & Row.

Goddard, H. H. (1912). *The Kallikak family: A study in the heredity of feeble-mindedness*. New York: MacMillan.

Godwin, J. (1978). *Murder USA: The ways we kill each other*. New York: Ballantine.

Godwin, M. (1999). *Hunting serial predators: A multivariate classification approach to profiling violent behavior*. Boca Raton, FL: CRC Press.

Goffman, E. (1986). *Stigma: Notes on the management of spoiled identity*. New York: Simon & Schuster.

Goring, C. (1913). *The English convict*. London: His Majesty's Stationery Office.

Greenberg, L. (1988). Constructive cognition: Cognitive therapy coming of age. *Counseling Psychologist, 16*, 235–238.

Groth, A., & Burgess, A. (1980). Male rape: Offenders and victims. *American Journal of Psychiatry, 137*, 806–810.

Groth, A., Burgess, A., & Holmstrom, L. (1977). Rape, power, anger and sexuality. *American Journal of Psychiatry, 134*, 1239–1243.

Haas, L., & Haas, J. (1990). *Understanding sexuality*. St. Louis, MO: C.V. Mosby.

Hagan, F. (1986). *Criminology*. Chicago: Nelson-Hall.

Hale, R. (1998). The application of learning theory to serial murder, or "you too can learn to be a serial killer." In R. Holmes & S. Holmes (Eds.), *Contemporary perspectives on serial murder*. Thousand Oaks, CA: Sage.

Haran, J., & Martin, J. (1984). The armed bank robber: A profile. *Federal Probation, 53*, 47–53.

Harris, G. (1994, March 10). Children still fascinate molester. *The Courier Journal*, pp. A1, A5.

Harris, T. (1981). *Red dragon*. New York: Putnam.

Harris, T. (1988). *The silence of the lambs*. New York: St. Martin's.

Harris, T. (1999). *Hannibal*. New York: Delacorte.

Harrison, S. (1993). *The diary of Jack the Ripper*. New York: Hyperion.

Harrison, S., & Maybrick, J. (1994). *The diary of Jack the Ripper*. London: Smith Gryphon.

Hazelwood, R. (1994, March). Lecture delivered at the Southern Police Institute, Ft. Lauderdale, FL.

Hazelwood, R., & Burgess, A. (1995). *Practical aspects of rape investigation: A multidisciplinary approach* (2nd ed.). Baton Rouge, LA: CRC Press.

Hazelwood, R., & Michaud, S. (2001). *The evil that men do: FBI profiler Roy Hazelwood's journey into the minds of sexual predators*. New York: Scribner.

Hazelwood, R., & Warren, J. (1989). The serial rapist: His characteristics and victims. *FBI Law Enforcement Bulletin, 58*(2), 18–25.

Hertica, M. (1991, February). Interviewing sex offenders. *Police Chief,* 39–43.

Hickey, E. (1991). *Serial murderers and their victims.* Pacific Grove, CA: Brooks-Cole.

Hickey, E. (2001). *Serial murderers and their victims* (2nd ed.). Pacific Grove, CA: Brooks-Cole.

Hippchen, L. (1981). Some possible biochemical aspects of criminal behavior. *Journal of Behavioral Ecology, 2,* 1–6.

Hippchen, L. (Ed.). (1978). *Ecologic-biochemical approaches to treatment of delinquents and criminals.* New York: Van Nostrand Rienhold.

Hirschi, T. (1969). *The causes of delinquency.* Berkeley: University of California Press.

Hirschi, T., & Hindelang, M. (1977). Intelligence and delinquency. *American Sociological Review, 42,* 571–587.

Holmes, R. (1983). *The sex offender and the criminal justice system.* Springfield, IL: Charles C Thomas.

Holmes, R., & Deburger, J. (1985a). Profiles in terror: The serial murderer. *Federal Probation, 39,* 29–34.

Holmes, R., & Deburger, J. (1985b). *Serial murder.* Beverly Hills, CA: Sage.

Holmes, R., & Deburger, J. (1988). *Serial murder.* Thousand Oaks, CA: Sage.

Holmes, R., & Holmes, S. (1992). Understanding mass murder: A starting point. *Federal Probation, 56,* 53–61.

Holmes, R., & Holmes, S. (1996). *Profiling violent crimes* (2nd ed.). Thousand Oaks, CA: Sage.

Holmes, R., & Holmes, S. (1998). *Serial murder* (2nd ed.). Thousand Oaks, CA: Sage Publications.

Holmes, R., & Holmes, S. (2000). *Murder in America* (2nd ed.). Thousand Oaks, CA: Sage.

Holmes, S., & Holmes, R. (2001). *Sex crimes* (2nd ed.). Thousand Oaks, CA: Sage.

Holmes, S., Tewksbury, R., & Holmes, R. (1999). Fractured identity syndrome: A new theory of serial murder. *Journal of Contemporary Criminal Justice, 115*(13), 262-272.

Holt, F. (1994, March). The arsonist profile. *Fire Engineering,* 127–128.

Home Box Office. (1984). Murder: No apparent motive. Stamford, CT: Vestron Video.

Howlett, J., Hanfland, K., & Ressler, R. (1986). The violent criminal apprehension program. *FBI Law Enforcement Bulletin, 55,* 14–18.

Jackman, T., & Cole, T. (1992). *Rites of burial.* New York: Pinnacle.

James, W., West, C., & Deters, K. (2000). Youth dating violence. *Adolescence, 35*(139), 455–465.

Jeffers, H. (1992). *Who killed precious?* New York: St. Martin's.

Jenkins, P. (1994). *Using murder: The social construction of serial homicide.* New York: Aldine de Gruyter.

Jenkins, M., Langlais, P., & Delis, D. (1998). Learning and memory in rape victims with posttraumatic stress disorder. *American Journal of Psychiatry, 155*(2), 278–279.

Johnson, I., & Sigler, R. (2000). Forced sexual intercourse among intimates. *Journal of Family Violence, 15*(1), 95–108.

Johnston, S., French, A., Schouweiler, W., & Johnston, F. (1992). Naivete and need for affection among pedophiles. *Journal of Clinical Psychology, 48*, 620–627.

Kelly, C. (1976). *Uniform crime reports: Crime in the United States*. Washington, DC: Government Printing Office.

Kennedy, D., & Nolin, R. (1992). *On a killing day*. New York: Bonus.

Kenney, J., & More, H. (1994). *Principles of investigation*. Minneapolis, MN: West.

Knight, R., Carter, D., & Prentky, R. (1989). A system for the classification of child molesters. *Journal of Interpersonal Violence, 4*, 3–23.

Knight, R., & Prentky, R. (1987). The developmental antecedents and adult adapatations of rapist subtypes. *Criminal Justice and Behavior, 14*, 403–426.

Kocsis, R., Orwin, H., & Hayes, A. (2000). Expertise in psychological profiling: A comparative assessment. *Journal of Interpersonal Violence, 15*(3), 311–331.

Kolarik, G. (1992). *Freed to kill: The true story of the serial killer Larry Eyler*. New York: Avon.

Kolko, D., & Kazdin, A. (1992). The emergence and recurrence of child firesetting: A one year perspective study. *Journal of Abnormal Child Psychology, 20*, 17–36.

Krassner, M. (1986). Diet and brain function. *Nutrition Reviews, 44*, 12–15.

Lange, J. (1929). *Crime as destiny*. Leipzig: Verlag.

Langer, W. (1972). *The mind of Adolf Hitler*. New York: New American Library.

LaVey, A. (1969). *The Satanic Bible*. New York: Avon.

Law, D. (1991, January). The pyromaniac vs. the hired torch. *Fire Engineering*, 50–53.

Leo, J. (1993, October 11). Pedophiles in the schools. *U.S. News and World Report*, 37.

Levin, J., & Fox, J. (1985). *Mass murder: America's growing menace*. New York: Plenum.

Lewis, N., & Yarnell, H. (1951). *Pathological firesetting (pyromaniac)* (Vol. 2). New York: Coopridge Foundation.

Lilly, J., Cullen, F., & Ball, R. (1995). *Criminological theory: Context and consequences* (2nd ed.). Thousand Oaks, CA: Sage.

Lilly, J. Cullen, F., & Ball, R. (2001). *Criminological theory: Context and consequences* (3rd ed.). Thousand Oaks, CA: Sage.

Linedecker, C., & Burt, W. (1990). *Nurses who kill*. New York: Windsor.

Linz, D. (1989). Exposure to sexually explicit materials and attitudes toward rape: A comparison of study results. *Journal of Sex Research, 26*, 50–84.

Lombroso, C. (1876). *Criminal man*. Milan: Torin.

Lombroso, C. (1917). *Crime, its causes and remedies*. Boston: Little.

Lunde, D. (1976). *Murder and madness*. New York: Norton.

Lynam, D., & Moffitt, T. (1995). Delinquency and impulsivity and IQ: A reply to Block. *Journal of Abnormal Psychology, 104*(2), 399–402.

Macy, J. (1979). *To the reader.* In *Arson: The federal role in arson prevention and control* [Report to Congress]. Washington, DC: Federal Emergency Management Association, U.S. Fire Administration, Office of Planning and Evaluation.

Mahoney, P., & Williams, L. (1998). Sexual assault in marriage: Prevalence, consequences, and treatment of wife rape. In J. Jasinski & L. Williams (Eds.), *Partner violence: A comprehensive review of 20 years of research*. Thousand Oaks, CA: Sage.

MASA. (2001, June 23). *Sexual assault statistics: Occurrence of rape* [On-line]. Available: http://sa.rochester.edu/masa/stats.html.

Merton, R. (1968). *Social theory and social structure*. Glencoe, IL: Free Press.

Michaud, S. (1986, October 26). The FBI's new psyche squad. *New York Times Magazine*, pp. 13-14.

Michaud, S., & Aynesworth, H. (1983). *The only living witness*. New York: Signet.

Moriarty, L., & Earle, J. (1999). An analysis of service for victims of marital rape: A case study. *Journal of Offender Rehabilitation, 29*(3/4), 171–181.

Morris, T. (1966). *The criminal area*. New York: Humanities Press.

Neisser, U. (1996). Intelligence: Knowns and unknowns. *American Psychologist, 51*, 77–101.

Neitzel, M. (1979). *Crime and its modification: A social learning perspective*. New York: Pergamon.

Norris, J., & Birnes, W. (1988). *Serial killers: The growing menace*. New York: Dolphin.

O'Brien, D. (1985). *Two of a kind: The Hillside Stranglers*. New York: Signet.

Okami, P., & Goldberg, A. (1992). Personality correlates of pedophilia: Are they reliable indicators? *Journal of Sex Research, 29*, 297–328.

Orr, J. (1989, July). Profiles in arson: The vanity firesetter. *American Fire Journal*, 24–47.

Paley, B. (1996). *Jack the Ripper: The simple truth*. London: Headline.

Pallone, N., & Hennessy, J. (1992). *Criminal behavior: A process psychological analysis*. New Brunswick, NJ: Transaction Books.

Palmiotto, M. (1994). *Criminal investigation*. Chicago: Nelson-Hall.

Park, R. (1952). *Human communities*. Glencoe, IL: Free Press.

Patterson, J. (2000). *Roses are red: A novel*. Boston: Little, Brown.

Peterson, M. (1997). Practical analytical techniques: A necessary addition to police education. *Journal of Criminal Justice Education, 8*(1), 19–35.

Pino, N., & Meier, M. (1999). Gender differences in rape reporting. *Sex Roles, 40*(11/12), 979–990.

Porter, B. (1983, April). Mind hunters. *Psychology Today*, 1–8.

Proulx, J., Cote, H., & Achille, P. (1993). Prevention of voluntary control of penile response in homosexual pedophiles during phallometric testing. *Journal of Sex Research, 30*, 140–147.

Queens Bench Foundation. (1976). *The rapist and his crime*. New York: John Wiley.

Quinsey, V., Chaplin, T., & Uphold, D. (1990). Arsonists and sexual arousal to firesetting: Correlation unsupported. *Journal of Behavior Therapy and Experimental Psychiatry, 20*, 203–209.

Rada, T. (1978). Alcoholism and forcible rape. *American Journal of Psychiatry, 32*, 444–446.

Redl, F., & Toch, H. (1979). The psychoanalytic explanation of crime. In H. Toch (Ed.), *Psychology of crime and criminal justice*. New York: Holt, Rinehart & Winston.

Ressler, R., Burgess, A., & Douglas, J. (1988). *Sexual homicide: Patterns and motives*. Lexington, MA: Lexington Books.

Ressler, R., & Shachtman, T. (1992). *Whoever fights monsters*. New York: St. Martin's.

Ressler, R., & Shachtman, T. (1997). *I have lived in the monster*. New York: St. Martin's.

Rice, M., & Harris, G. (1991). Firesetters admitted to maximum security psychiatric institution. *Journal of Interpersonal Violence, 6*, 461–475.

Rider, A. (1980a). The firesetter: A psychological profile [Part 1]. *FBI Law Enforcement Bulletin, 49*, 2–17.

Rider, A. (1980b). The firesetter: A psychological profile [Conclusion]. *FBI Law Enforcement Bulletin, 49*, 5–11.

Roche, P. (1958). *The criminal mind: The study of communication between criminal law and psychiatry*. New York: Grove.

Rossmo, D. (1994). Place, space, and police investigations: Hunting serial violent killers. In J. Eck & D. Weisburd (Eds.), *Crime prevention studies* (Vol. 4). Monsey, NY: Criminal Justice Press.

Rossmo, D. (1995). Targeting victims: Serial killers and the urban environment. In T. O'Reilly-Flemming & S. Egger (Eds.), *Serial and mass murder: Theory, research and policy*. Toronto: University of Toronto Press.

Rowe, D. (1985). Sibling interaction and self-reported delinquency behavior: A study of 265 twin pairs. *Criminology, 23*, 223–240.

Rumbelow, D. (1988). *The complete Jack the Ripper*. New York: Penguin.

Russell, D. (1982). *Rape in marriage*. New York: MacMillan.

Sakeheim, G., & Osborn, E. (1986). A psychological profile of juvenile firesetters in residential treatment: A replication study. *Child Welfare, 65*, 495–503.

Sakeheim, G., Vigdor, M., Gordon, M., & Helprin, L. (1985). A psychological profile of juvenile firesetters in residential treatment. *Child Welfare, 64*, 453–476.

Samenow, S. (1984). *Inside the criminal mind*. New York: Time Books.

Sanders, L. (1981). *The third deadly sin*. New York: Putnam.

Sanders, W. (1983). *Criminology*. Reading, MA: Addison-Wesley.

Sandford, J. (1994). *Winter prey*. New York: Berkley Books.

Sandford, J. (1995). *Mind prey*. New York: Putnam.

Sandford, J. (1997). *Sudden prey*. New York: Berkley Books.

Sandford, J. (1998). *Secret prey*. New York: Putnam.

Sandford, J. (1999). *Certain prey*. New York: Putnam.

Sandford, J. (2000). *Easy prey*. New York: Putnam.

Sandford, J. (2001). *Chosen prey*. New York: Putnam.

Sapp, A., Huff, T., Gary, G., Icove, D., & Horbert, P. *A report of essential findings from a study of serial arsonist*. Unpublished manuscript.

Savitz, L. D. (1972). Introduction. In G. Lombroso-Ferrero (Ed.), *Criminal man*. Montclair, NJ: Patterson-Smith.

Schechter, H. (1990). *Deranged*. New York: Pocket Books.

Schiller, L. (1999). *Perfect murder perfect town: JonBenet and the city of Boulder*. New York: Harper Collins.

Schuessler, K., & Cressey, D. (1950, March). Personality characteristics of criminals. *American Journal of Sociology, 55*, 476–484.

Schwendinger, J., & Schwendinger, H. (1983). *Rape and inequality*. Beverly Hills, CA: Sage.

Sears, D. (1991). *To kill again*. Wilmington, DE: Scholarly Resources.

Sheldon, W., Hartl, E., & McDermott, E. (1949). *Varieties of delinquent youth: An introduction to constitutional psychiatry*. New York: Harper.

Sheldon, W., & Stevens, S. (1940). *The varieties of human physique*. New York: Harper.

Sheldon, W., & Stevens, S. (1942). *The varieties of temperament*. New York: Harper.

Shook, L. (1990). Sexual glossary. In L. Shook (Ed.), *Investigation of variant sex styles*. Montgomery, AL: Auburn University Press.

Smith, C., & Guillen, T. (1990). *The search for the Green River killer*. New York: Onyx.

Stack, A. (1983). *The lust killer*. New York: Signet.

Sullivan, T., & Maiken, P. (1983). *Killer clown*. New York: Pinnacle.

Sutherland, E. (1937). *The professional thief*. Chicago: University of Chicago Press.

Tarde, G., & Clark, T. (1969). *On communication and social influence: Selected papers*. Chicago: University of Chicago Press.

Tarde, G. D., & Parsons, E. W. C. (1903). *The laws of imitation*. New York: Holt.

Terry, M. (1999). *The ultimate evil*. New York: Barnes and Noble Books.

Teten, H. (1995). Offender profiling. In W. Bailey (Ed.), *The encyclopedia of police science*. New York: Garland.

Thomas, S., & Davis, D. (1999). *JonBenet: Inside the Ramsey murder investigation*. New York: St. Martin's.

Tracey, S., & Chorpita, B. (1997). Empirical evaluation of DSM-IV generalized anxiety disorder criteria in children and adolescents. *Journal of Clinical Child Psychology, 26*(4), 404–415.

U.S. Department of Justice. (1988). *Report to the nation on crime and justice.* Washington, DC: Government Printing Office.

U.S. Department of Justice. (1991). *Criminal victimization in the United States.* Washington, DC: Government Printing Office.

U.S. Department of Justice. FBI. (1993). *Uniform crime reports: Crime in the United States, 1992.* Washington, DC: Government Printing Office.

Vito, G. F., & Holmes, R. M. (1994). *Criminology: Theory, research and policy.* Belmont, CA: Wadsworth.

Vold, G., & Bernard, T. (1986). *Theoretical criminology* (3rd ed.). New York: Oxford University Press.

Vorpagel, R. (1998). *Profiles in murder: An FBI legend dissects killers and their crimes.* New York: Dell.

Warming, E. (1969). Plant communities. In R. Park & E. Burgess (Eds.), *Introduction to the science of sociology* (pp. 175–182). Chicago: University of Chicago Press.

Warren, J., Reboussin, R., & Hazelwood, R. (1998). Crime scene and distance correlates of serial rape. *Journal of Quantitative Sociology, 14*(1), 35–39.

Webb, N., Sakeheim, G., Towns-Miranda, L., & Wagner, C. (1990). Collaborative treatment of juvenile firesetters: Assessment and outreach. *American Journal of Orthopsychiatry, 60,* 305–309.

Wilson, J., & Hernstein, R. (1985). *Crime and human nature: The definitive study of the causes of crime.* New York: Simon & Schuster.

Yochelson, S., & Samenow, S. (1976). *The criminal personality.* New York: Jason Aronson.

INDEX

Abrahamsen, D., 58
Ainsworth, P., 48
Alienist, The, 23
Angel of Darkness, The, 23
Anger retaliation rapists:
    interviewing strategy and, 150
    rape process and, 149-150, 149 (table)
    self-perception of, 148-149
    social core variables, 148, 148 (table)
Anomie, 58, 66, 123
Anti-social personality, 55-56
Aquino, M., 188
Arson, 85-87, 86-87 (tables)
    arsonists' characteristics, 89-90, 90
        (table), 95, 96-98 (table)
    crime concealment and, 102-103
    excitement arsonists, 101
    firesetting experience, 98-100
    organized vs. disorganized personalities
        and, 104-107, 107 (table)
    profit motivation and, 103-104
    revenge, 101-102
    search warrant suggestions, 106-107
        (table)
    serial arson, 90, 91-95 (table)
    social/behavioral traits, 105 (table)
    statistics on, 87-88, 88-89 (tables)
    vandalism, 100
Autoeroticism, 172-173, 184
    aquaeroticism, 175
    asphyxiation, 174
    chemical eroticism, 175
    crime scene indicators of, 179-181
    definition of, 173-174
    habitual practice, evidence of, 182-184
    practitioner characteristics, 176-179
    suffocation, 176
Automated Reports and Consummated
    Orders System (ARCOS), 277

Berdella, Robert, 114
Berkowitz, David, 193
Berkowitz, L., 53
Bianchi, Ken, 113, 115
Biological factors:
    born criminal type, 61-62, 62 (table)
    chemical/hormonal influences, 64-65
    mental deficiency, 54
    physical characteristics, 62-64, 64 (table)
Black Notice, 24
Blindfolds, 130-131
Body disposal, 128, 132-133
Bondage, 134
Born criminal typology, 61-62, 62 (table)
The Boston Strangler, 43
Brintingham, P., 214
Brooks, P., 278
Brownmiller, S., 139
Brudos, Jerry, 8-9, 113, 116, 133, 269
Bundy, Carol, 133
Bundy, Ted, 76, 78, 80, 111, 127, 133, 155,
    156, 211, 212, 269, 271
Buono, Angelo, 113
Burg, B., 167
Burgess, A., 161

Carignan, Harvey, 112, 133
Carr, C., 23
Carter, D., 168
Casey-Owens, M., 276
Cason, H., 55
Certain Prey, 24
Charles Manson family, 193
Chase, R. T., 1
Child, I., 63, 64
Child sexual abuse. *See* Pedophilia
Chosen Prey, 24
Church of Satan. *See* Satanism
Clark, Douglas, 133

Cleckley, H., 55
Comfort-oriented serial murderer, 114, 129
   (table)
Computerized analysis:
   drug tracking systems, 277
   geographic profiling, 216, 220-222
   homicide tracking systems, 277-278
   profiling process and, 279
   violent crime analysis, 278
Constitutional theories, 60-61
   born criminal typology, 61-62, 62 (table)
   chemical/hormonal influences, 64-65
   physical characteristics, crime and, 62-64,
      64 (table)
Cornwell, P., 24
Cortes, J., 63, 64
Cressey, D., 52
Crime:
   addiction to, 42
   psychological profiling and, 3-4, 4 (table),
      10
   serial crime, 42-43, 51
   victimology and, 5
   See also Serial crime; Serial murder;
      Structural-functionalist perspective
Crime scene analysis, 71-72
   crime scene comparison, 80-82, 81 (table)
   disorganized asocial offenders, 72-76, 73
      (table)
   interpretation and, 7
   organized nonsocial offenders, 76-80, 77
      (table)
   personality peculiarities and, 40, 41-42
   physical evidence, 5-6
   satanic rituals, 202-206, 203 (table), 204
      (figure), 206 (table)
   serial murder cases, 127-130, 128 (fig-
      ure), 129 (table)
   staging and, 135
   victim-offender relationship, 82-84
Criminal Geographic Targeting (CGT), 220-
   221
Criminological theories, 47-49
   individual-level explanations, 50-65
   social/structural theories, 65-69
   source/nature of crime, 49

strain theory, 48, 54
Crowley, A., 186
Cult-related murder. *See* Satanism

Dahmer, Jeffrey, 114, 211
Deductive assessments, 5-7
DeGrimston, M. A., 188
DeGrimston, R., 188
DeSalvo, Albert, 43
Dismemberment, 134
Disorganized asocial offenders, 72
   arson and, 104-107, 107 (table)
   crime scene characteristics, 80-82, 81
      (table)
   interviewing techniques for, 75-76
   personal characteristics of, 72-74, 73
      (table)
   postoffense behavior, 74-75
   serial murderers, 127
   victim-offender relationship, 82-84
Do, 193
Dodd, Westley, 166, 168
Dollard, J., 53
Domination. *See* Power-control serial
   murderer
Douglas, J., 2, 101, 102, 103, 104, 105, 107,
   135
Drug Abuse Warning Network (DAWN),
   277
Durkheim, E., 65, 66, 67

Egger, S., 110
Evidence:
   crime scene evidence, 5-6
   offenders' possessions, 8-9
   See also Crime scene analysis
Eyler, Larry, 111
Eysenck, H., 51

Fantasy, 7, 126-127, 170, 180
Fictional profiling cases:
   Alienist, The, 23
   Angel of Darkness, The, 23
   Black Notice, 24
   Certain Prey, 24
   Chosen Prey, 24
   From Potter's Field, 24

Post-Mortem, 24
Red Dragon, 18-20
Roses Are Red, 24
Secret Prey, 24
Sherlock Holmes and, 16-18
Silence of the Lambs, The, 20-21
Third Deadly Sin, The, 21-22
Fish, Albert, 166
Fixated child molesters, 167, 168 (table), 169
Fox, J., 275
Fractured identity syndrome, 51
Freud, S., 56, 57, 58, 59
From Potter's Field, 24

Gacy, John Wayne, 111, 114, 160-161
Gatti, F., 63, 64
Gerberth, V., 14, 15
Gem, Ed, 111
Geographic profiling, 208
    alternative routes and, 211
    boundaries/barriers, effects of, 210-211,
        219
    computerized analysis, 216, 220-222
    crime location types, 217-218, 217 (table)
    displacement, criminal activity and, 220
    distance, perception of, 209, 209 (table),
        211
    elements of, 215-220, 216-217 (tables)
    familiar paths, choice of, 210
    land use information, 219
    mobility, level of, 212-214
    neighborhood demographics and, 219
    process of, 221-222
    spatial mental imaging, 211-212, 212
        (table)
    transportation modes, 209
    travel routes, preferences in, 210, 218
    victim activities, 219-220
    victim selection and, 214-215, 215
        (figure)
Gilbert, J., 86, 87
Gleuck, E., 52, 64
Glueck, S., 52, 64
Godwin, J., 275
Goldberg, A., 168
Goring, C., 48

Greenberg, L., 54
Groth, A., 161

Haas, J., 165
Haas, L., 165
Haran, J., 276
Harris, T., 18-21
Hazelwood, R., 2, 44
Hedonistic serial murderer, 113-114
Hertica, M., 157
Hickey, E., 111
Hirschi, T., 68
Historic profiling:
    Hitler, Adolph, 25-30
    Metesky, George, 30-31
    Miller, Charlene L., 32-35
    serial rape cases, 31-32
Hitler, Adolph, 25-30
Holmes, R., 51, 163
Holmes, S., 51, 163
Holmes, Sherlock, 16-18, 223
Holstrom, L., 161
Homicide Assessment and Lead Tracking
    System (HALT), 277, 278
Homicide Investigative Tracking System
    (HITS), 278
Homicides, 3, 4, 109-110
    See also Serial Murderers

Individual theories of crime, 50
    constitutional theories, 60-65
    personality characteristics and, 51-56
    psychiatric explanations, 56-60
    psychological explanations, 50-51
Inductive assessments, 5-7
Interviewing:
anger retaliation rapists, 150
    disorganized asocial offender, 75-76
    organized nonsocial offender, 79-80
    power assertive rapists, 153
    power reassurance rapists, 147-148
    profile information and, 9-10
    sadistic rapists, 157
Investigatory process, 3, 4, 45-46

Jack the Ripper, 223-224
    Chapman, Annie, 228-231, 230 (table)

Eddowes, Catharine, 234-236, 236
    (table), 237 (table)
Kelly, Mary, 236-240, 238-239 (tables)
Nichols, Mary Ann ("Polly"), 224-228,
    226-228 (tables)
profile of, 240, 242
Stride, Elizabeth, 231-234, 232-233
    (tables)
suspect list, 241 (table)
victim list, 225 (table)
Jenkins, P., 110, 137
Jukes, Ada, 60-61

Kasso, Ricky, 194-195
Kemper, Edmund, 79, 133
Knight, R., 145, 168
Koresch, David, 193

Langer, W. C., 25, 26, 28, 29
La Vey, A., 185, 187, 188, 200
Learned criminal behavior, 67-68
Levin, J., 275
Lombroso, C., 61, 62
Lucas, Henry, 111, 193
Lust murders, 4, 113-114, 129 (table)

Macy, J., 86
Martin, J., 276
Mental deficiency, 54, 74
Merton, R., 66
Metesky, George, 30-31, 45
Miller, Charlene L., 32-35
Mission serial murderer, 112-113, 129 (table)
Modus operandi (MO), 3, 42-43
Morally indiscriminate child molester, 163,
    164 (table)
Mudgett, H. W., 114
Mutilation murders, 4, 113-114
    See also Serial murder
Mysoped child molester, 165-167

Naive/inadequate child molester, 163, 164
(table)
Neitzel, M., 51

Offenders:
    disorganized asocial offenders, 72-76, 73
        (table)

interviewing strategies and, 9-10
methods of operation, 42-43
organized nonsocial offenders, 76-80, 77
    (table)
possessions, psychological evaluation of,
    8-9
signatures of, 44
See also Personality characteristics; Serial
    murderers
Okami, P., 168
Organized nonsocial offenders, 72
    arson and, 104-107, 107 (table)
    crime scene characteristics, 80, 81 (table)
    interviewing techniques for, 79-80
    personal characteristics, 76-79, 77 (table)
    postoffense behavior, 79
    serial murderers, 127
    victim-offender relationship, 82-84

Park, R., 67
Patterson, J., 24
Pedophilia, 158
    child pornography and, 170
    computer use and, 170
    definition of, 158-161, 160 (box)
    fixated offender, 169
    immature/regressed offenders, 169-170
    preferential child molester, 165-167
    sadistic offender, 168-169
    situational child molester, 161-165, 164
        (table)
    typology of, 167-171, 168 (table)
    women and, 161
Personality characteristics, 51-52
    anti-social personality, 55-56
    criminal tendencies and, 52-53
    criminal thinking patterns, 54-55
    mental deficiency, 54
    somatyping theory and, 63-64, 64 (table)
    See also Crime scene analysis
Personality profiling, 37
    biological inheritance, 38
    commonalities, 39
    crime scene and, 40, 41-42
    cultural influences, 38
    environmental experiences, 38-39

unique experiences, 39
Police agencies, 4, 216
Positivist theory of criminality, 61-62
Post-Mortem, 24
Power assertive rapists, 150
   interviewing strategy, 153
   rape process and, 151-152, 152 (table)
   social core variables, 151, 151 (table)
Power-control serial murderer, 114-115, 129
   (table)
Power reassurance rapist, 145
   backgrounds of, 145
   interviewing strategy, 147-148
   rape process and, 146-147, 147 (table)
   sexual aberrations of, 145
   social core variables of, 145-146, 146
     (table)
Preferential child molesters, 165
   child pornography and, 170
   fixated child molesters, 167
   mysoped child molesters, 165-167
Prentky, R., 145, 168
Profiling rationale:
   crime scene, offender personality and, 40,
     41-42
   method of operation, static nature of, 42-
     43
   personality, core of, 44
   personality factors and, 37-39
   psychological profiling, reliability/validity
     of, 45-46
   signature uniqueness and, 44
Psychiatric model of criminality, 56-57
   anomie and, 58
   guilt and, 59
   psyche, elements of, 57-58, 57 (figure)
   psychoanalytic treatment and, 59-60
Psychological profiling, ix-x, 1-3
   accuracy in, 3, 45-46
   art of, 13-15
   crimes, profiling suitability of, 3-4, 4
     (table), 10
   fictional accounts of, 16-24
   goals in, 7-10
   historical cases of, 25-35
   homicide investigation and, 3

inductive vs. deductive profiling, 5-7
   police cooperation and, 4
   social core variables, x, 41
   training/education for, 276-277
   utility of, 275-276
   See also Jack the Ripper; Profiling ratio-
     nale; Ramsey, JonBenet
Psychopathology, 3, 4, 55-56, 111-112, 114-
   115
Puente, Dorothea, 114

Ramirez, Richard, 194
Ramsey, JonBenet, 11-13, 12-14 (figure),
   243
   autopsy report, 255-266
   crime/discovery time line, 247-248, 252-
     255, 253 (figure)
   emergency 911 call transcript, 253
     (figure)
   evidentiary items, 266
   external exam, 257-261
   family/friends of, 243-245
   internal exam, 261-266
   law enforcement officials, 245-246
   ransom note analysis, 248-252 (figures)
Rape, 31-32, 139
   anger retaliation rapist, 148-150, 148-149
     (tables)
   definitions of, 139-140
   posttraumatic stress disorder and, 142
   power assertive rapist, 150-153, 151-152
     (tables)
   power reassurance rapist, 145-148, 146-
     147 (tables)
   psychological elements in, 143-144
   rapists' characteristics, 142
   sadistic rapist, 153-157, 154-155 (tables),
     165 (figure)
   statistics on, 140-142
   victim precipitation of, 139
Red Dragon, 18-20, 131, 210
Regressed child molester, 162-163, 164
   (table)
Ressler, R., 1, 2, 109
Rider, A., 90, 176
Rossmo, D., 214, 215

Sadistic child molesters, 168-169, 168 (table)
Sadistic rapists, 153
  interview strategies, 157
  rape process and, 154-156, 155 (table),
      156 (figure)
  social core variables, 153-154, 154 (table)
Samenow, S., 55
Sanders, L., 21-22, 144
Sanford, J., 23-24
Sapp, A., 90, 91-95
Satanism, 185-186
  ceremonies in, 200-202
  crime scene elements, 202-207, 203
      (table), 204 (figure), 206 (table)
  hell, hierarchy in, 197
  historical development of, 186-187
  human sacrifice and, 196-197
  Masses, types of, 199-200
  May Day rite, 202
  night of the beast, 200-201
  Passover rite, 201-202
  personal involvement, tiers of, 188-195,
      191 (table), 192 (figure)
  ritual devices, 197-199, 198 (table)
  satanic bible, 187-188, 187 (table)
  terminology in, 188, 189-190 (table)
  trinity in, 195-196
Schuessler, K., 52
Secret Prey, 24
Serial crime, 4
  arson, 90, 91-95 (table)
  child molestation, 170
  fractured identity syndrome and, 51
  law enforcement linkage blindness, 110
  method of operation, static nature of, 42-
      43
Serial murder, 126-127
  blindfolds and, 130-131
  body disposal, 128, 132-133
  body positioning, 134-135
  bondage, 134
  crime scene evaluation, 127-130, 128
      (figure), 129 (table), 135
  dismemberment, 134
  duct tape and, 135
  facial attacks, 131-132

killing process, windows in, 127, 128
      (figure), 132
  souvenirs and, 136
  staging, crime scene and, 135
  trophies in, 136
  weapons in, 133
  See also Jack the Ripper
Serial murderers, 109-110
  characteristics of, 115-116
  comfort-oriented, 114
  fantasy and, 126-127
  hedonistic type, 113-114
  mind-images of, 120-121
  mission type, 112-113
  perspective of, 116
  power-control type, 114-115
  spatial mobility of, 111, 111 (table)
  thought process of, 124-126, 125 (figure)
  victim selection, 110, 117-119
  victims, objectification of, 119-122, 130,
      131
  violence, perception of, 122-124
  visionary type, 111-112
Serial rape, 31-32
Sexual gratification, 113-114, 127, 131-132,
      134
  anger retaliation rapists and, 149-150
  power reassurance rapists and, 145, 146
  sadistic rapists and, 153-154
  See also Autoeroticism; Pedophilia
Sheldon, W., 62, 63, 64
Signature patterns, 44
Silence of the Lambs, The, 20-21
Simmons, Beoria, 133
Situational child molesters, 161, 164 (table),
      165
  morally indiscriminate child molesters,
      163
  naive/inadequate child molesters, 163
  regressed child molesters, 162-163
Social bond theories, 68-69
Social core variables, x, 41, 90, 91-95 (table)
  anger retaliation rapists and, 148, 148
      (table)
  power reassurance rapists and, 145-146,
      146 (table)

Social/structural theories. *See* Structural-
functionalist perspective
Sociopaths, 78-79, 114-115, 125, 168
Sociopsychological assessment, x, 7-8
Somatyping theory, 63-64, 64 (table)
Stevens, S., 62
Strain theory, 48, 54, 66
Structural-functionalist perspective, 65, 67
anomie and, 66
cultural transmission theories, 68
industrialized society and, 65-66
learned criminal behavior, 67-68
social bond theories, 68-69
social-individual strain, 66-67
Sutherland, E., 68

Tarde, G. D., 67, 68
Tewksbury, R., 51
Third Deadly Sin, The, 21-22
Thrill murders, 113-114, 129 (table)
Toole, Otis, 115, 193

Victim-offender relationships, 82-84
Victimology, 5, 268

activities prior to crime, 273
court history, 273
educational experience, 271
marital status, 269-270
medical history, 272
occupation, 270-271
personal demographics, 271-272
personal lifestyle, 270
physical traits, 268-269
psychosexual history, 272-273
Victim selection, 117-119, 214-215, 215
(figure)
Violent Criminal Apprehension Program
(VICAP), 278
Visionary serial murderer, 111-112, 129
(table)
Vorpagel, R., 1

Weapons, 133
Wilder, Chris, 111
Williams, Wayne, 111
Wuornos, Aileen, 114

Yochelson, S., 55

ABOUT THE AUTHOR

Ronald M. Holmes is Professor of Justice Administration at the University of Louisville. Author of several books—among them Profiling Violent Crimes, Sex Crimes, and Serial Murder—he has also written more than 50 articles appearing in scholarly publications. He is Vice President of the National Center for the Study of Unresolved Homicides and has completed more than 500 psychological profiles for police departments across the United States. He received his doctorate from Indiana University.

Stephen T. Holmes is Assistant Professor of Criminal Justice at the University of Central Florida. Prior to this position, he was a social science analyst for the National Institute of Justice in Washington, D.C. He has authored 6 books and more than 15 articles dealing with policing, drug testing, probation and parole issues, and violent crime. He received his doctorate from the University of Cincinnati.